Revision for
EDEXCEL

G C S E
MODERN
EUROPEAN &
WORLD
history

Steve Waugh

Ben Walsh

Wayne Birks

Hodder Murray
A MEMBER OF THE HODDER HEADLINE GROUP

In the same series:
Revision for AQA GCSE Modern World History   0 7195 7738 1
Revision for OCR GCSE Modern World History   0 7195 7740 3

Words printed in SMALL CAPITALS are defined in the Glossary on page 235.

© Steve Waugh, Ben Walsh, Wayne Birks 2002

First published in 2002
by Hodder Murray, a member of the Hodder Headline Group
338 Euston Road
London NW1 3BH

Reprinted 2004, 2006

Layouts by Janet McCallum
Illustrations by Mike Humphries
Typeset in Rockwell Light by Wearset Ltd, Boldon, Tyne and Wear
Printed and bound in Spain

A CIP catalogue entry for this title can be obtained from the British Library

ISBN-10: 0 7195 7737 3

ISBN-13: 978 0 7195 7737 6

Contents

Acknowledgements

Thanks are due to the following for permission to reproduce copyright photographs:

Cover *all* Corbis; **p.119** David King Collection; **p.122** David King Collection; **p.123** David King Collection; **p.126** Peter Newark's Military Pictures; **p.148** Peter Newark's Military Pictures; **p.151** Imperial War Museum, London (Q53446); **p.168** Peter Newark's American Pictures; **p.170** Peter Newark's American Pictures; **p.171** Peter Newark's American Pictures; **p.174** AKG London; **p.187** AKG London; **p.190** Mary Evans Picture Library; **p.212** Novosti Photo Library, London; **p.215** The Art Archive/Imperial War Museum; **p.227** UPI Radiophoto, Popperfoto; **p.229** Topham Picturepoint; **p.232** Corbis.

Examination questions are reproduced on the following pages, with kind permission from Edexcel: 11–12, 30–31, 35, 48–50, 54, 70–71, 75, 96–98, 106, 118–121, 126, 146–152, 156, 166–169, 174, 186–191, 194, 210–216, 219, 227–233. Edexcel accepts no responsibility whatsoever for the accuracy or method of working in the answers given.

Every effort has been made to contact copyright holders, but if any have been inadvertently overlooked the publishers will be pleased to make the necessary arrangements at the earliest opportunity.

Introduction

You will soon be taking your GCSE in Modern European and World History. Your aim is to get the best grade that you can. Our aim in this book is to help you to get that grade.

To improve your grade you need to:

- get organised – this book will help you make a revision plan and stick to it
- know the content – this book will help you learn the core content for your course
- apply your knowledge – this book will help you apply what you know to actual examination questions.

How to revise

There is no single way to revise. But there are some golden rules everyone should follow:

1 *Know the objectives of your course*: ask your teacher for full details of the specification. This book is geared to Edexcel's specification A, Modern European and World History.
2 *Make a revision plan and stick to it*: start your revision early – the earlier the better. Revise regularly – regular short spells are better than panicky six-hour slogs until 2a.m.
3 *Revise actively*: be a scribbler; make notes as you learn. You will need an exercise book for most of the revision tasks but you can also write in this book.

The rest of this introduction is about how to apply these rules to your revision and make sure that you get the grade you are aiming for.

1 Know the objectives of your course

Assessment objectives for GCSE History

GCSE History has assessment objectives. These are similar in all GCSE History syllabuses. In the Edexcel examination these objectives are:

- AO1 *recall, select, organise and deploy knowledge of the specification content to communicate it through description, analysis and explanation of:*
  - *the events, people, changes and issues studied*
  - *the key features and characteristics of the periods, societies or situations studied.*

  This means using sources and your own knowledge to judge whether you agree with a particular view or interpretation of a past event or person.
- AO2 *use historical sources critically in their context, by comprehending, analysing, evaluating and interpreting them.*

  This means reading sources carefully, making sure you know what they mean, comparing sources with each other and with your own knowledge. It also means judging a source's 'utility' or usefulness to a question.

- AO3 *comprehend, analyse, and evaluate, in relation to the historical context, how and why historical events, people, situations and changes have been interpreted and represented in different ways.*
  This means using your knowledge (what you have learned) to describe, explain or analyse. It does not mean 'writing all you know' about a topic, but selecting and organising the relevant parts to answer a specific question.

Although the assessment objectives are expressed separately, they are not entirely distinct.

The most important thing to remember is that the examiner is not just interested in finding out what you know but finding out *how far you understand and can apply your knowledge*: how far you can think for yourself about history.

2 Make a revision plan

You will not only need to plan your revision for history. You will also need to fit in your history revision with your revision for all your other GCSE subjects.

You could use this kind of table to plan your overall revision:

Dates		Revision targets and deadlines			
Month	Week	History	Science	English	Others
Jan	4	Key points summary card for Russia			
Feb	2		Test on metals		
Mar				Mock oral	

You could construct a table like the one below to plan your history revision. In your plan, aim to come back to each topic several times so that you revise in stages:

Stage 1: Put the date normal school-based work on a topic will be/was completed.
Stage 2: Put the target date for finishing your own summary of the key points for each topic.
Stage 3: Give yourself memory tests.
Stage 4: Fine tuning (e.g. final memorising and/or practice examination questions).

History topics	Date	Key points summary	Memory test	Fine tuning
1 Stalin's Five Year Plans
2 Collectivisation
3		March	April	2000 Question–May

3 Revise actively

Most students say when faced with revising for GCSE History:

The ideas in this book are all aimed at helping you to remember.

Use the revision tasks in this book

We believe the best way to remember information is to use it – to revise actively. To take an everyday example: to start with it is difficult to remember a new telephone number, but the more you use it the easier it is to remember it.

Throughout this book therefore we have provided revision tasks for you to do. Don't miss them out. If you do the tasks you will have to use the information in the book. If you use the information you will remember it better. The more you use the information the better you will remember it.

Use the key words method

Think of your brain as being like a computer. To read a file on a computer you need to know the name of the file. The file name is the key, and if you do not have this key you cannot get to the file, even though the computer has the file in its memory.

Your brain works rather like a computer. When you read something it goes in.

But to get the information out again you have to have the keys to unlock your memory.

So one approach to jog your memory is to use a key words method. This is how it works:

1 As you read through each paragraph, highlight one or two key words. For example:

What were the main political and economic features of the USA during the Cold War period?

- It had a *democratic system of government*. The President and Congress of the USA were chosen in free democratic elections.
- It had a *capitalist economy*. Business and property were privately owned. Individuals could make profits in business or move jobs if they wished. However, they might also go bankrupt or lose their jobs.
- The USA was the world's wealthiest country, but under capitalism there were always *great contrasts* – some people were very rich, others very poor.

2 You can then use cue cards, or the revision plan at the end of each chapter, to summarise your key words for each subheading. That way you can have a whole topic summarised on one sheet.

3 Later on, return to your revision plan and see if you can recall or rewrite important paragraphs using just the key words to jog your memory.

Other revision ideas

Different people revise in different ways and you may have your own ideas on how to work. Here are some other techniques that students have used:

- summarising events in diagrams or pictures – see page 15 for an example
- recording the text on to a cassette and playing it back
- using acronyms or mnemonics – see page 140 for an example
- working with friends:
  - testing each other
  - comparing your answers to practice questions.

How to use this book

Chapters 1–5 of this book cover the skills and content of the most popular Outline Studies for Edexcel Paper 1. Chapter 1 explains the style of questions and skills required for Paper 1. You will need to revise the two Outline Studies you have studied during the course.

Chapters 6–12 concentrate on the skills and content of the most popular Depth Studies for Paper 2. Chapter 6 explains the style of questions and source skills you will need. Again, you need to revise the two Depth Studies you have covered during the course.

Each chapter has the same features. The opening page outlines the topic. It gives a summary of:

- the KEY CONTENT that you need to know for that topic
- the KEY THEMES: the historical issues and themes that you need to understand and be aware of in order to tackle examination questions.

The key content

The next part is the largest section in each chapter. This is the part where the key content is described in detail. This is what you need to revise.

Important terms are highlighted in capital letters like this: APPEASEMENT. They are included in a glossary at the back of the book.

Comment

At various points you will also see short comment paragraphs like this:

● *Self-determination sounds fine in theory but in practice it would be very difficult to give the peoples of eastern Europe the chance to rule themselves because they were mixed and scattered across many countries. However the countries were reorganised, some people of one ethnic group were bound to end up being ruled by people from another.* ●

The examiner wants you to have an opinion on history and to make your own balanced judgements. These comment paragraphs are supposed to help you do that. Sometimes they will give you ideas about how to interpret the events described in that part of the chapter. At other times they try to show how one event links with another, or to show the views of people involved in events at the time. These boxes will also help you if you find it difficult to produce a balanced answer, because they give both sides of an argument or conflicting interpretations.

Revision tasks

These tasks help you to revise actively. They help you to highlight important words, names, dates, etc., and note them down. They also help you to think for yourself about the content.

Revision session

At the end of each chapter we take an examination question apart, and look at what should go into a good answer. We have called it a revision session because you can tackle it with another student or on your own. This feature will particularly help you if you find your answers sometimes miss the point, or if they are too long or too short.

In answering the examination questions you should always be guided by the number of marks on offer. Don't be tempted to write pages and pages for a question worth only four marks. The most important thing is to answer the question directly, so keep your writing relevant and concise and keep your eye on the time!

Summary and revision plan

This summarises the content covered in the chapter. Use this as a check-list to make sure you are familiar with the content. Using the key word approach, this page could provide a complete summary of the chapter. You could also use it as a 'prompt sheet' when you are testing yourself.

Exam Skills: How to succeed in Edexcel Paper 1

Format of Paper 1

For Edexcel Paper 1 you have to answer questions from two Outline Studies. This could be two from:

- The Road to War: Europe, 1870–1914
- Nationalism and Independence in India, c.1900–49
- The Emergence of Modern China, 1911–76
- The Rise and Fall of the Communist State: the Soviet Union, 1928–91
- A Divided Union? The USA, 1941–80
- Superpower Relations, 1945–90
- Conflict and the Quest for Peace in the Middle East, 1948–95

We have covered only the most popular options in this book. The Outline Study is divided into two sections.

Section A

There are four sub-questions worth relatively low marks which include:

- a brief *three-mark* causation or definition question
- two questions, each worth *five marks*, usually on key features, causation or consequence
- a *seven-mark* question which again could be causation, key features or consequence.

Section B

There are two essay-type questions on change, key features or causation.

- The first is worth *ten marks*.
- The second, worth *fifteen marks*, includes a four-point plan to help you answer the question.

Advice on Section A

1 The first question – brief causation or definition

Give ONE reason to explain why Stalin ended the New Economic Policy.   *(3 marks)*

- This question is only worth three marks so keep your answer brief. A paragraph is enough.
- Give your reason/definition.
- Explain the reason/definition with relevant knowledge.

2 Brief causation/consequence question

This can be worth five or seven marks.

Why were so many members of the Soviet army and the Communist Party purged in the 1930s?   *(5 marks)*

- You need to write two or three causes/consequences.
- Begin each paragraph with the cause/consequence and then explain it.
- Make links between each cause/consequence.
- Write a brief conclusion summing up the causes/consequences.

3 Brief key features question

This can be worth five or seven marks.

Describe the key features of the women's movement in the USA in the 1960s.   *(7 marks)*

Key features means the main or important developments.

- You need to write about two or three key features.
- Begin your paragraph with the key feature and then explain it.
- Try to link each of your key features.

Advice on Section B

1 Causation questions

Why did President Gorbachev face many problems when he became leader of the Soviet Union in 1985?
     (10 marks)

- Begin your answer with an introduction explaining the meaning of the question and what problems he faced.
- You will need to explain at least three problems faced by Gorbachev.
- Begin each paragraph by giving a problem and then explain it.
- Make links between each problem.
- Write a conclusion in which you summarise the reasons for these problems and make a judgement on which you think was the most important reason.

Make a copy of the following table and use it to plan causation questions.

	Explanation
Introduction	
First reason	
Link	
Second reason	
Link	
Third reason	
Link	
Conclusion	

2 Key features questions

Describe the key features of President Johnson's 'Great Society' in the USA in the years 1963–68. *(10 marks)*

Remember, key features means the main or important developments.

- Begin your answer with an introduction explaining the meaning of the question and what the main features were.
- You will need to explain at least three features.
- Begin each paragraph by giving a feature and then explain it.
- Make links between each feature.
- Write a conclusion in which you summarise the key features and make a judgement on which you think was the most important.

Make a copy of the following table and use it to plan key features questions.

	Explanation
Introduction	
First feature	
Link	
Second feature	
Link	
Third feature	
Link	
Conclusion	

3 Change questions

In what ways did the 'Scramble for Africa' change relations between the major European powers in the late nineteenth and early twentieth centuries? *(10 marks)*

- Begin with an introduction that explains the question and identifies the changes you intend to explain.
- Begin each paragraph with a change and then explain it.
- You need to explain at least three important changes.
- Write a conclusion in which you summarise the changes and make a judgement. This could be linking the changes, explaining the most important change or explaining the overall pattern of change during the period.

Make a copy of the following table and use it to plan the important changes.

	Explanation
Introduction	
First change	
Why a change?	
Second change	
Why a change?	
Third change	
Why a change?	
Conclusion	

4 The question with a plan

In what ways were the Soviet Union and the lives of its people changed by the Five Year Plans in the years 1928–41?

You may use the following information to help you with your answer:

- modernisation of industry
- control of the workforce
- growth of heavy industry
- production of consumer goods.

(15 marks)

- Once again you need an introduction that explains the meaning of the question.
- Explain each of the four factors mentioned in the question but try to add at least one of your own.
- Begin each paragraph with a factor and make it answer the question. For example, it could be a question about change, causation or key features. Then explain the factor.
- Try to link each factor.
- Write a conclusion that makes a judgement. This could be deciding which is the most important factor.

Make a copy of the following table and use it to plan your answer.

	Explanation
Introduction	
First factor	
Link	
Second factor	
Link	
Third factor	
Link	
Fourth factor	
Link	
Fifth factor	
Link	
Conclusion	

The Road to War: Europe, 1870–1914

In 1871 the French were defeated by Prussia and a new united German empire emerged. The years that followed brought increasing rivalry between the Great Powers, culminating in the outbreak of the First World War in 1914.

To answer questions on the period 1870–1914 leading to the First World War you need to be familiar with both the key content and the key themes of the period.

Key content You will need to show that you have a good working knowledge of these key areas:

A The Franco-Prussian War, 1870–71: its effect on France and Germany
B The expansion of the German empire, 1871–1914
C International rivalries and alliances, 1873–1914
D The changing balance of power in the Balkans, 1876–1914
E The Moroccan Crises, 1905–11
F The Balkan Crises, 1908–14
G The development of rivalry between Britain and Germany, 1890–1914

Key themes As with all examination questions, you will not be asked simply to learn this content and write it out again. You will need to show your understanding of some key themes from the period. These are:

● Why did an alliance system emerge?
● What effects did it have on international relations?
● What were the main causes of rivalry between the European powers?
● Why was there a struggle for control of the Balkans?
● How did this affect relations between the European powers?
● Why did Britain and Germany become rivals at the beginning of the twentieth century?
● What were the causes and effects of the international crises of 1905–13?
● Why did the assassination at Sarajevo in June 1914 lead to a general European war?

For example, look at the question below which is adapted from Specimen Paper 1 by permission of Edexcel.

a) This question is about problems in the Balkans during the years 1877–1914.

The map opposite shows the Balkans after the Treaty of San Stefano (1878).

Look at the map and then answer all the questions which follow.

   i) Give ONE reason to explain why the Treaty of San Stefano was disliked by the Great Powers of Europe.   *(3 marks)*

This question is asking you to show your knowledge and understanding of this topic.

   ii) Describe the key features of the Treaty of Berlin (1878).   *(5 marks)*

You will need to know the events leading to, and the terms and results of the Treaty of Berlin.

   iii) Why was there a crisis over Bulgaria in the years 1885–86?   *(5 marks)*

For this question you need to know the causes of this crisis, especially Russo-Bulgarian rivalry.

   iv) Why did tension in the Balkans increase in the years 1908–13?   *(7 marks)*

If you look carefully at the question you will see that you need to know about these important areas:

   · *Austro-Serbian rivalry*
   · *the Bosnian Crisis, 1908–09*
   · *the creation of the Balkan League*
   · *the two Balkan Wars, 1912–13, and their consequences.*

We will look at this question in detail at the end of this chapter.

b) i) Explain the main aims of Bismarck's policies towards France in the years 1879–90.

(10 marks)

We will look at this question in more detail at the end of the chapter.

ii) In what ways did France try to develop a system of defensive alliances in the years 1894–1914?

You may use the following information to help you with your answer:

- 1890s improved relations with Russia
- 1900s improved relations with Britain
- 1905 and 1911 Moroccan Crises
- 1907 Triple Entente. *(15 marks)*

We will look at this question in more detail at the end of the chapter.

A The Franco-Prussian War, 1870–71: its effect on France and Germany

1 Causes of the war

Rivalry built up between Prussia and France.

- Napoleon III was concerned at the success of Prussia in the wars against Denmark (1864) and Austria (1866) and did not want a powerful, united Germany.
- Bismarck wanted to encourage the south German states to join the North German Confederation and complete German unification.
- The immediate cause was the problem of the Spanish succession. Napoleon III was alarmed when a relative of William I of Prussia, Leopold of Hohenzollern, was put forward as a candidate. Napoleon asked William to withdraw his candidate.
- Bismarck, to provoke war, published the Ems telegram, in which William apparently rejected Napoleon's demands. Napoleon declared war.

2 The events of the war

- In August von Moltke, the commander of the Prussian troops, moved into Lorraine and defeated the right wing of the French army at Worth.
- The French army, under Marshal Bazaine, withdrew in confusion to the fortress of Metz which was besieged by the Prussian armed forces.
- A second French army, under Marshal MacMahon, sent to relieve the siege of Metz, was defeated at Sedan on 1 September.
- The Prussian army then laid siege to Paris which held out from October 1870 to January 1871.

3 Reasons for Prussian victory

- Isolation of France. Napoleon had been provoked by Bismarck into declaring war and was seen as the aggressor.
- Favourable circumstances. The British prime minister, William Gladstone, believed in isolation and did not want to get involved. The Tsar of Russia was preoccupied with trying to make gains in the Black Sea.

- Weaknesses of the French army. The French mobilisation was slow and confused and the French armies poorly led and badly organised. The French cavalry was no match for the superior Prussian armed forces.
- The Prussian armed forces were far superior. They had needle guns (an improved type of rifle) and the new Krupps field guns which mowed down the French cavalry. The Prussian troops were quickly mobilised and transported to the front in less than three weeks. They had experience and confidence as a result of the wars against Denmark (1864) and Austria (1866).
- Superior communications. The Prussian armed forces made effective use of the railway system.

4 The Treaty of Frankfurt, 1871

Bismarck gave way to pressure from his military leaders and forced France to agree to a harsh peace treaty. The French had to:

- hand over the provinces of Alsace–Lorraine
- pay a fine of £200 million. Parts of France were occupied by German troops until some of the fine was paid.

5 Results of the war

- In France it led to the fall of the empire of Napoleon III and the setting up of a French Republic.
- German unification. The war had fanned patriotic feelings and brought the southern states into the war on the side of Prussia. They agreed to join the North German Confederation. On 18 January 1871 King William of Prussia was proclaimed Emperor of Germany.
- Franco-German rivalry. The French were furious with the peace terms imposed upon them, especially the loss of Alsace–Lorraine. This was to be a long-term cause of the First World War.

● *Bismarck regretted the harsh peace treaty with France and was especially concerned about Alsace–Lorraine. He did not want to humiliate the French. The Prussian generals, however, were determined to make the French pay and forced their views upon Bismarck. The peace treaty was to create long-term rivalry between the two countries and forced Bismarck to set up the alliance system.* ●

● *Revision tasks*

1 Make a list of key words to summarise the following causes of the Franco-Prussian War:
   a) Bismarck's aims
   b) Napoleon's attitude
   c) The Spanish throne
   d) The Ems telegram.
2 Copy and complete the table below, using the information in this section to summarise the reasons for Prussia's victory in 1870–71.

French weaknesses	Prussian strengths	Favourable circumstances

3 Do you think that Bismarck was right to punish France so harshly in 1871?

B The expansion of the German empire, 1871–1914

1 Bismarck's aims

- He wanted to isolate France. He realised that the French would want revenge for the defeat and losses of the Franco-Prussian War and was determined to prevent France from gaining allies.
- This, in turn, meant that Germany would need to get on well with the other Great Powers of Europe, especially Britain, Russia and Austria–Hungary.
- He wanted to keep the peace in the Balkans and prevent rivalry between Russia and Austria–Hungary which might lead one of them to form closer relations with France.
- Bismarck had little interest in colonies or an empire abroad.

2 Bismarck's policies, 1871–90

- He launched the alliance system in order to keep France isolated (see pages 18–19).
- In 1875 he created a 'war scare' in an attempt to warn off the French. There were rumours that France was building up its armed forces ready for revenge. Bismarck authorised an article in a German newspaper entitled 'Is War in Sight?' in an attempt to warn off the French with the threat of a German preventative war. This backfired on him as both Britain and Russia announced that they would not allow a second French defeat.
- Bismarck tried to act as the 'honest broker' during crises in the Balkans, especially in 1878 and 1885–86 (see pages 21–23) but only succeeded in upsetting the Russians.
- To further isolate France, Bismarck encouraged the French to occupy Tunis in 1881, realising that this would bring them into rivalry with Italy which also wanted this area. In the following year he encouraged the British occupation of Egypt, knowing that this would infuriate France and drive a wedge between the two nations, leaving Britain dependent on German support.
- Between 1883 and 1885 Germany gained colonies in Africa, including the Cameroons, German South West Africa and German East Africa, and in the Far East. Although he was not interested in colonies, Bismarck agreed to this in order to win over German public opinion which was strongly in favour of sharing in the 'Scramble for Africa'. It was also a way of working with France against Britain.

3 The aims of Kaiser William II

In 1888 William II became Emperor (Kaiser) of Germany and within two years Bismarck had resigned. William II had different aims.

- He wanted Germany to gain 'a place in the sun' – to expand the German empire by gaining as many colonies as possible.
- This, in turn, would help the expansion of the German economy by providing raw materials for Germany and a market for German manufactured goods.
- William wanted closer relations with Austria–Hungary but not with Russia.
- He was determined to build a German navy to protect his empire and trade.

4 William's policies, 1890–1914

- Relations with Russia soon cooled and in 1894 Russia signed the Dual Alliance with France.
- William became involved in the 'Scramble for China' in the 1890s and in 1897 gained the Chinese port of Kiaochow.

- He was interested in expanding German interests in the Turkish empire and persuaded the Sultan of Turkey to agree, in 1898, to the construction of the Berlin to Baghdad railway. This upset Britain and Russia which both had interests in this area.
- In 1898 Germany began a programme of naval building which brought serious rivalry with Britain (see page 28).
- The Kaiser frequently interfered in the affairs of other nations. For example, during the Boer War (1899–1902) between the Dutch settlers of South Africa and the British, he expressed his sympathy for the Boers. In 1905 and 1911 he tried to prevent French expansion into Morocco. This provoked two serious international crises (see pages 24–25).

● *It is generally thought that William II was responsible for driving Russia into the arms of France when he refused to renew the Reinsurance Treaty (see page 18). In fact Bismarck had found it very difficult to keep close relations with both Austria and Russia. As early as 1889, before Bismarck's resignation, the Russians were seeking loans from France.* ●

● Revision tasks

1 Draw two spider diagrams like the ones shown below, comparing the aims and policies of Bismarck and the Kaiser. Try to make links between the aims and policies.

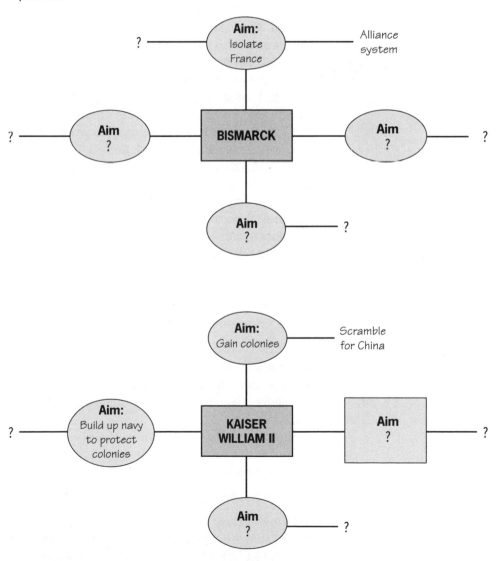

2 'The Kaiser totally changed the policies of Bismarck.' How far do you agree with this statement? Make a list of key words to summarise 'for' and 'against' arguments.

C International rivalries and alliances, 1873–1914

1 Rivalries between the Great Powers

- Great Britain, ruled by Queen Victoria. Britain was Europe's leading industrial power with an empire that covered a quarter of the world and included India, Australia and much of Africa. This empire was protected by the British navy. Britain was suspicious of any country that tried to build up its navy. Until 1900 Russia and France had seemed to present the greatest threat to Britain. Germany's decision to build up its navy changed the situation and brought increasing rivalry between Britain and Germany.
- France, a republic ruled by a President. France had been defeated by Germany in 1871 and lost the two provinces of Alsace and Lorraine. Many of the French wanted revenge on Germany and the return of these provinces and were known as the *Revanchists*. In 1894 France allied with Russia in what was known as the Dual Alliance.
- Germany, ruled by Kaiser (Emperor) William II. Germany was becoming a rival to Britain because of its fast-growing industry and determination to build up an empire. The Kaiser also wanted to build up the German navy. This brought increasing rivalry with Britain over the navy and with France over Morocco in North Africa. The Kaiser felt threatened by the Triple Entente (see pages 18–19) and felt that Germany was being surrounded by its rivals. He was, therefore, keen to back up his major ally, Austria, in its conflict with Serbia.
- Austria–Hungary, ruled by Emperor Franz Josef. This was a huge empire in the centre of Europe with many different Slav nationalities including Serbs, Croats, Czechs and Bosnians. Many of these nationalities wanted their independence. The Serbs in the empire wished to join with the state of Serbia. Austria–Hungary feared this would spark the break-up of its empire and was determined to crush Serbia.
- Russia, ruled by Tsar (Emperor) Nicholas II. Russia had the largest army and population in Europe. The Tsar wanted the empire of Austria–Hungary to break up and be replaced by independent states controlled by Russia. Russia was the protector of the Slav peoples of eastern Europe, especially Serbia and those in the Austro-Hungarian empire.
- Italy had only recently (1861) become a united country and wanted to be seen as a great power.

2 The Scramble for Africa

This was the name given to the expansion of European countries into Africa. It was due to:

- economic motives: the African colonies were a source of raw materials and a market for manufactured goods
- prestige: the acquisition of colonies increased the standing and prestige of a country
- strategic reasons: for example, Egypt was vital to Britain's links with India
- humanitarian motives: the desire to 'civilise' the African peoples
- religious reasons: to bring Christianity to these peoples.

The Scramble brought rivalry between the powers of Europe.

- There was rivalry between Britain and France in North and West Africa. The French were furious when the British occupied Egypt in 1882. They competed for control of the Sudan and West Africa. At first the British opposed French attempts to extend their influence into Morocco at the turn of the century.

- There was rivalry between Britain and Germany for influence and control over South West and East Africa after Bismarck's decision to join the race for colonies in the early 1880s.
- The British and Italians were rivals for control of the Sudan and Abyssinia. Italian attempts to expand into Abyssinia ended in defeat at the Battle of Adowa, 1896.

The division of Africa into colonies by 1914

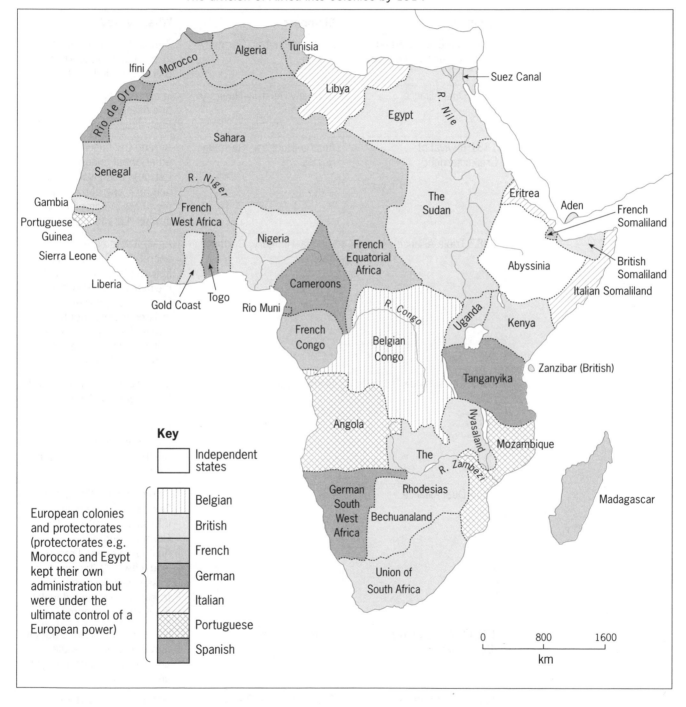

Key

Independent states	

European colonies and protectorates (protectorates e.g. Morocco and Egypt kept their own administration but were under the ultimate control of a European power)

- Belgian
- British
- French
- German
- Italian
- Portuguese
- Spanish

0   800   1600
km

3 The alliance system

By 1907 Europe was divided into two armed camps or rival gangs. These were the Triple Alliance of Germany, Austria–Hungary and Italy, and the Triple Entente of Britain, France and Russia.

This system of ALLIANCES had started under Bismarck. He feared the French desire for revenge after the loss of Alsace–Lorraine and wanted to keep the French isolated from the other GREAT POWERS.

Alliance	Members	What agreed
1873 The Dreikaiserbund (Three Emperors' League)	Austria–Hungary, Germany, Russia	Agreed to co-operate to keep peace especially in Balkans. Ended in 1875.
1879 Dual Alliance	Germany, Austria–Hungary	In secret they agreed that if one of them was attacked by Russia the other would help.
1881 Revival of Dreikaiserbund	Austria–Hungary, Germany, Russia	Agreed to consult each other about changes in Balkans. Each would remain neutral if one of the other members became involved in war with a fourth country.
1882 Triple Alliance	Austria–Hungary, Germany, Italy	Again it was agreed in secret that Germany and Italy would help one another if either was attacked by France. Italy, however, insisted it would not be involved in war against Great Britain. It feared the strength of the Royal Navy.
1887 Reinsurance Treaty	Germany, Russia	Each would remain neutral if the other was at war with a third power but not if Germany attacked France or Russia attacked Austria–Hungary. Ended in 1890.
1894 Dual Alliance	France, Russia	If France was attacked by Germany, Russia would help. If Russia was attacked by Germany and/or Austria–Hungary, France would help. At this point Russia was desperate for a foreign loan to help develop the Russian economy.
1904 Entente Cordiale (Dual Entente)	France, Britain	Not a military alliance but an agreement which settled areas of difference in Egypt and Morocco.
1907 Triple Entente	Russia, France, Britain	Not an alliance but an agreement to try to settle areas of difference between the three.

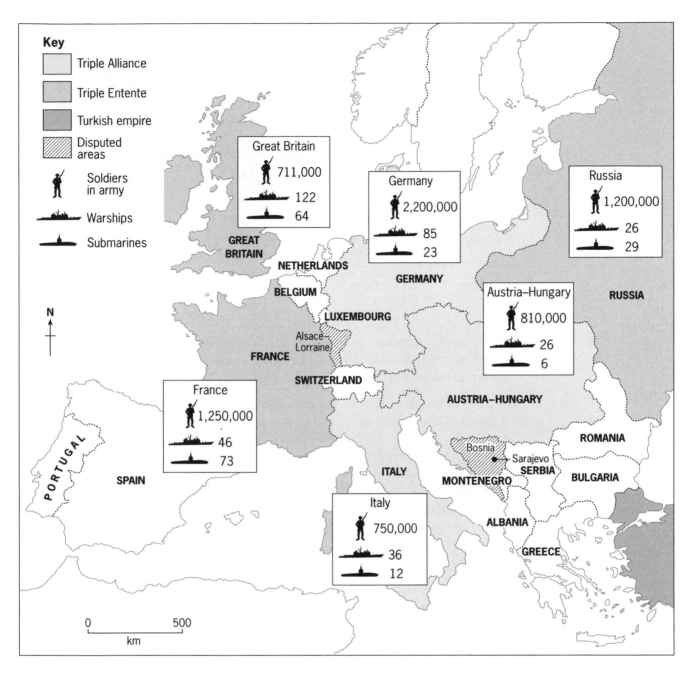

Key

- Triple Alliance
- Triple Entente
- Turkish empire
- Disputed areas
- Soldiers in army
- Warships
- Submarines

Great Britain
711,000
122
64

GREAT BRITAIN

NETHERLANDS

BELGIUM

LUXEMBOURG

Alsace-Lorraine

FRANCE

SWITZERLAND

Germany
2,200,000
85
23

GERMANY

Russia
1,200,000
26
29

RUSSIA

Austria–Hungary
810,000
26
6

France
1,250,000
46
73

PORTUGAL

SPAIN

ITALY

AUSTRIA–HUNGARY

Bosnia

Sarajevo

SERBIA

MONTENEGRO

ROMANIA

BULGARIA

Italy
750,000
36
12

ALBANIA

GREECE

N

0   500
km

The Triple Alliance and the Triple Entente in 1914

The alliance system brought war nearer for several reasons:

- It created two armed camps or rival gangs in Europe – the Triple Alliance against the Triple Entente.
- A dispute between two countries in different camps could well involve the other members of the two camps. This would turn a war between two countries into a major war between all six.
- Although the agreement between them was not as formal as that of a military alliance, relations between France and Britain drew much closer after the establishment of the Entente Cordiale in 1904. The two countries even planned together how to fight a future war against Germany.

● *The alliance system has often been seen as one of the major reasons for the outbreak of the First World War because it divided Europe into two armed camps. In fact, when you examine more closely the sequence of events that took place in 1914 after the assassination of the Archduke Franz-Ferdinand, you find that most of the Great Powers did not go to war because of their alliance commitments.* ●

4   The arms race

This means the rivalry between the Great Powers to build up the size of their armed forces. Every major power in Europe except Britain used a programme of CONSCRIPTION to build up their armies. These armies could be mobilised (called-up) at a moment's notice. In the period 1900–14 the main European powers more than doubled their spending on their armies.

	Military personnel (excluding reserves)		
	1900	**1910**	**1914**
France	0.7 m	0.8 m	0.9 m
Britain	0.6 m	0.55 m	0.5 m
Russia	1.1 m	1.3 m	0.8 m
Austria–Hungary	0.25 m	0.3 m	0.35 m
Germany	0.5 m	0.7 m	1.5 m
Italy	0.25 m	0.3 m	0.35 m

Guns, shells, bullets and other weapons had been stockpiled in case of war. More destructive weapons, such as the machine gun and field guns, were being developed and improved. The arms race brought war nearer because:

- it increased tension between the Great Powers. It had a rolling snowball effect. If one power increased its army, another would follow suit
- it made war more likely. As each country increased its army and weapons it became more confident of success in a future war and more willing to test out its armed forces
- in 1904 the Germans had devised a plan for a future war. It was drawn up by the Chief of Staff, Alfred von Schlieffen, to enable Germany to fight a war on two fronts: to the east against Russia, and in the west, against France.

D   The changing balance of power in the Balkans, 1876–1914

The Balkans is a peninsula in south-east Europe. This area was controlled by the Turkish or Ottoman empire. This empire was then known as the 'sick man of Europe', since it was weak and in decline. The Balkans was inhabited by Slav peoples such as the Serbs, Bosnians, Bulgarians and Romanians. Many of them wanted to be able to rule themselves and belonged to the movement for Pan-Slavism. The Slavs were mainly Christians who had little in common with the Turkish religion of Islam.

1   The interests of the Great Powers

- Russia, primarily inhabited by Slavs, regarded itself as the protector of the Slavs and saw the Balkans as an area of influence and expansion.
- Austria–Hungary was an empire of many nationalities similar to those of the Balkans. The Austrians wanted to prevent the emergence of strong Balkan states, especially Serbia, which might encourage the break-up of their own empire. They feared Russian influence and expansion into the area.
- Great Britain wanted to prop up the Turkish empire in the Balkans to prevent Russian expansion and keep links with its own empire in Asia, especially India.
- Germany, under Bismarck, had no direct interest in the Balkans except to try to prevent problems in the area causing conflict between Austria–Hungary and Russia.

2 The Balkan Crisis, 1875–78

There was a series of events during this period which increased rivalry between the Great Powers.

a) The Turkish empire and the Russian attack in 1877

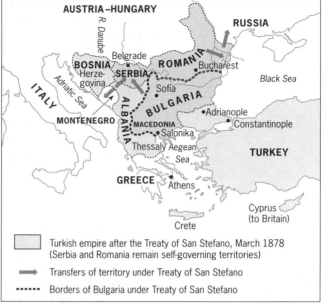

b) The Turkish empire after the Treaty of San Stefano, 1878

c) The Turkish empire after the Treaty of Berlin, 1878

- In July 1875 the province of Bosnia-Herzegovina rebelled against Turkish rule and appealed to the Great Powers for support. Germany, Austria–Hungary and Russia presented the Sultan of Turkey with the Andrassy Note and Berlin Memorandum, requesting reforms in the province.
- In 1876 the rebellion spread to Bulgaria which was supported by Serbia and Montenegro. The Turks retaliated by massacring thousands of Bulgarians. The Great Powers met at a conference at Constantinople in December 1876 and made the Sultan, Abdul Hamid, agree to self-government for the Bulgars. When the conference broke up, Abdul Hamid went back on his word.
- Alexander II of Russia, as protector of the Balkan Christians, declared war on Turkey in April 1877. The Russian armies drove the Turks back to the fortress of Plevna where they fiercely held out until December 1877.

- In March 1878 the Tsar forced the Turks to sign the Treaty of San Stefano. This created an enlarged Bulgaria which stretched from the River Danube to the Aegean Sea and was to be supervised by Russia. Russia also gained the ports of Kars and Batumi on the Black Sea.
- Britain and Austria–Hungary, alarmed by Russian influence in Bulgaria, forced the Tsar to agree to a congress.
- The Congress of Berlin, with Bismarck as chairman, met in June 1878.
  - Serbia and Romania were given independence from the Turks.
  - Bosnia and Herzegovina, although still part of the Turkish empire, were to be administered by Austria–Hungary.
  - Britain was given the island of Cyprus.
  - The enlarged Bulgaria was split into three. The south and south-west were restored to the Sultan, cutting Bulgaria off from the Aegean Sea. A second part, Eastern Rumelia, was also restored to Turkey but allowed a Christian governor. The Bulgaria that remained was little more than one-third of the original country.
- The Congress did not end the problems of the Balkans. Within seven years there was another crisis over Bulgaria. The Russians were furious with the outcome of the Congress. They had fought a war and yet had been forced to give way over Bulgaria. They blamed Bismarck, who was supposed to be the 'honest broker' at the Congress, for siding with Austria–Hungary. The result was that relations between Russia and Germany were very strained.

3   The Bulgarian Crisis, 1885–86

This was caused by:

- the division of Bulgaria at the Congress of Berlin
- developments in Bulgaria. The Bulgarians soon resented Russian influence. The Russians had supported Alexander of Battenberg as the first Prince of Bulgaria but the Prince was quick to identify himself with Bulgarian rather than Russian interests. The Bulgarian prime minister, Stefan Stambolov, who had been born in Rumelia, persuaded Alexander in 1885 to annexe Eastern Rumelia.

The Russians opposed this but got no support from the other powers which now realised that Bulgaria was not a Russian SATELLITE after all.

The Prince was kidnapped in 1886, with Russian connivance, and forced to abdicate, but further Russian action was prevented by the opposition of Austria–Hungary and Britain. The Bulgarians elected Ferdinand of Saxe-Coburg as their new Prince in 1887 and continued to resist Russian influence.

The Bulgarian crisis had several effects:

- Russia resented Austrian opposition and once again believed Bismarck had not helped their interests in the area. The Dreikaiserbund broke up.
- The Serbs, resentful of the union of Bulgaria and Eastern Rumelia, invaded Bulgaria in 1885. The Serbs were beaten but Serbo-Bulgarian rivalry now became a feature of Balkan affairs.

4   Austro-Serbian rivalry

This was the major development in the area at the turn of the century. It was caused by:

- Serbian nationalism. In 1903 King Alexander of Serbia, who was friendly towards Austria–Hungary, was assassinated and replaced by a king who was friendly to Russia. Russian influence now dominated Serbia. Serbian nationalism grew and the Serbs set up patriotic clubs in the neighbouring states of Bosnia and Herzegovina. The Serbs wished to create a greater

Serbia which would include those Serbs living in the Austro-Hungarian empire as well as those in Bosnia and Herzegovina (governed by Austria–Hungary since 1878).

- This brought rivalry with Austria–Hungary which feared that NATIONALISM would spread to the other Slavs in its empire and hasten its break-up.
- Russia saw itself as the protector of the Slavs in this area and saw Serbian nationalism as an opportunity to extend its influence into a neighbour of Austria–Hungary.

● *The Balkans were certainly the major trouble spot in Europe in the late nineteenth and early twentieth centuries. There were several wars, including the Russo-Turkish war of 1877–78 and the Serbo–Bulgarian war of 1885. There was also a bitter rivalry between the Austrians and the Serbs that had its roots in Serbian nationalism.* ●

● *Revision tasks*

1 Copy the table below and list the differences between the Treaty of San Stefano and the Treaty of Berlin.

Treaty of San Stefano	Treaty of Berlin

2 Using a few key words explain the reactions of the following powers to the Treaty of Berlin:
   a) Germany
   b) Austria–Hungary
   c) Britain
   d) Russia.
3 Why was there a further crisis over Bulgaria, 1885–86?

E The Moroccan Crises, 1905–11

1 Crisis, 1905–06

In 1904 Britain and France agreed the Entente Cordiale (Dual Entente) which gave freedom of action to Britain in Egypt and France in Morocco. The Kaiser, however, decided to interfere in Morocco. He wanted to test the strength of the Entente. He did not believe Britain would stand by France over Morocco. He did not want to see France extend its North African empire. In 1905 the Kaiser paid a visit to the Moroccan port of Tangiers. There he made a speech in which he declared that Morocco should remain independent of France. This sparked off a crisis. France, supported by Britain, refused to back down but did agree to the Kaiser's demand for an international meeting or conference to discuss the future of Morocco.

The conference took place at Algeciras in Spain. It was a disaster for the Kaiser. Only Austria–Hungary backed his demands for Moroccan independence. Britain supported the French. This crisis increased tension because:

- although the conference confirmed Morocco's independence, it accepted France's role in maintaining order in the country
- the Kaiser had suffered an embarrassing defeat, which he blamed on the British and their support for France
- it strengthened the Entente Cordiale, as Britain had fully supported France.

2 The second Moroccan or Agadir Crisis, 1911

In 1911 there was a second crisis in Morocco. Early in 1911 the Sultan, the ruler of Morocco, asked the French for help in crushing a revolt led by rebel tribesmen. Germany was certain that this would be followed by a French take-over. As soon as the French occupied Fez, in Morocco, the Kaiser sent a gunboat, the *Panther*, to the Moroccan port of Agadir.

- Once again he was trying to break the Entente Cordiale.
- He was also seeking compensation from France in the form of the whole of the French Congo in Central Africa.

Germany's action misfired. Britain was even more determined to support France and oppose Germany. The British believed that Germany was trying to set up a naval base in Morocco. It seemed to be another attempt by the Kaiser to break up the Entente. Britain's fleet was even prepared for war. In the end, Germany backed down rather than risk war.

Once again a crisis had brought the Great Powers to the brink of war and increased tension:

- It drew Britain and France closer together. France was again very pleased at Britain's support against Germany. The two countries began secret joint naval manoeuvres and discussed military co-operation should war break out.
- It had again humiliated the Kaiser, who blamed the British. He was unlikely to back down again.

● *In many respects the two Moroccan crises are more important for their effects on relations between Britain and Germany. Yes, they certainly increased rivalry between France and Germany. The Kaiser, however, on both occasions was far more furious with the British for the way in which their support for the French led to German diplomatic defeats.* ●

● Revision tasks

1 Using a few key words explain why there was rivalry between the following countries in the period 1873–1914:
   a) France *v* Germany
   b) Austria–Hungary *v* Russia
   c) Britain *v* Germany.
2 Using the map on page 17 showing the Scramble for Africa, make a list of the main areas acquired by the following powers:
   a) Germany
   b) France
   c) Britain
   d) Italy.
3 Make your own table to show the agreements and alliances which led to the formation of the two armed camps, the Triple Alliance and the Triple Entente.
4 Why did the arms race make war more likely at the beginning of the twentieth century? Make a list of key words to summarise the main reasons.
5 Why did the two Moroccan crises worsen relations between:
   a) France and Germany
   b) Germany and Britain?

F The Balkan Crises, 1908–14

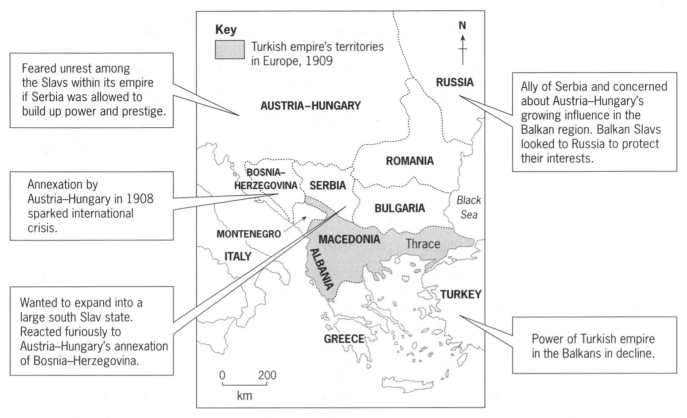

Feared unrest among the Slavs within its empire if Serbia was allowed to build up power and prestige.

Annexation by Austria–Hungary in 1908 sparked international crisis.

Wanted to expand into a large south Slav state. Reacted furiously to Austria–Hungary's annexation of Bosnia–Herzegovina.

Ally of Serbia and concerned about Austria–Hungary's growing influence in the Balkan region. Balkan Slavs looked to Russia to protect their interests.

Power of Turkish empire in the Balkans in decline.

Key — Turkish empire's territories in Europe, 1909

The Balkans in 1909

1 The Bosnian Crisis, 1908–09

In 1908 Austria–Hungary added Bosnia–Herzegovina to its empire. This created a second international crisis.

- The Serbs were furious as they had hoped to make Bosnia part of a greater Serbian state. They appealed to Russia for help. Russia's answer was to call for an international conference to discuss Austria–Hungary's action. Austria–Hungary refused to attend and was backed by Germany.
- Germany demanded that Russia accept the Austro-Hungarian seizure of Bosnia–Herzegovina. Russia had little choice but to back down. Russia's armies were no match for the German forces.

This crisis again increased tension:

- Serbia was furious with Austria–Hungary and wanted revenge.
- Russia was humiliated but was unlikely to back down in another crisis.
- Germany was now fully committed to supporting Austro-Hungarian policy in the Balkans even if it led to war.
- Russia drew even closer to France and Britain.

2 The Balkan Wars, 1912–13

Between 1912 and 1913 there were two wars in the Balkans. These, again, increased tension and brought a major European conflict nearer.

- Ever since the Bosnian crisis of 1908–09, Russia had tried to get the Balkan states to form an alliance. In this way Russia hoped to block an Austro-Hungarian take-over of the Balkans. In 1912 Serbia, Greece, Bulgaria and Montenegro formed a group called the Balkan League.

- In October the armies of this League attacked the Turks to drive them out of the small area of the Balkans they still controlled. They were very successful and drove Turkey out of Europe.
- This alarmed Austria–Hungary, especially as Serbia had come out as the strongest Balkan state. The Austrian generals now wanted a quick war to crush Serbia once and for all. This could well trigger off a wider European war.
- The Great Powers stepped in and forced a peace settlement on the victorious Balkan states. At the peace conference of 1913 Serbia gained much territory when Turkey's European territory was shared out among the Balkan League. Albania became an independent state.
- Within a month the Balkan League had fallen out and there was a second Balkan war. Bulgaria quarrelled with Serbia and Greece. In June 1913 the Bulgarians attacked their former allies. They were, however, quickly defeated. In the peace settlement that followed, Bulgaria surrendered nearly all the lands it had won in the first war to Greece and Serbia. Serbia gained even more land.

The Balkan Wars brought war one step nearer because:

- Serbia became almost twice as large. It was even more determined to unite with the Serbs in the Austro-Hungarian empire.
- Serbia was now a much greater threat to Austria which was more determined than ever to crush the Serbs. On the other hand, Russia was more determined than ever to support Serbia.
- The Germans had restrained Austria–Hungary during this period but knew that in any subsequent crisis they would have to support Austrian action.
- Bulgaria was determined to have revenge on Serbia and Greece.

a) The Balkans before the first Balkan War in 1912

b) The Balkans after the second Balkan War in 1913

3 The assassination of Franz-Ferdinand

This was the immediate cause of the First World War. On 28 June 1914 the Archduke Franz-Ferdinand, who was heir to the throne of Austria–Hungary, and his wife, Sophie, paid a state visit to Sarajevo, the capital of Bosnia. They were both assassinated by Gavrilo Princip, a member of a Serbian terrorist group known as the 'Black Hand'.

The news of the assassination shocked the world and set off a chain of events that culminated in a major war. Austria–Hungary was furious and blamed the Serbs but did nothing for nearly one month. The Austrians needed to be certain of German support. If they invaded Serbia it might well lead to war with Russia. On 5 July the Kaiser gave his support to the Austrian ambassador.

23 July The Austrians delivered an ultimatum which they knew the Serbs would reject. It included ten demands which meant the virtual end of Serbian independence. Surprisingly the Serbs accepted all but one.

28 July Austria declared war on Serbia. Serbia appealed to Russia for help.

29 July Russia mobilised its armed forces in support of Serbia.

30 July The Kaiser warned the Tsar of Russia to stop mobilising.

31 July Germany gave Russia a threatening ultimatum.

1 Aug When Russia did not reply, Germany declared war and began to mobilise. France, which was an ally of Russia, now mobilised its army.

2 Aug Germany presented an ultimatum to Belgium asking for a passage through Belgium.

3 Aug Germany declared war on France. Britain sent an ultimatum demanding that Germany respect Belgian neutrality.

4 Aug Germany declared war on Belgium. Britain declared war on Germany.

● *There was no one reason for the outbreak of war in 1914. It was a combination of long-term causes such as the arms race, the alliance system and the rivalry in the Balkans, and the tension created by the crises that occurred over Morocco and the Balkans in the years before 1914. These rivalries and tensions could not withstand the shock and repercussions of the assassination in Sarajevo.* ●

● *Revision tasks*

1 Copy the table below and complete it with relevant information from this section.

Crisis	Causes	Events	Results
Bosnian Crisis 1908–09			
First Balkan War 1912			
Second Balkan War 1913			
Assassination of Franz-Ferdinand			

2 Make a key word summary of the reasons why the following European powers became involved in war in August 1914:
a) Germany
b) Austria–Hungary
c) France
d) Russia.

G The development of rivalry between Britain and Germany, 1890–1914

1 The role of Kaiser William II

The Kaiser is often seen as one of the reasons for rivalry between Britain and Germany. In British eyes, William II was both menacing and ridiculous.

- He decided to build up a powerful navy which began a naval race between the two countries.
- His desire for 'a place in the sun' led to clashes with Britain in Africa, the Far East and the Turkish empire.
- He upset the British public during the Boer War of 1899–1902 when he openly sympathised with the Boers and tried to set up an anti-British COALITION of European powers.
- In 1908 he gave an interview to the *Daily Telegraph* in which he again showed lack of tact. He told the paper's readers that although he himself was friendly towards Britain, the German people were not.
- His interference in Morocco in 1905 and 1911 alienated the British government and public.

2 Anglo-German naval rivalry

Although Britain only had a small professional army, its Royal Navy was the most powerful in the world. It outgunned and outnumbered all other navies. The navy was vital to Britain. It protected the empire and trade, prevented invasion and guaranteed Britain's position as a great power.

Germany already had the world's best army. In 1898 it began a fleet of battleships to rival the British navy. This was because the Kaiser had always had more interest in the navy than the army and it would help to build up and protect German trade and colonies.

At first this was not of major concern to Britain. The Royal Navy was far superior and it would take Germany many years to catch up. All this changed with the launch of the British super-battleship, Dreadnought, in 1906. This made all previous battleships obsolete or out of date. It was faster, bigger and had a much greater firing range than existing battleships. A race developed between the two countries to see who could build the most Dreadnought-class battleships. In 1909 Britain had eight Dreadnoughts to Germany's seven.

This naval race, more than anything else, poisoned relations between the two countries.

- Britain feared German world domination if the Kaiser had both the strongest navy and the strongest army.
- Germany resisted British attempts in the years before 1914 to slow down the building of Dreadnought-class battleships. Indeed, the Kaiser could not understand British concerns.

3 Other causes of rivalry

These included:

- economic competition. Britain had been the first industrialised nation and, until the late nineteenth century, had led the world. The German economy rapidly expanded in the period 1871–1914 and began to provide serious competition in iron, steel and coal, and in the competition for markets abroad. Indeed Germany led the way in the chemical and electrical industries.

- colonial rivalry. The two countries were competing for COLONIES and influence in Africa and China.
- the Turkish empire. For many years Britain had been the protector of the Sultan and had dominated trade with the Turks. The Berlin–Baghdad railway showed the extent of the Kaiser's influence in the area by 1897. Germany was now a serious rival for markets in the Turkish empire.
- Belgium and the 'scrap of paper'. This was the immediate reason for British entry into the First World War. In 1839 Britain and the other Great Powers signed the Treaty of London which guaranteed the neutrality of Belgium in a future war. This was the 'scrap of paper'. Britain did not want a major country to occupy Belgium and use it as a base to invade Britain. The German Schlieffen Plan, however, meant that Germany would have to invade France through Belgium. The Germans gambled that either the British would not go to war over Belgium or, if they did, they would arrive in France too late to make any difference to the outcome. The German invasion of Belgium angered the British people and the vast majority supported the British declaration of war.

4 Why did Britain go to war in 1914?

Rivalry with Germany was certainly important, especially the naval race and the German threat to Belgium. There were other reasons:

- Britain was closely allied to France and to a lesser extent to Russia. The British felt they had to help France and Russia.
- The consequences of not intervening would be bad for Britain. If Germany defeated France then it would dominate Europe and be a greater threat to Britain. If France won, the French would no longer trust Britain, which would be left with no allies.

● *Revision tasks*

1 Copy the table below and use it to decide how important each factor was in causing rivalry between Britain and Germany. Use key words to explain your choices.

	Unimportant	**Quite important**	**Important**	**Decisive**
Attitude of Kaiser				
Naval race				
Economic rivalry				
Colonial rivalry				
Turkish empire				

2 Why did Britain go to war in 1914?

Revision session

The aim of this session is for you to see how you can apply your knowledge of the content of this chapter to the kind of questions you will face in your exams.

Examination questions

Examination questions on this topic appear on Paper 1. In the following examples we will look at questions adapted by permission of Edexcel from the Specimen Paper.

a) This question is about problems in the Balkans during the years 1877–1914.
The map shows the Balkans after the Treaty of San Stefano (1878).
Look at the map and then answer all the questions which follow.

i) Give ONE reason to explain why the Treaty of San Stefano was disliked by the Great Powers of Europe.

(3 marks)

What is required?	This is a simple test of your knowledge and memory. A simple factual answer will do. It is only worth three marks.
Ideas for your answer	You could write about the reduction in the size of Turkey or Russia's desire to expand.

ii) Describe the key features of the Treaty of Berlin (1878). *(5 marks)*

What is required?	This question is asking you to identify and describe at least two important features. Identify each feature and then describe it as precisely as possible.
Ideas for your answer	You could describe the following two key features: 1 The main terms of the Treaty, especially in relation to Bulgaria. 2 The role of Bismarck at the Congress and the reactions of the Great Powers, especially Austria–Hungary and Russia.

iii) Why was there a crisis over Bulgaria in the years 1885–86? *(5 marks)*

What is required?	This is a causation question and is asking you to identify and explain at least two causes.
Ideas for your answer	1 Your first cause could be the problems left by the Treaty of Berlin, especially the division of Bulgaria into three and the rivalry of Bulgaria and Serbia. 2 Your second cause could be developments in Bulgaria itself, more especially its anti-Russian stance and the reactions of Russia.

iv) Why did tension in the Balkans increase in the years 1908–13? *(7 marks)*

What is required? Again this is causation and you need to identify and explain as precisely as possible at least three causes of tension. At the start of each paragraph give the reason and then explain it. Try to make links between each paragraph/reason, for example Austro-Serbian rivalry could be easily linked to the next reason/paragraph on the Bosnian Crisis 1908–09.

Ideas for your answer
1 Austro-Serbian rivalry and how this brought tension in both 1908–09 and 1912–13.
2 The consequences of the Bosnian Crisis 1908–09, especially for Austro-Serbian and Austro-Russian relations.
3 The creation of the Balkan League and the outbreak of the First Balkan War.

b) i) Explain the main aims of Bismarck's policies towards France in the years 1879–90. *(10 marks)*

What is required? This question is asking you to identify and explain the key features of Bismarck's policies towards France. A low-level answer (1–2 marks) would make brief, simple statements such as Bismarck feared France because of the results of the 1870–71 war. An answer at the next level (3–5 marks) would describe at least two reasons but in a way that is not well organised and without directly relating them to the question. To reach level 3 (6–8 marks) you must identify at least three aims and policies backed up by appropriately selected knowledge. Begin each paragraph with the aim and then explain fully the aim and policy. If possible, make links between each aim/paragraph. For the highest level, level 4 (9–10 marks), you will need to do the same as level 3 but structure your answer with a relevant introduction and conclusion in which you could try to link all the policies mentioned to Bismarck's aim of isolating France.

Ideas for your answer Here are some aims and policies you could discuss.

1 The war scare of 1875. Here Bismarck's aim was to warn off the French who had recovered very quickly from the defeat of 1871. Bismarck used a newspaper article to threaten a preventative war.
2 The Dreikaiserbund set up in 1873 and revived in 1881 as a means of keeping France isolated by allying with both Austria–Hungary and Russia.
3 The Congress of Berlin, 1878. Here Bismarck tried to act as the honest broker in order to prevent rivalry between Austria–Hungary and Russia and to prevent the Russians from allying with France.
4 These could be linked in with the basic aim of Bismarck's foreign policy, which was to isolate the French through his alliance system. You will need to explain the impact of the Treaty of Frankfurt of 1871, the French loss of Alsace–Lorraine and the desire for revenge.

ii) In what ways did France try to develop a system of defensive alliances in the years 1894–1914? You may use the following information to help you with your answer:

- 1890s improved relations with Russia
- 1900s improved relations with Britain
- 1905 and 1911 Moroccan Crises
- 1907 Triple Entente.

(15 marks)

What is required? This is a question about change. You will need to identify and explain at least the four major changes in French policy during the period mentioned in the question. If your explanation is relevant and precise this would be enough for level 3 (9–12 marks). For a top-level answer (13–15 marks) you would need to ensure that your whole answer relates to change and has an introduction and a conclusion that sums up the main pattern of change during the given period. Draw a table like the one on page 32 and use it as a check-list to plan your answer. Remember, change means a key turning point.

Ideas for your answer   Complete the table and use this as a basis for your answer. One section has been done for you.

Change	Cause	Nature	Scope
Relations with Russia	Isolation and Russian need for loan	Alliance which brought much closer relations	Major shift in French policy and end of isolation
Relations with Britain			
Moroccan Crises			
Triple Entente of 1907			

Now write your answer. Remember:

1 an introduction setting the scene for your answer by identifying the main areas of change

2 a paragraph on each change – try to link one change to the next; for example, closer relations with Britain in 1904 led to British support during the two Moroccan Crises

3 an explanation of at least one other change not mentioned in the question; for example, military talks with Britain 1906–14

4 a conclusion in which you summarise the main points and pick out the major change or trend in French foreign policy in this period.

Practice questions

Now have a go at the following questions without any guidance. Remember to bear in mind how many marks each question is worth before deciding on the length of your answer.

a) i)   Give ONE reason why Russia and France signed the Dual Alliance of 1894.   *(3 marks)*

ii)   Describe the key features of the Agadir Crisis of 1911.   *(5 marks)*

iii)   Why was there a crisis over Bosnia in 1908?   *(5 marks)*

iv)   Why was there naval rivalry between Britain and Germany in the period 1900–14?   *(7 marks)*

b) i)   Explain the main features of the Franco-Prussian War of 1870–71.   *(10 marks)*

ii)   Describe the changes that took place in the Balkans as a result of the crises between 1875 and 1913. You may use the following information to help you with your answer:
- the crisis of 1875–78
- the Bulgarian Crises 1885–86
- Austro-Serbian rivalry and the Bosnian Crisis 1908–09
- the Balkan Wars 1912–13.   *(15 marks)*

Summary and revision plan

Below is a list of headings which you may find helpful. Use this as a check-list to make sure that you are familiar with the material featured in this chapter. Record your key words alongside each heading.

A The Franco-Prussian War, 1870–71: its effects on France and Germany
- ❏ Causes of the war
- ❏ The events of the war
- ❏ Reasons for Prussian victory
- ❏ The Treaty of Frankfurt, January 1871
- ❏ Results of the war

B The expansion of the German empire, 1871–1914
- ❏ Bismarck's aims
- ❏ Bismarck's policies, 1871–90
- ❏ The aims of Kaiser William II
- ❏ William's policies, 1890–1914

C International rivalries and alliances, 1873–1914
- ❏ Rivalries between the Great Powers
- ❏ The Scramble for Africa
- ❏ The alliance system
- ❏ The arms race

D The changing balance of power in the Balkans, 1876–1914
- ❏ The interests of the Great Powers
- ❏ The Balkan Crisis, 1875–78
- ❏ The Bulgarian Crisis, 1885–86
- ❏ Austro-Serbian rivalry

E The Moroccan Crises, 1905–11
- ❏ Crisis, 1905–06
- ❏ The second Moroccan or Agadir Crisis, 1911

F The Balkan Crises, 1908–14
- ❏ The Bosnian Crisis, 1908–09
- ❏ The Balkan Wars, 1912–13
- ❏ The assassination of Franz-Ferdinand

G The development of rivalry between Britain and Germany, 1890–1914
- ❏ The role of Kaiser William II
- ❏ Anglo-German naval rivalry
- ❏ Other causes of rivalry
- ❏ Why did Britain go to war in 1914?

The Rise and Fall of the Communist State: the Soviet Union, 1928–91

The communist government set up by Lenin survived until 1991. During this period the government of the Soviet Union was dominated by four leading figures: Stalin, Khrushchev, Brezhnev and Gorbachev.

To answer questions on the Soviet Union 1928–91 you will need to be familiar with both the key content and key themes of the period.

Key content

You will need to show that you have a good working knowledge of these key areas:

A The nature of Stalin's dictatorship
B Changes in industry and agriculture and their impact; the changing role of women
C Khrushchev's rise to power and de-Stalinisation
D Khrushchev's attempts at modernisation and growing unpopularity
E The rule of Brezhnev, 1964–82
F Gorbachev's reforms
G The decline and fall of Gorbachev and the communist state

Key themes

As with all examination questions, you will not be asked simply to learn this content and write it out again. You will need to show your understanding of some key themes from the period. These are:

● How did Stalin establish his dictatorship in the 1930s?
● Why did Stalin carry out the purges of the 1930s and what effects did they have?
● What motives did he have for industrialisation and collectivisation? Did they benefit the USSR?
● Why was Khrushchev able to achieve power by 1957 and how did he attempt to reform the Soviet Union?
● What was de-Stalinisation?
● What changes occurred under Brezhnev?
● Why and with what results did Gorbachev try to modernise the Soviet Union?
● Why did the Soviet Union break up and Gorbachev resign?

For example, look at the questions below which are adapted from Specimen Paper 1 by permission of Edexcel.

a) i) Give ONE reason to explain why Stalin introduced the show trials in the 1930s.

(3 marks)

This question is asking you to show knowledge and understanding of the topic.

ii) Describe the key features of the cult of personality. *(5 marks)*

You will need to explain the meaning of the cult of personality and describe the main methods used to create this cult.

iii) In what ways did Stalin control education and religion in the years 1928–45? *(5 marks)*

For this question you will need to know the methods Stalin used to control education, his anti-religious propaganda and changes after 1941.

iv) What were the effects of the purges on the Soviet Union in the years to 1941? *(7 marks)*

If you look carefully at this question you will see that you have to know about these important effects:

· short-term effects on people, party and army leaders
· more long-term effects on Stalin's control, the economy and the Soviet Union during the Second World War.

b) i) Why was there so much opposition to collectivisation in the 1930s? *(10 marks)*

We will look at this question in more detail at the end of the chapter.

ii) In what ways was the Soviet Union and the lives of its people changed by the Five Year Plans in the years 1928–41?
You may use the following information to help you with your answer:

- modernisation of industry
- control of the workforce
- growth of heavy industry
- production of consumer goods. *(15 marks)*

We will look at this question in more detail at the end of the chapter.

A The nature of Stalin's dictatorship

Stalin had established a dictatorship by the end of the 1930s. This was achieved by the following means.

1 The cult of personality

Stalin expected love and worship, not just respect and obedience. He made sure everyone knew about his successes.

- Huge rallies were held in his honour.
- Many photographs were published showing him meeting children and ordinary workers.
- Soviet artists produced paintings showing Stalin opening factories.
- The Soviet people were told that he could do no wrong. He was described as a superman, a genius at everything.
- Stalin rewrote the history of Russia and the USSR in a way that indicated he was much more important than he really had been before he came to power.

2 Education

Education was the key to ensuring that the whole population became communist and accepted Stalin's dictatorship. Stalin sought to control what people were taught.

- Teachers and professors who were considered not to be teaching in the way the Communist Party wanted were arrested.
- Children were taught that Stalin was the 'Great Leader'.
- Education became stricter because Stalin wanted schools to produce useful citizens. He insisted on uniforms, tests and examinations and prescribed the subjects and information that children should learn.

3 Religion

Stalin continued the attack on religion started after the Bolshevik Revolution.

- Christian leaders were imprisoned and churches closed down.
- Muslim mosques and schools were closed and pilgrimages to Mecca banned.
- This persecution eased between 1941 and 1945 as Stalin tried to keep the support of all religions and nationalities in the USSR during the struggle against Nazi Germany. He allowed religious worship and teaching again and restored the Church to its former position. Some churches were reopened and some bishops restored to office.

4 The purges

Radical policies like Stalin's were bound to cause concern. Criticism within the party grew because of the human cost of Stalin's policies.

In 1934 Stalin's ally Sergei Kirov was murdered. Stalin saw this as evidence of a conspiracy and began a series of political purges (imprisonment and execution).

Historians are now fairly sure that Stalin planned Kirov's murder to give him an excuse to purge the USSR of opponents, whom Stalin saw as traitors to himself and the USSR. From 1934 to 1938 thousands were arrested, imprisoned, murdered or simply disappeared. They came from all areas of Soviet life.

- The Communist Party: the number of party members fell from 3.5 million in 1934 to 2 million in 1935.

- Leading party members such as Zinoviev, Kamenev and Bukharin were tortured and their families threatened. Then at show trials, they 'confessed' and were executed. These show trials against political opponents were publicly and elaborately staged. They were used to create an atmosphere of fear and a sense that there were enemies and spies everywhere.
- Many less important opponents (or even supporters who were not enthusiastic enough) were arrested and executed or sent to labour camps.
- In 1937 around 25,000 army officers (including the Commander of the Red Army, Marshal Tukhachevsky) were purged.

The effects of the purges were mixed. Stalin was certainly secure. His new secret police (the NKVD) ruled the population with terror. Over 8 million had been killed or sent to labour camps.

However, Stalin had weakened the USSR. Many of those purged had been skilled or educated (for example, managers, army officers) and industrial progress slowed down. The army was seriously weakened and suffered badly against the Germans in 1941.

The Constitution

Stalin made himself more secure still in 1936 with the USSR's new constitution. At first sight it seemed more democratic – all citizens voted for members of the Supreme Soviet. However, it had no real power and decisions were still made by Stalin and his closest supporters.

5 The culture of Stalin's USSR

Stalin's USSR was disciplined and seemingly full of fear. Some real advances in industry were made, but at a cost:

- Freedom of speech was denied to Soviet citizens.
- Education improved basic standards for most Russians, but it was heavily controlled by the NKVD.

> **Source 1** Nadezhda Mandelstam, a Russian writer
> *She showed us her school textbooks where the portraits of party leaders had thick pieces of paper pasted over them as one by one they fell into disgrace – this the children had to do on instructions from their teacher . . . With every new arrest, people went through their books and burned the works of disgraced leaders in their stoves.*

- Artists, writers, musicians and performers had to please Stalin with their work, get out of the USSR or face being purged. Posters, radio broadcasts and the press all constantly pressed home the need for loyalty to the party and to Stalin. However, Lenin's ideals of a classless society did not seem to match the realities. High-ranking party officials and the military seemed to enjoy a much higher standard of living than most Soviet citizens.

6 The gulags

This was the name given to the labour camps which were set up in the worst areas of the USSR such as Siberia.

- Prisoners were made to work in terrible conditions and as many as 12 million died due to the cold and harsh treatment.
- Stalin also used the labour camps to provide labour for unpleasant or dangerous projects in areas where ordinary workers did not want to go.

● *Stalin was able to achieve his dictatorship by a variety of methods. Most textbooks stress his use of fear and terror through the purges of the 1930s. Stalin also made effective use of propaganda, especially the 'cult of personality', to ensure long-term support for his policies.* ●

● Revision tasks

1 What was meant by the cult of personality under Stalin?
2 Using key words explain Stalin's policies towards education and religion.
3 Copy and complete the summary table below on the purges using key words.

Reasons for purges	Short-term effects	Long-term effects

4 List three ways in which freedom was restricted in Stalin's USSR.

B Changes in industry and agriculture and their impact; the changing role of women

Stalin believed that the USSR was under threat from non-communist states. He also believed that the only way for the USSR to make itself secure was to become a modern, industrial country. His aim was to force the USSR to make 50 years' progress in 10 years. There were two key aspects of Stalin's plans:

- the need to expand heavy industry (Five Year Plans)
- the need to improve food production (COLLECTIVISATION).

1 The Five Year Plans

Stalin seems to have had several clear reasons for industrialising the USSR:

- security
- to create a showpiece of success for the outside world
- to carry out his idea of 'SOCIALISM in one country'.

In order to achieve his aims he came up with two Five Year Plans for the development of the USSR. The Five Year Plans were incredibly ambitious targets for industrial production which had to be achieved in five years.

Few targets were met (see page 39) but even so industries made huge advances.

From 1928 Stalin set about creating a command economy, in which each factory and industrial works was set targets by Gosplan, which was based in Moscow. Specially trained workers in Shock Brigades showed how new ideas could be put into practice.

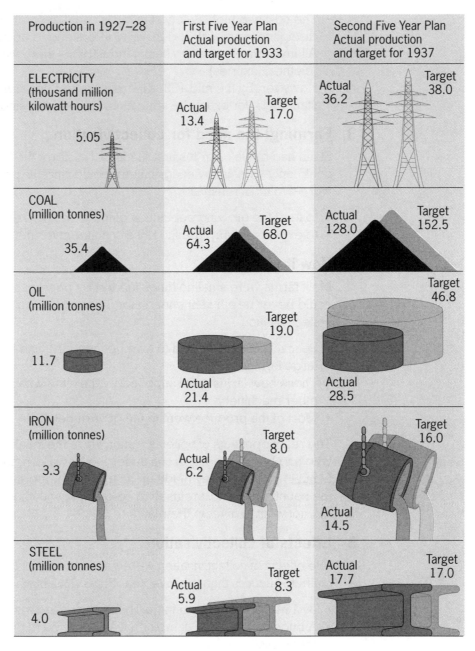

Production in 1927–28	First Five Year Plan Actual production and target for 1933	Second Five Year Plan Actual production and target for 1937
ELECTRICITY (thousand million kilowatt hours) 5.05	Actual 13.4 — Target 17.0	Actual 36.2 — Target 38.0
COAL (million tonnes) 35.4	Actual 64.3 — Target 68.0	Actual 128.0 — Target 152.5
OIL (million tonnes) 11.7	Target 19.0 — Actual 21.4	Target 46.8 — Actual 28.5
IRON (million tonnes) 3.3	Actual 6.2 — Target 8.0	Target 16.0 — Actual 14.5
STEEL (million tonnes) 4.0	Actual 5.9 — Target 8.3	Actual 17.7 — Target 17.0

Targets and actual production for the Five Year Plans

2 Effects of the Five Year Plans

Historians disagree about the aims and the effects of the Five Year Plans. One thing on which all historians do agree is that the USSR was transformed.

- The main aim was achieved – by 1940 the USSR was in the 'first division' of industrial powers, along with Britain, Germany and the USA.
- Vast projects like the Belomor Canal, the Dnieper Dam, and the metalworks at Magnitogorsk were completed with amazing speed.
- Huge towns and factories were built from nothing, deep inside the USSR to protect them from invasion.
- Foreign technicians were brought in and enormous investment was put into education and training to produce skilled workers.
- Great pressure was put on workers to meet targets and to be 'Stakhanovites'. Stakhanov was a miner who managed to produce over 100 tons of coal in one shift, and was held up as a model to inspire all workers.

- The cost was high. Safety standards came second to meeting targets, discipline was harsh and many workers ended up in labour camps (gulags). All investment went into heavy industries – there were few consumer goods (clothes, luxuries).
- However, by the mid 1930s there were definite signs of improved living standards (for example, education, welfare, housing).

3 Farming: the need for collectivisation

Stalin had made clear his ambitions to transform the USSR. The Five Year Plans could only work if Soviet agriculture could raise its production massively. There were two main reasons:

- to feed the growing population of industrial workers
- to export any surpluses to raise cash for investment in industry.

4 How it worked

Most farms were smallholdings tended by peasant families. These holdings could never be efficient enough for Stalin's plans so he introduced the policy of collectivisation.

- Peasants effectively had to give up their land and join other families on very large farms.
- These new farms were supplied by the state with seed, tools, tractors and other machinery.
- Most of the produce went to the government.

The real opponents of collectivisation were the kulaks. Kulaks were peasants who had become prosperous under the New Economic Policy introduced by Lenin in 1921 and they made up a large and important part of the population of the countryside. Most refused to co-operate with the new policy, because they did not want to give up their land.

5 Effects of collectivisation

The effects of collectivisation were very mixed, but this policy certainly had less claim to success than the Five Year Plans. This is what happened:

- By 1941 almost all land in the USSR was collectivised.
- A huge propaganda campaign was launched to persuade peasants to modernise.
- Kulaks were murdered or sent to labour camps – many killed their animals or burnt their crops rather than let the government have them.
- Much of the countryside was devastated by struggles between Stalin's agents and the kulaks.
- Although collectivisation was achieved, food production fell dramatically. In the Ukraine there was famine in the early 1930s and yet at the same time food was being exported.

The long-term result of this struggle was that the peasants were battered into submission and never again seriously threatened the communist regime.

● *Most Western historians have criticised Stalin's economic policies, especially the human cost. They stressed the purge of the kulak class, the famine of 1932–33 and the suffering of the workers in industry, especially in new towns such as Magnitogorsk. Some have now begun to stress the more long-term achievements of both collectivisation and the Five Year Plans. Stalin created an economy which enabled the Soviet Union to survive the German invasion of 1941 and eventually defeat the Nazis.* ●

6 The position of women

For the first time in the Soviet Union, women achieved some form of equality.

- The Five Year Plans needed all the workers they could get. Factories were provided with nurseries so that women with young children could go to work. Some 80 per cent of new workers in the second Five Year Plan were women. In 1928, 28 per cent of industrial workers were women; and by 1937 it was 40 per cent.
- Women began to attend university and many of the new doctors trained in the Soviet Union were women.
- Women were also needed to replace the many people, mainly men, who disappeared during the purges.

● *Revision tasks*

1 Draw a table like the one below and use the information and evidence in this section to complete it.

	Five Year Plans	Collectivisation
Aims		
Methods		
Successes/failures		
Costs		

2 Using a few key words, explain how the position of women changed under Stalin.

C Khrushchev's rise to power and de-Stalinisation

1 Why did Khrushchev emerge as the new leader?

Stalin's successor was expected to be Georgi Malenkov. When Stalin died Malenkov became prime minister and party secretary. He was soon persuaded to give up one post and chose to be prime minister. Khrushchev was made party secretary. From 1953 the Soviet Union was governed by a committee but by 1956 it was clear that Khrushchev was the main man in power.

- A possible rival, Lavrenti Beria, who was hated by all the other leaders, was arrested and shot in December 1953.
- The post of party secretary gave Khrushchev control of the party machinery.
- He was able to isolate the other leaders by playing one off against the other.
- His part in the defence of Stalingrad during the war had won him the support of the army, and especially of Marshal Zhukov.
- He promised reforms, especially improvements in the standard of living.
- His attack on Stalin in 1956 won him much support in his bid for the leadership. He seemed a completely different character from Stalin.

2 De-Stalinisation

In February 1956 Khrushchev attacked Stalin in the so-called 'Secret Speech', made to a closed session at the Twentieth Party Congress. He attacked Stalin's cult of personality, his dictatorial methods, the purges of the 1930s and his mistakes during the Second World War. Khrushchev made the speech because:

- it gave him an advantage over his rivals for the leadership
- it would clear the way for him to carry out economic reforms
- it enabled him to distance himself from Stalin's dictatorship. He had been a key figure in Stalin's regime and had carried out purges in the Ukraine.

The speech led to the de-Stalinisation of the USSR.

- Statues and pictures of Stalin were removed.
- Stalingrad was renamed Volgograd. Other places and streets were also renamed.
- The size and power of the secret police were reduced, and the death penalty was abolished.
- Millions of political prisoners were released from the labour camps. Many party members who had been expelled under Stalin were reinstated.
- Freedom of expression was increased a little. Some writers who had been banned under Stalin were permitted to publish again, especially if they criticised Stalin. The party, however, continued to control what they published.
- Some performers were allowed to travel abroad to give shows.
- National minority languages were allowed to develop again, but every citizen had to become fluent in Russian as well.

3   Results of de-Stalinisation

De-Stalinisation did cause problems for Khrushchev.

- Abroad it was misunderstood and encouraged unrest in Hungary and Poland.
- It encouraged criticism of the Soviet government. Therefore in 1961 the death penalty was reintroduced and 10,000 churches were closed down.
- Khrushchev got rid of all his leading opponents, with the exception of Bulganin. In 1957 Malenkov, Molotov and Kaganovich were dismissed.

● *Revision tasks*

1 Using a few key words, give three reasons why Khrushchev was able to achieve control of the Soviet Union by 1956.
2 Copy the summary table below on de-Stalinisation and use key words to complete it.

Khrushchev's motives	Features of de-Stalinisation	Effects

D Khrushchev's attempts at modernisation and growing unpopularity

Khrushchev decided on reform to modernise agriculture and industry in order to produce more food and consumer goods. He believed there was far too much central control of the economy and wanted to encourage local initiative.

1   Reforms in agriculture

He introduced three main policies:

- He amalgamated collective farms into gigantic units, like farm cities. He also cancelled all the debts of collective farms and closed the motor tractor stations.
- Maize was introduced as animal fodder at many farms to allow wheat to be used for human consumption.
- He also introduced the Virgin Lands Scheme whereby large areas of Kazakhstan, Western Siberia and the Urals were ploughed up in order to provide more food for the towns.

His agricultural policies were not a success:

- Khrushchev believed he was an expert on agriculture and interfered too much. He would not allow the new amalgamated farms to use much initiative. Most were controlled by Communist Party officials who knew little of agriculture.
- Maize was planted in unsuitable areas and did not grow.
- There was not enough use of fertilisers and pesticides.
- The Virgin Lands Scheme failed badly. The topsoil was left unprotected and millions of tonnes of it was stripped away by the wind, especially in Kazakhstan.
- Much of the wheat was sown in areas which were unsuitable.
- The result was a shortage of food and food riots took place in some areas. Food rationing eventually had to be introduced.

2 Industry

Khrushchev also tried to modernise industry.

- A seven-hour working day was introduced and workers were allowed to change their jobs. Pensions and other social welfare benefits were greatly increased.
- Large-scale building work was undertaken to provide more houses and to build spectacular public buildings.
- Regional economic councils, called *sovnarkhozy*, were set up to control industrial production in their area.

These reforms did not work.

- Khrushchev would not allow the regional councils to use the chance of making profits as an incentive to increase productivity. The managers had been used to strict central control and did not believe they could make decisions.
- From 1956 he spent far too much on the space programme. Production of consumer goods suffered. In 1962 there were strikes and demonstrations against price rises.

3 Khrushchev's resignation

In October 1964 Khrushchev resigned. He was called back from holiday to be told that neither the government nor the Central Committee had confidence in him. This was due to the following factors:

- He had failed to keep his promises. There were still food shortages and rising prices.
- Many old Stalinists disliked his policy of de-Stalinisation.
- Others thought his behaviour was wrong; for example, at the United Nations in 1960 he took off his shoe and banged the table to get attention.
- The main reason was that he had been forced to back down to Kennedy over the Cuban missile crisis.

● *Revision tasks*

1 Copy and complete the table below using a few key words.

	Khrushchev's main policies	Successes	Failures
Agriculture			
Industry			

2 List the main reasons why Khrushchev was forced to resign in 1964.

E The rule of Brezhnev, 1964–82

1 Lack of progress

Leonid Brezhnev was the opposite of Khrushchev. He was not interested in reform and, like other party members, had become alarmed at the changes brought about by Khrushchev. Brezhnev was far more interested in foreign policy. He reversed much of what Khrushchev had done and the Soviet Union made little or no progress during this period. Brezhnev suffered a stroke in 1976 which left him an invalid for the next six years.

- Brezhnev clamped down on any criticisms of the government and party. Writers and intellectuals were arrested and some were put on trial.
- The powers of the KGB, the secret police, were increased. It was placed under the control of Yuri Andropov.
- Corruption increased, with Brezhnev's own daughter heavily involved. Andropov tried to reduce corruption but was unable to do anything against her until after Brezhnev's death.
- The black market flourished due to the shortages of consumer goods such as cars and televisions.
- Far too much Soviet spending went on the space programme, the arms race and helping other communist countries such as Cuba. The Soviet invasion of Afghanistan increased this spending and proved unpopular with many Soviet citizens.
- The Soviet economy could not cope with the strains imposed by such spending. The USSR needed to sell goods abroad to finance its foreign policy. All it could sell was grain and yet it could not produce enough for its own people.
- Brezhnev refused to allow the various national minorities in the Soviet Union to develop their own culture and language, especially in the Ukraine. There were riots in Georgia.

2 The Soviet Union, 1982–85

Brezhnev died in 1982. He was succeeded by Andropov, who died of kidney disease in February 1984. The next leader, Konstantin Chernenko, was already seriously ill when he came to power and died in March 1985. Both leaders continued Brezhnev's cautious policies and the Soviet Union continued to stagnate.

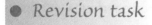 *Revision task*

1 Why did the Soviet Union stagnate under Brezhnev's leadership in the period 1964–82? (Use six to eight key words to summarise your main points.)

F Gorbachev's reforms

Mikhail Gorbachev succeeded Chernenko as leader of the Soviet Union in 1985. He was determined to bring about major reforms before it was too late. The twin themes of his policies were *perestroika* and *glasnost*. He did not want to end communist control of the Soviet Union.

1 *Perestroika*

This means 'restructuring'. Gorbachev was convinced that central control of the economy was not working. He wanted to end state monopolies, and encourage competition and some free enterprise.

* Prices were no longer subsidised by the state.
* Workers were allowed to set up co-operatives and small family businesses were encouraged.

2 *Glasnost*

This meant 'openness' both within the Soviet Union and with the West. Gorbachev realised that to revive the economy he needed to encourage foreign investment and reduce Soviet spending on arms and foreign policy.

* He allowed more freedom of expression in the media. Thought control was abandoned and dissidents were no longer locked up in mental hospitals. In 1986 the leading dissident Dr Andrei Sakharov was released from internal exile.
* The political system was reorganised with the introduction of free elections for local government.
* The powers of the KGB were restricted and it was later abolished. Its records were made public. The Lubianka prison that housed KGB prisoners was closed.

3 Why did attempts at reform fail?

Gorbachev's reforms did not solve the problems of the Soviet Union.

* The problems of the economy were too great. When he took over, most state enterprises were running at a loss with the black market accounting for as much as 30 per cent of the output of Soviet industry. In the 1980s the annual budget deficit was running at 35,000 million roubles.
* Gorbachev introduced his plans hastily and was impatient for change.
* The Soviet people were used to being told what to do. They had no experience of democracy and freedom and could not cope with it.
* Many traditional party members were alarmed at his reforms.
* Gorbachev had hoped for much help and large-scale investment from the West in return for arms limitation. The West gave little help.

● *Gorbachev tried to ensure the survival of communism in the Soviet Union and eastern Europe through his policies of* glasnost *and* perestroika. *However, his reforms had the opposite effect. They brought an end to Communist Party rule in the countries of eastern Europe and the break-up of the Soviet Union. Gorbachev had tried to do too much too quickly.* ●

● *Revision tasks*

1 Copy and complete the following chart using key words for each column.

	Meaning	**Main features**
Perestroika		
Glasnost		

2 List three reasons why Gorbachev's policies did not work.

G The decline and fall of Gorbachev and the communist state

Gorbachev's reforms brought a wave of criticisms and unrest which eventually brought his downfall and an end to the Soviet Union.

1 The break-up of the Soviet Union

- *Glasnost* simply encouraged greater criticism and a demand for even more change.
- *Perestroika* did not revive the economy nor improve living standards. Shortages continued and Gorbachev was booed in the streets of Moscow. The ailing economy seemed to be getting worse. More and more people grew tired of communism, of few consumer goods and food shortages.
- The Chernobyl disaster of 1986, in which a nuclear reactor caught fire, releasing high levels of radioactive emissions across the Soviet Union and Scandinavia, was a great embarrassment to the government. It highlighted how out of date the Soviet economy was.
- *Glasnost* also encouraged unrest in the republics making up the Soviet Union. They wanted to run their own affairs. They were further encouraged by events in 1989 when the countries of eastern Europe threw off communism.

Independent states formed following the break-up of the Soviet Union

The Baltic states of Lithuania, Estonia and Latvia were the first to demand more freedom. In 1989 Gorbachev was forced to withdraw Soviet troops from these states. In 1991 they declared their independence from the Soviet Union, followed soon after by the other republics. They agreed to join the Commonwealth of Independent States (CIS). This meant that the Soviet Union had now been replaced by a group of independent nations.

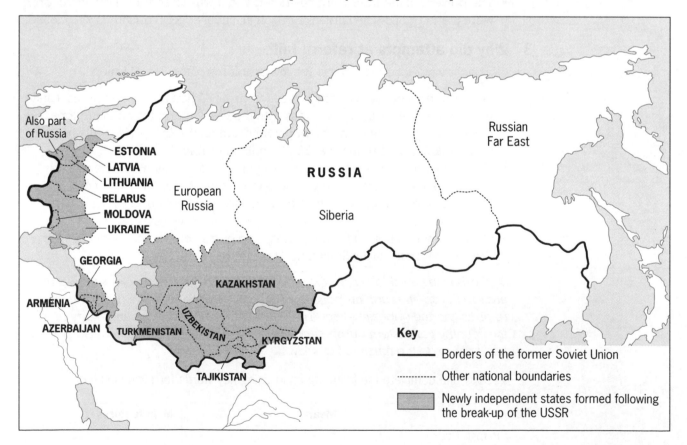

2   The end of Gorbachev's rule

Gorbachev's reforms had brought opposition from both sides in the Soviet Union.

- Party hard-liners had been alarmed by the nature and pace of his reforms.
- When he tried to stop criticism of his changes in 1990, he lost the support of reformers such as Edward Shevardnadze, who resigned as foreign secretary.
- He also faced opposition from the more RADICAL Boris Yeltsin, who criticised him for the economic crisis in the Soviet Union. He called for Gorbachev's resignation. Yeltsin became even more powerful when he was elected President of Russia in June 1990.

In August 1991 Gorbachev was placed under house arrest by party hard-liners as tanks rolled on to the streets of Moscow. Gorbachev was saved by the bravery of Yeltsin who stood on one of the tanks and dared the troops to mutiny. He was supported by the workers of Moscow. After three days the tanks left and the *coup* had failed.

Although Gorbachev was reinstated as leader he had little power and support.

- Yeltsin was the real hero and held the power.
- Some of Gorbachev's closest advisers had been involved in the *coup*.
- Gorbachev totally lost face when the Baltic states declared their independence from the Soviet Union.

Gorbachev resigned in December 1991.

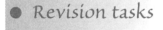 *Revision tasks*

1 Make a timeline for the key events of 1986–1991 which brought an end to the Soviet Union. You could start with the Chernobyl disaster of 1986 and end with Gorbachev's resignation in December 1991.
2 Was Gorbachev's resignation due only to the popularity of Boris Yeltsin? Make a note of your answer.

Revision session

The aim of this session is for you to apply your knowledge of the content of this chapter to the kind of questions you will face in your exams.

Examination questions

Examination questions on this topic appear on Paper 1. In the following examples we will look at questions adapted by permission of Edexcel from the Specimen Paper.

---

a) i) Give ONE reason to explain why Stalin introduced the show trials in the 1930s. *(3 marks)*

What is required? This is a simple test of your knowledge and memory. A simple factual answer will do. It is only worth three marks. Keep your answer brief – a maximum of two sentences.

Ideas for your answer You could write about Stalin's paranoia and his use of the trials to justify the purges.

---

ii) Describe the key features of the cult of personality. *(5 marks)*

What is required? This question is asking you to identify and describe at least two important features. Identify the feature and then describe it as precisely as possible. Try to make links between the two key features you describe.

Ideas for your answer You could describe the following two key features:

1 use of pictures and posters and re-naming of places
2 rewriting of history.

Try to make links between the two. What was the common aim of each feature?

---

iii) In what ways did Stalin control education and religion in the years 1928–45? *(5 marks)*

What is required? This question is asking you to identify and describe at least two important features, one on education and the other on religion. Identify the feature and then describe it as precisely as possible. Try to make links between the two key features you describe.

Ideas for your answer You could describe two of the following key features:

1 methods of control in education
2 persecution of religion before 1941
3 easier attitude to religion 1941–45.

What links are there between control of education and control of religion? (Clue: dictatorship.)

---

iv) What were the effects of the purges on the Soviet Union in the years to 1941? *(7 marks)*

What is required? This question is asking you to explain the consequences of Stalin's purges. Simple and brief statements of consequence will score one or two marks. An example of this type of answer would be simply listing consequences without explaining them; for example, 'many party members were removed'.

To aim for the next level (3–5 marks) you will need to explain fully at least three consequences. Give the consequence and then give a developed explanation. To achieve the highest level (6–7 marks) your answer will have to be more analytical. For example, you might distinguish clearly between immediate and more long-term consequences.

Ideas for your answer

1 More short-term effects you could discuss include:

- the impact on the party, especially the removal of the old Bolsheviks
- the wider consequences for the people of the Soviet Union – fear and the numbers arrested and sent to labour camps
- the impact on the army 1937–41 – who was purged.

2 More long-term effects could include:

- the establishment of Stalin's dictatorship by the removal of rivals
- the disastrous impact on the army shown by the early success of Hitler's invasion in 1941
- the effect on Soviet industry of the loss of so many technicians and skilled workers.

b) i) Why was there so much opposition to collectivisation in the 1930s? *(10 marks)*

What is required?

This question is about causation. You will need to identify at least three major reasons for opposition to collectivisation. If your explanation is relevant and precise this would be enough for level 3 (6–8 marks). For a top-level answer (9–10 marks) you will need to ensure that your whole answer relates to causation. You will also have to include an introduction that discusses the meaning of the question and how you will tackle it and a conclusion that sums up and possibly links the main reasons for opposition.

For your introduction, think about the following:

- What is the question asking?
- Which causes will I discuss?

Draw a table like the one below and use it as a check-list to plan your answer.

The causes	What is the cause?	Explain the cause	Link to next cause
First cause	Attitude of kulaks	Resented loss of land and status and opposed collectivisation	Even poorer peasants not keen on pooling land and resources
Second cause			
Third cause			

For your conclusion, think about the following:

- What were the key causes of opposition?
- Which do you think was the most important and why?

Ideas for your answer

You could explain the following reasons:

1 The attitude of the kulaks – why did they oppose collectivisation and what happened to them?
2 Members of the Communist Party – why were some against collectivisation?
3 Other peasants – why did they resent and oppose collectivisation?
4 General opposition – those who believed the USSR was regressing, that collectivisation was not working.

For your conclusion you can link the opposition of the kulaks and peasants to the general opposition.

ii) In what ways was the Soviet Union and the lives of its people changed by the Five Year Plans in the years 1928–41?

You may use the following information to help you with your answer:

- modernisation of industry
- control of the workforce
- growth of heavy industry
- production of consumer goods.

(15 marks)

What is required?

This is a question about change. A change means a key turning point. In other words, for each change you are comparing what went before the event, in this case the Five Year Plans, with what followed. You will need to identify and explain at least the four major changes in the Soviet Union during the period mentioned in the question. If your explanation of each is relevant and precise and you can link some of the changes this would be enough for level 3 (9–12 marks). For a top-level answer you will need to do this and ensure that:

- your whole answer focuses on changes to the Soviet Union and its people brought about by the Five Year Plans
- you write an introduction that explains the meaning of the question and the key changes you intend to discuss
- you write a conclusion that sums up the changes and gives a balanced judgement. You could discuss whether overall the changes were for the better or worse, and/or contrast the immediate changes with more long-term changes
- you write about the four changes mentioned in the question and, if possible, add one or two of your own.

Ideas for your answer

Some of the changes or key turning points in the Soviet Union during this period as a result of the Five Year Plans were:

1 modernisation of industry – here you could compare methods of production before and after the Plans

2 control of the workforce – explain the increased state control of the workforce including the use of forced labour and restrictions on the freedom of movement

3 the growth of heavy industry – compare production before and after each of the Plans and discuss the impact of the Plans on the production of machinery, tractors and machine tools

4 the production of consumer goods – explain why this was not a priority and the limited achievement.

Further changes you could write about include:

5 changes in the role of women – again, compare the role of women before the introduction of the Plans and the need for female workers due to the demands of industrialisation after the Plans were introduced.

6 the impact of the Stakhanovite movement

7 links between the Stakhanovite movement and increased production

8 living conditions – explain the problems of housing and living conditions in the new industrial centres, and the better welfare and educational opportunities.

For your conclusion you could contrast the more unfortunate short-term changes, such as the poor living conditions in the new industrial centres, with the long-term benefits including the strong position of Soviet heavy industry by 1941, which enabled the Soviet Union to sustain the war against Germany.

Practice questions

Now have a go at the following questions without any guidance. Remember to look at the number of marks for a question before deciding how much time you spend answering it and the length of your answer.

a) **i)** Give ONE reason why Khrushchev became leader of Russia by 1956. *(3 marks)*

    ii) Describe the key features of de-Stalinisation. *(5 marks)*

    iii) In what ways did Khrushchev change industry and agriculture in the period 1956–64? *(5 marks)*

    iv) What were the effects of Brezhnev's policies on the Soviet Union in the period 1964–82? *(7 marks)*

b) **i)** Why did Gorbachev introduce his policies of *glasnost* and *perestroika* in the Soviet Union in the 1980s?
(10 marks)

    ii) In what ways were the Soviet Union and the lives of its people changed by the policies of Gorbachev in the period 1985–91?
You may use the following headings to help you with your answer:

- economic problems
- over-spending
- need to restructure economy
- need to encourage foreign investment. *(15 marks)*

Summary and revision plan

Below is a list of headings which you may find helpful. Use this as a check-list to make sure that you are familiar with the material featured in this chapter. Record your key words alongside each heading.

A The nature of Stalin's dictatorship
- ❏ The cult of personality
- ❏ Education
- ❏ Religion
- ❏ The purges
- ❏ The culture of Stalin's USSR
- ❏ The gulags

B Changes in industry and agriculture and their impact; the changing role of women
- ❏ The Five Year Plans
- ❏ Effects of the Five Year Plans
- ❏ Farming: the need for collectivisation
- ❏ How it worked
- ❏ Effects of collectivisation
- ❏ The position of women

C Khrushchev's rise to power and de-Stalinisation
- ❏ Why did Khrushchev emerge as the new leader?
- ❏ De-Stalinisation
- ❏ Results of de-Stalinisation

D Khrushchev's attempts at modernisation and growing unpopularity
- ❏ Reforms in agriculture
- ❏ Industry
- ❏ Khrushchev's resignation

E The rule of Brezhnev, 1964–82
- ❏ Lack of progress
- ❏ The Soviet Union, 1982–85

F Gorbachev's reforms
- ❏ *Perestroika*
- ❏ *Glasnost*
- ❏ Why did attempts at reform fail?

G The decline and fall of Gorbachev and the communist state
- ❏ The break-up of the Soviet Union
- ❏ The end of Gorbachev's rule

A Divided Union?
The USA, 1941–80

The Second World War greatly benefited the USA, which emerged as the leading economy of the world. There were, however, many tensions within US society during the war which later led to great unrest and upheaval, and in particular to the movements for civil rights. The USA was also greatly divided by McCarthyism and the fear of communism, and by the students' and women's movements of the 1960s.

To answer questions on 'A divided union?' you need to be familiar with the key content and key themes of the period.

Key content   You need to show that you have a good working knowledge of these key areas:

A The impact of the Second World War on the US economy and society
B McCarthyism and the Red Scare
C The growth of the civil rights movement in the 1950s
D The civil rights movement in the 1960s
E The achievements of Kennedy and Johnson
F The protest movements of the 1960s and early 1970s
G The Watergate scandal and its impact

Key themes   As with other topics you will be expected to do more than simply write out all the content you have learnt about the USA 1941–80. The questions you face will be asking you to show your understanding of these key themes from the period:

● Why did the US economy benefit so much from the war?
● What impact did the Second World War have on the lives of black Americans, Japanese immigrants and women?
● Why did McCarthyism emerge and what impact did it have on US society in the 1950s?
● What brought about the growth of the civil rights movements in the 1950s and 1960s?
● How important were the roles of Martin Luther King and Malcolm X?
● How successful were the civil rights movements by 1970?
● What were the aims of Kennedy and Johnson in their reforms of the 1960s and how far were they achieved?
● Why were there so many protest movements in the 1960s and what impact did they have on US society?
● Why was there a Watergate scandal and what impact did it have upon the presidency of Nixon and upon US society?

For example, look at the questions below which are adapted by permission of Edexcel from the Specimen Paper for Paper 1.

a) i) What was meant by 'New Frontier'? *(3 marks)*

> *The question is asking you to show knowledge and understanding of the topic.*

ii) Why did President Kennedy face problems in his attempts to improve civil rights in the years 1961–63? *(5 marks)*

> *For this question you will need to explain at least two reasons why Kennedy faced problems.*

iii) Why was President Johnson unable to build his 'Great Society' in the years 1963–68? *(5 marks)*

> *Again you will need to explain at least two reasons.*

iv) In what ways did President Johnson improve civil rights in the years 1963–68? *(7 marks)*

> *For this question you need to explain at least two important changes in the area of civil rights.*

b) i) Describe the main features of the Watergate scandal in the USA. *(10 marks)*

> *We will look at this question in more detail at the end of the chapter.*

ii) Why was the fear of communism so strong in the USA in the years 1945–54?
You may use the following information to help you with your answer:

- spread of communism
- Korean War 1950–53
- Hiss and Rosenberg cases
- McCarthyism. *(15 marks)*

> *We will look at this question in more detail at the end of the chapter.*

A The impact of the Second World War on the US economy and society

1 The impact on the economy

The Second World War greatly benefited the US economy.

- The achievements of the American war economy were staggering. Between 1941 and 1945, American factories produced 250,000 aircraft, 90,000 tanks, 350 naval destroyers, 200 submarines and 5600 merchant ships. By 1944 the USA was producing almost half the weapons being made in the world.
- American industry was also providing food, clothing, vehicles, rubber tyres, engines and engine parts, and countless other items.
- The war created 17 million new jobs and overtime was often available. With extra wages in their pockets, Americans were able to buy more goods and so boost demand which, in turn, created more jobs. The war effort ended unemployment.
- More than half a million new businesses started up during the war. Many people became rich as a result of war contracts.

- Even American farmers, after almost twenty years of depressed prices and economic crises, began to enjoy better times as the US exported food to help its allies.
- Ordinary Americans invested their income in bonds. They effectively lent money to the government by buying war bonds, on a promise that the war bonds would be paid back with interest. Ordinary Americans contributed $129 billion to the war effort.
- The War Production Board was set up in January 1942 to improve wartime production. The government became more involved in the lives of its citizens and employed about 4 million civilian workers by 1945.

2 The impact on women

In some respects the war had a positive effect on the position of women.

- Before the war there were 12 million working women. During the war 300,000 women joined the armed forces and another 7 million joined the workforce.
- Women were given many new tasks, such as flying all types of warplane in tests and delivery runs, and difficult welding jobs. One in three aircraft workers and one in two workers in the munitions and electronic industries were women.
- Many managers believed women did a better job than men and the image of women workers was boosted by a government poster campaign.
- The confidence gained meant that many continued to work after the war as secretaries, clerks and shop assistants.

There was, however, the negative side.

- Women workers were not always welcomed by their male colleagues or by trade unionists who felt that women were a threat to their jobs and to pay levels.
- Factories made little or no effort to provide childcare facilities.
- Women were refused equal pay to men in the armed forces.
- After the war most women left their wartime jobs. They had to, since they had been doing 'men's jobs'. Some resented the loss of the independence that their wage packet had given them.

● *Revision tasks*

1 Make a list of the benefits that the war brought to the US economy.
2 Draw a table like the one below on the impact of the Second World War on the position of women, and use key words to complete three entries under each heading.

Positive effects of the Second World War on women	Negative effects of the Second World War on women

3 Internment of Japanese-Americans

The US had a large Japanese immigrant population. The Japanese attack on Pearl Harbor aroused much anti-Japanese feeling which was further whipped up by official propaganda. In 1942, under General John de Witt, US security forces rounded up 110,000 Japanese-Americans living on the West Coast. It was a brutal policy:

- They were transported to bleak internment camps in remote areas of the USA and most were kept there until 1945.
- Many of them lost most of their property, or were forced to sell it at very low prices.

- There was no differentiation between people who were Issei (immigrants born in Japan) and Nisei (children of immigrants born in the USA).
- Elsewhere in the USA, Japanese people were abused and even murdered.
- Many Chinese-Americans suffered because they looked Japanese.

This was an unfair and unnecessary policy. Only the Japanese immigrants were targeted, not those who were from Germany or Italy. Yet, in 1943 when Congress allowed Japanese-Americans to serve in the armed forces, 17,600 immediately joined up.

4 Black Americans

Black Americans made a major contribution to the US war effort but still faced prejudice and discrimination in the armed forces:

- black soldiers usually served in black-only units with white officers
- many black women served as nurses but could only treat black soldiers
- there were fighter squadrons of black-only pilots
- discrimination was worst in the navy. By the end of the war only 58 black sailors had risen to the position of officer. It was exclusively black sailors who were given the dangerous job of loading ammunition on to ships, and in July 1944 a horrific accident killed 323 of them.

Similarly, in the workplace:

- black workers generally earned half of what white workers did
- in 1942, at the Packard electronics company, 3000 white workers walked out when three black workers had their jobs upgraded.

There were race riots in 47 cities during the war, the worst of which was in Detroit during June–July 1943. The war years, however, did see some progress.

- As the war developed, racially integrated units became more commonplace because General Eisenhower was a supporter of them. Such units performed with distinction at the Battle of the Bulge in December 1944.
- The number of black officers greatly increased.
- The war gave black Americans the opportunity to press for equality of civil rights. The black press set up the 'Double V' campaign. This campaign pushed President Roosevelt into action. In 1941 he issued Executive Order 8802 which ordered employers on defence work to end discrimination. The Fair Employment Practices Committee was set up to investigate violations of that Order.
- In 1942 black leaders set up the Congress of Racial Equality (CORE).
- Membership of the National Association for the Advancement of Colored People (NAACP) increased tenfold between 1940 and 1946.

● *The Second World War had mixed effects on the USA. In some ways there was progress, especially in women's rights and the economy. In other areas there seemed little or no progress. The treatment of Japanese-Americans was not that of an advanced nation. There was very little progress in equal rights for black Americans. Segregation remained commonplace, especially in the southern states.* ●

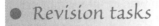

● *Revision tasks*

1 Using key words, what criticisms can you make of the treatment of Japanese-Americans during the war?
2 Draw up a balance sheet like the one below using key words to show discrimination against and gains made by black Americans during the war.

Gains made by black Americans	Discrimination against black Americans

B McCarthyism and the Red Scare

1 Why was there a Red Scare?

In the 1950s the USA was in the grip of extreme anti-communism. If you were thought to be communist you could be 'blacklisted', sacked or even attacked. This anti-communism came about for several reasons.

- It was partly the influence of the early Cold War. Relations between the USA and USSR had turned sour. US agents were spying on the USSR – so it was reasonable for Americans to believe that the Soviet Union was doing the same to them. In 1950 the USA became involved in the war in Korea, supporting the South Koreans in their resistance against the communist north. This involvement worsened anti-communist feeling.
- The Federal Bureau of Investigation (FBI) had a strongly anti-communist director, J. Edgar Hoover. In 1947, under the Federal Employee Loyalty Program set up by President Truman, the FBI investigated government employees to see if they were current or former members of the Communist Party. From 1947 to 1950 around 3 million were investigated. Nobody was charged with spying.
- From the 1930s, the US Congress had the House Un-American Activities Committee (HUAC), which had the right to investigate anyone suspected of doing anything un-American. 'Un-American' mostly meant communism. In 1947 HUAC became big news. The FBI had evidence that a number of prominent Hollywood writers, producers and directors were members of the Communist Party. The so-called 'Hollywood Ten' were brought before the HUAC. They were doing nothing illegal as they were not government employees and refused to answer questions, pleading the First Amendment. They were jailed for one year for contempt of court and 'blacklisted'. All this made front-page news.
- In 1948 a man called Whittaker Chambers faced the HUAC and admitted being a communist. He also said that Alger Hiss, a high-ranking member of the US State Department, was a communist. Hiss denied this and said he did not know Chambers. President Truman dismissed the case. Richard Nixon, a young member of the HUAC, investigated further and showed that Hiss had known Chambers. In 1950 Hiss was imprisoned for five years for perjury.
- In 1951 Julius and Ethel Rosenberg were found guilty of spying for the USSR and passing on atomic secrets. Two years later they were executed. The evidence against the Rosenbergs was flimsy, although coded telegrams between the Rosenbergs and Soviet agents were later discovered.

The Hiss and Rosenberg cases led Congress to pass the McCarran Act, which required that all communist organisations had to be registered with the US government. No communist was allowed to carry a US passport or work in the defence industries.

2 Joseph McCarthy

In 1950 Joseph McCarthy was a young Republican senator in search of a headline. He decided to take advantage of the anti-communist hysteria that was building up in the USA.

- He claimed, using FBI loyalty board investigations, that he had a list of over 200 communists in the State Department.
- This brought widespread publicity. Democrat Senator Millard Tydings declared that the charges lacked foundation. McCarthy accused Tydings of being a communist.

In the 1952 elections the Republicans did very well, winning many seats. Tydings lost his seat to a supporter of McCarthy.

- As chairman of a Senate committee, McCarthy began to investigate communist activities in the government. Throughout 1952 and 1953, McCarthy extended his investigations and turned his committee into a weapon to increase his personal power. He targeted high-profile figures and accused them of communist activities. One was General George Marshall who had been responsible for the Marshall Plan of 1947. Marshall was accused of being at the centre of a gigantic communist conspiracy against the USA.
- Thousands of lives were ruined by McCarthy's witch-hunt. False accusations led to people being 'blacklisted', which meant they could not find work. Over 100 university lecturers were fired due to McCarthy, and 324 Hollywood personalities were 'blacklisted'.

3 The end of McCarthyism

McCarthyism ended in 1954 for several reasons.

- There was much influential opposition to McCarthy's activities. Many senators and some top Hollywood stars spoke up against his activities. Quality newspapers such as the *Washington Post* and *New York Times* produced reports which seriously challenged McCarthy's activities.
- In 1954 McCarthy went too far. He accused 45 army officers of being communist agents. The hearings that followed were televised. McCarthy was rude, abusive and had a bullying manner. In contrast the army's attorney, Joseph Welch, was polite and humiliated McCarthy. McCarthy's popularity fell dramatically. He had become an alcoholic and died three years later.

McCarthyism was important for several reasons.

- It showed the extent of anti-communism in the USA.
- It brought great suffering to those accused of communist activities and sympathies.
- It showed that many Americans wanted to return to the traditional values that had been disrupted by the chaos of the 1920s and 1930s and then the war years. Supporters of McCarthy would have liked women to stay in the home, black people to be content with their lowly place in society, and all rock-and-roll music to be banned.

● *McCarthyism took place at a time when the USA was the leader of the 'free' Western world in its struggle to stop the spread of communism. Yet the witch-hunt which was a key feature of the McCarthy period showed the sort of intolerance supposed to be typical of communist-controlled countries.* ●

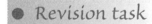
Revision task

1 Copy the table below on McCarthyism and use key words to complete each section.

Reasons for McCarthyism	Key features of McCarthyism	Reasons why it died out	Importance of McCarthyism

C The growth of the civil rights movement in the 1950s

1 Racism in the 1950s

Although some progress had been made during the Second World War, racism was still an everyday experience for black people, particularly in the southern states of the USA.

- Most southern states fully enforced the 'Jim Crow' laws which segregated everyday facilities such as parks, buses and schools.
- Black Americans had officially been given the vote in the early years of the twentieth century but violence often prevented black Americans from voting.
- Black Americans faced official and legal discrimination in areas such as employment and education. In the south, white teachers earned 30 per cent more than black teachers.
- The best universities were closed to black people.

2 The struggle for equal education

For decades it had been legal in the USA for states to have separate schools for black and white children. Schools for black children were always less well equipped.

- The National Association for the Advancement of Colored People (NAACP) and the black civil rights lawyer Thurgood Marshall had brought a series of complaints about segregated schools in the 1940s. Judge Julius Waring ruled that states had to provide equal education for black and white students but said nothing about integration.
- The *Brown v Board of Education of Topeka* case of 1954 showed further progress in education. In 1952 the NAACP brought a court case against the Board of Education of Topeka in Kansas on behalf of a black student, Linda Brown, who had to walk a considerable distance to get to school because she was not allowed to attend the whites-only school near her home. In May 1954 Chief Justice Earl Warren ruled in favour of Brown and stated that segregated education could not be equal because black students had inferior facilities. He ordered the southern states to set up integrated schools 'with all deliberate speed'.

Challenging inequality through the legal system was the method favoured by the NAACP civil rights campaigners. They took an individual case all the way to the Supreme Court, which decided in their favour, thus forcing the states to act.

This method was also used at Little Rock in Arkansas. By 1957 Arkansas had not introduced integrated education. In 1957 the Supreme Court ordered the Governor, Orval Faubus, to let nine black students attend a white school in Little Rock. He brought out state troops to stop the nine attending, insisting he was using the troops to protect the children. Faubus only backed down when President Eisenhower sent federal troops to protect the children.

3 The Montgomery bus boycott

This took place in Montgomery, Alabama, in 1955 and is normally seen as the beginning of the civil rights movement.

- In Montgomery a local law stated that black Americans were only allowed to sit on the back seats of buses and had to give up those seats if white people wanted them.
- Rosa Parks, an NAACP activist, deliberately refused to give up her seat and was arrested and convicted of breaking the bus laws.

- Local civil rights activists set up the Montgomery Improvement Association (MIA), led by Martin Luther King. They boycotted the buses and organised private transport for people. This was a great success and the first example of non-violent direct action. It showed how powerful black people could be if they worked together.
- Civil rights lawyers fought Rosa Parks' case in court. In December 1956 the Supreme Court declared Montgomery's bus laws illegal.

This was the beginning of non-violent mass protests by the civil rights movement.

4 Direct action gathers pace

In the winter of 1959–60 civil rights groups stepped up their campaigns.

- They organised marches, demonstrations and boycotts to end segregation in public places. In February 1960 in Nashville, Tennessee, 500 students organised sit-ins in restaurants, libraries and churches. Their college expelled them but then backed down when 400 teachers threatened to resign. By May 1960 the town had been desegregated.
- In May 1961 both white and black members of the Congress of Racial Equality (CORE) began a form of protest known as 'freedom rides' in the southern states. They deliberately rode on buses run by companies that were ignoring laws banning segregation. They faced much violence and opposition. By September, 70,000 students had taken part and 3600 had been arrested. Over 100 cities in 20 states were affected.

By 1961 the civil rights movement had become a national movement. Many Americans were becoming aware of the unfair way in which black people were treated, especially in the southern states.

● *Revision tasks*

1 Use key words to list four ways in which black Americans were treated as second-class citizens in the 1950s.
2 Draw a table like the one below and complete each section using key words.

Dispute	Reason for dispute	Court decision	Importance
Brown v Topeka			
Little Rock			
Montgomery bus boycott			

3 Draw your own timeline to show the progress made in the period 1959–61 in the campaign for civil rights.

D The civil rights movement in the 1960s

1 Martin Luther King

King became the leading figure in the civil rights movement until his assassination in 1968. He believed passionately in non-violent protest and favoured actions such as the bus boycott and sit-ins. He won increased support for the civil rights movement by appealing to students. From this emerged, in April 1960, the Student Non-violent Co-ordinating Committee (SNCC). Many SNCC workers dropped out of their studies to work full-time in those areas that were most resistant to integration.

- In the summer of 1961 the main civil rights groups – SNCC, CORE and NAACP – met with the Attorney-General, Robert Kennedy, brother of the new president, John F. Kennedy. Together they devised the Voter Education Project, which aimed to get more black people registered to vote.
- In April 1963 King organised a march on Birmingham, Alabama, as the city had still not been desegregated. The aim of the march was to turn attention on Birmingham and expose its policies to national attention. Police Chief Bull Connor ordered police and fire officers to turn dogs and fire hoses on the peaceful protesters. The police arrested over 1000 protesters, including King. King's tactics worked, as President Kennedy forced Governor George Wallace to release the protesters and desegregate Birmingham.
- In August 1963 King staged his most high-profile event. Over 200,000 black and 50,000 white Americans marched together to Washington to pressure Kennedy to introduce a civil rights bill. There was no trouble and King gave his famous 'I have a dream' speech.

2 The Civil Rights Act and events 1964–65

In November 1963 Kennedy was assassinated. His successor, Lyndon Johnson, was just as committed to civil rights. On 2 July 1964 he signed the Civil Rights Act. The Act made it illegal for local government to discriminate in areas such as housing and employment. The summer of 1964 was known as the 'freedom summer'. King and the SNCC continued to encourage black Americans to register to vote. In the twenty months that followed the Civil Rights Act, 430,000 black Americans registered to vote.

King continued to target areas where discrimination was worst. In 1965 he organised a march through Selma, Alabama, which had a notoriously racist sheriff called Jim Clark, to protest against the violence being used to stop black voters from registering. The authorities banned the march but 600 people went ahead and were brutally attacked. The media called it 'Bloody Sunday'. King organised a second march but compromised with the authorities by turning back after a certain distance. This lost King the support of the more radical black activists, but nevertheless helped President Johnson to push through a Voting Rights Bill in 1965 which finally became law in 1968. The Act allowed government agents to inspect voting procedures to make sure that they were taking place properly. It also ended the literacy tests that voters had previously had to complete before they voted. After 1965 five major cities had black mayors.

In April 1968 King was assassinated, probably by a hired killer, although it has never been proved which of King's enemies hired the assassin.

● *Martin Luther King did not invent the tactic of direct action. This had developed as a result of the key education and transport cases of the 1950s and early 1960s. He did, however, provide national leadership for such action and ensured massive publicity for the cause of civil rights within and beyond the USA.* ●

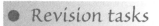 **Revision tasks**

1 Using key words explain the importance of each of the following in the civil rights movement of the 1960s:
   a) SNCC
   b) Voter Education Project
   c) the Birmingham and Washington Marches of 1963.
2 Make a list of gains made by the civil rights movement in the 1960s.

3 Black nationalism and black power

Black nationalism became more popular in the 1960s and won much support. Most black nationalists rejected the non-violence of the civil rights movement. They felt violence was justified to achieve full equality. Some even wanted complete separation from the rest of the USA. One of the groups that called for this was the Nation of Islam, led by Elijah Mohammad. This group attracted high-profile figures such as the boxer Cassius Clay (later known as Muhammad Ali).

- One member of the Nation of Islam was Malcolm Little, better known as Malcolm X. He was bitterly critical of King's methods and believed the civil rights movement held black Americans back. He wanted to see black people rise up and use force if necessary to set up their own separate state in the USA. He was assassinated in 1965.
- The SNCC became more radical when the black student Stokely Carmichael was elected chairman in 1966. He talked of 'black power' and criticised King.
- An even more radical group was the Black Panthers. They had around 2000 members and were a political party and a small private army. They believed that black Americans should arm themselves and force the white Americans to give them equal rights. They clashed many times with the police, killing nine police officers between 1967 and 1969.

Between 1965 and 1967 American cities suffered a wave of race riots.

- This was mainly due to poor relations between the police, who were mainly white, and black people. Many black working-class people did not feel they got the same protection from crime as white people.
- Many black rioters were influenced by the radical black nationalists.
- Others joined the riots because of their frustration with the way they were treated in the USA.

The most serious riots were in the Watts area of Los Angeles in August 1965 and in Detroit in July 1967.

Revision tasks

1 Use a few key words to describe the aims of the black nationalists in the 1960s.
2 Using a few key words, explain the part played by the following in the 1960s:
   a) Elijah Mohammad
   b) Malcolm X
   c) Stokely Carmichael
   d) the Black Panthers.
3 Why were there race riots in the USA, 1965–67? Make a list of the causes.

E The achievements of Kennedy and Johnson

1 Kennedy and the 'New Frontier'

Kennedy narrowly defeated Richard Nixon in the presidential election of 1960. He was the youngest-ever US president and put the emphasis on youth and idealism. He talked about the USA being at the edge of a New Frontier. This was at first a slogan but then became a series of reforms. He wanted to make the USA a better, fairer place for all Americans. He wanted to spread these ideas abroad and asked Americans to join him in being 'new frontiersmen'. He urged Americans to 'Ask not what your country can do for you, but what you can do for your country'. He asked them to help attack 'tyranny, poverty, disease and war itself'. The New Frontier included social reforms to help poor Americans.

To tackle deprivation and ensure that poor Americans had the opportunity to help themselves:

- Kennedy increased the minimum wage
- the Area Redevelopment Act enabled poor communities to get loans and grants to start new businesses or build roads, etc.
- the Housing Act helped people in run-down inner-city areas to get loans to improve their housing
- the Social Security Act made more money available for payments to the elderly and unemployed
- the Manpower Development and Training Act retrained the unemployed.

Kennedy also reformed the economy. He wanted the US economy to be the strongest in the world.

- He cut income tax to give people more money to spend.
- Grants were given to companies to invest in hi-tech equipment and train their workers.
- He increased spending on defence.
- He made $900 million available to businesses to create new jobs.
- He massively increased spending on space technology.

Kennedy was also active in the area of civil rights. He was determined to achieve equality for black Americans.

- In September 1962 he made a major speech committing himself to the cause of civil rights.
- He made high-level black appointments, including Thurgood Marshall (see page 59) as the first black US circuit judge.
- He stood up to the governors of the southern states, who were opposed to civil rights, and tried to force them to defend the freedom riders (see page 60).
- In October 1962 he sent 23,000 troops to ensure that one black student, James Meredith, could study at the University of Mississippi without being hounded by racists.

2 The achievements of 'New Frontier'

How successful were Kennedy's reforms?

- His social reforms had limited effects. The minimum wage did not help those out of work and slum clearance led to housing shortages in the inner cities. The housing loans did not help the poorest people who could not afford the loans.
- The economy grew quickly, but technology did not help to reduce unemployment in traditional industries. In fact, fewer workers were needed. Critics said the boom was too dependent on government spending – what would happen when it was cut back?

- In certain respects the situation of black Americans worsened under Kennedy. The rate of black unemployment was twice that of white unemployment. Many poor black families from the south moved to northern cities where they experienced poverty and racial tension. Worried southern congressmen blocked many of Kennedy's attempts at civil rights reform. Many members of his own party represented the southern states and opposed civil rights legislation.

Kennedy was assassinated in November 1963 after less than three years as president. He remains one of the great 'what ifs' of history, having achieved only a small part of what he set out to do.

● **Revision tasks**

1 Using key words explain the meaning of 'New Frontier'.
2 Draw a table like the one below on Kennedy's reforms, and use key words to complete each section.

Area of reform	Aim	Main reforms	Criticisms
Social policy			
Economic policy			
Civil rights policy			

3 Johnson and the 'Great Society'

Vice-President Lyndon Johnson became president when Kennedy was assassinated. He talked in terms of a 'Great Society' and of taking Kennedy's reforms further with an 'unconditional war on poverty' and an immediate end to racial injustice. He was very good at politics and much more successful than Kennedy in getting measures passed by Congress. Johnson tackled areas that Kennedy had not been able to tackle, for example 'medicare', which provided free medical care for the poor. He does not get the credit that he deserves for his domestic achievements because:

- he was not a showman like Kennedy and did not work well with the whizz-kid advisers used by Kennedy
- the conservatives in Congress attacked him for spending too much on welfare reform
- the liberals criticised him for increasing American involvement in the Vietnam War.

Johnson's achievements in civil rights included:

- the 1964 Civil Rights Act (see page 61)
- the appointment of the first-ever black American to the White House cabinet and the Supreme Court: Thurgood Marshall became US Solicitor General in 1965 and a Supreme Court judge in 1967.
- the Immigration Act of 1965, which ended the system of racial quotas for immigrants into the USA.

Despite these reforms there was racial tension and rioting in several cities in the summer of 1968.
  Johnson's war on poverty involved a range of measures:

- In 1965 two government funded health-care programmes, Medicare and Medicaid, were set up for elderly people and families on low incomes.
- The minimum wage was increased from $1.25 to $1.40 per hour.
- The funding of the Aid to Families with Dependent Children (AFDC) scheme was increased. This gave financial help to 745,000 families on low incomes.

- The VISTA programme tried to create work in poor inner-city areas.
- The Elementary and Secondary Education Act of 1965 for the first time put federal funding into improving education in poorer areas.
- The Model Cities Act (1966) linked to the other inner-city employment programmes by clearing slums and providing parks and sports facilities.

4 Johnson and the economy

Johnson also made improvements to the economy.

- He cut taxes which helped the better off.
- He improved transport links such as railways and highways and increased funding for universities, all of which directly benefited the middle class.
- Johnson also introduced a range of consumer laws. These meant that manufacturers and shops had to label goods fairly and clearly.

On the other hand, unemployment and inflation increased, with the real reason for this being the huge cost of the war in Vietnam.

● *Kennedy was very much the popular cult leader of the 1960s. For a generation after his assassination, historians stressed his aims and achievements and played down those of Johnson. Johnson was, in certain ways, simply finishing off what Kennedy had started. There were, however, other achievements which have been overlooked.* ●

● *Revision tasks*

1 What was Johnson's 'Great Society'? Make a list of the main features using key words.
2 Why does he not get much credit for his domestic reforms? Make a note of your answer.
3 **a)** Draw up and complete a summary table like the one below, comparing the measures introduced by Kennedy and Johnson.
   b) Decide which president achieved the most in the three main areas, using key words to explain your decision.

Area of reform	Measures introduced by Kennedy	Measures introduced by Johnson
Civil rights		
The economy		
Poverty		

F The protest movements of the 1960s and early 1970s

The campaign for black civil rights encouraged other protest movements including those campaigning for women's rights and the student movement.

1 The women's movement

This was not one single organisation but thousands of different groups all with similar aims – to raise the status of women and end discrimination against women in all areas of life. This movement emerged for several reasons.

- Inequality in employment: the number of women in employment had continued to increase in the years after the Second World War, but a commission on the status of women at work reported in 1963 that 93 per cent of company managers and 88 per cent of technical workers were men and only 4 per cent of lawyers and 7 per cent of doctors were female. Work for women was overwhelmingly low paid, with many earning only 50 per cent of the wages of men for doing the same job.
- In 1963 Betty Friedan wrote a best-seller called *The Feminine Mystique*. This was her term for a set of ideas that said that women's happiness came from being wives and mothers. Friedan challenged this notion, insisting that many married women needed employment to avoid frustration and boredom. She wrote of hundreds of college-educated women who felt little better than domestic servants.
- Women's attitudes also changed because of the introduction of the contraceptive pill in 1960. This changed women's attitudes to sexual relations and gave them much greater independence and control of their lives.

Women's rights received a boost from the federal government, which passed a number of important measures, and from the Supreme Court. In 1963 the Equal Pay Act required employers to pay women the same as men for the same work. This, however, did not stop discrimination against female employment. The following year the Civil Rights Act made it illegal to discriminate on grounds of gender. In 1972 the Educational Amendment Act outlawed sex discrimination in education, and courses had to be rewritten to ensure that gender stereotyping did not occur in the curriculum. In 1973 the Supreme Court's ruling in the *Roe v Wade* case made abortion legal.

2 Women's organisations

Various organisations emerged in the 1960s.

- In 1966 Betty Friedan set up the National Organisation for Women (NOW) which had 40,000 members by the early 1970s. It co-operated with a wide range of women's movements, such as the National Women's Caucus and the Women's Campaign Fund. It used similar tactics to the civil rights movement, campaigning in the streets of American cities and challenging discrimination in court. NOW, however, was not an extreme organisation and still believed in traditional families and marriage.
- In contrast, there were younger feminists with more radical aims and different methods. They became known as the Women's Liberation Movement (Women's Lib). They used more extreme methods to get across their views, such as bra-burning, since bras were seen as a symbol of male domination. In 1968 radical women picketed the Miss World beauty contest in Atlantic City. They said that the contest treated women like objects rather than women. To make their point, they crowned a sheep as Miss World.

The women's movement achieved much publicity and support, with several important laws passed. However, there were limitations:

- Support was lost because of the extreme methods of the Women's Lib Movement which some believed ridiculed the position of women.
- Anti-feminist organisations were set up, with the most famous, STOP ERA, led by Phyllis Schafly. ERA stood for Equal Rights Amendment, which was a proposal to amend the US Constitution to outlaw sex discrimination. Schafly led a successful campaign to prevent it becoming law as late as the 1980s.
- Despite legislation, few women had achieved top posts in Congress, business or industry by the end of the 1970s.

● *Revision tasks*

1 Use four to six key words to describe the main aims of the women's movement.
2 Why did the following encourage the women's movement:
   a) the 1963 commission report on the status of women at work
   b) *The Feminine Mystique*
   c) the contraceptive pill?

3 The student movement

The 1960s was a decade of social unrest and this spread to the USA's youth, especially in universities and colleges. Student protest emerged for several reasons:

- Students were deeply involved in the black civil rights campaign and also the women's movement. Idealistic young students were appalled at the injustices experienced by black people.
- The death of President Kennedy in 1963 came as a great shock to the American people, especially the young who had been inspired by his brief presidency.
- The war in Vietnam united student protest. Half a million young Americans were fighting in a war that was very unpopular with students. The anti war protests reached a peak between 1968 and 1970.
- The 1960s saw the pop music explosion and the popularity of the protest singer. This was epitomised by the singer/songwriter Bob Dylan whose lyrics attacked war and racism.
- The 1960s was also a time of student unrest across the world, especially in Paris in 1968.

4 Student activities

There were many different groups involved in student protest. One of the main organisations was Students for a Democratic Society, set up in 1959. It aimed to get more say for students in how their colleges and universities were run and had 100,000 members by the end of the 1960s.

- In 1964 radical students in many colleges organised rallies and marches to support the civil rights campaign. They tried to expose racism in their own colleges. Some universities tried to ban their protests. The students responded with a Free Speech Movement. Student groups also backed campaigns for nuclear disarmament and criticised US involvement in South America.
- During the first half of 1968 there were over 100 demonstrations against the Vietnam War involving 40,000 students. Anti-war demonstrations often ended in violent clashes with the police. The worst incident came in 1970 at Kent State University, Ohio, where students organised a demonstration against President Nixon's decision to invade Cambodia. The National Guards panicked and fired on the students, killing four.

- Some young people took up an entirely different kind of protest. They 'dropped out' and became hippies. They opted out of the society their parents had created. They decided not to work or study. They grew their hair long, talked of peace and love, and experimented with sex and drugs.

● *We tend to look at the protest movements of the 1960s separately. This does not give us a real idea of what was happening. Many individuals were not campaigning only for women's rights, or for an end to the war in Vietnam or for civil rights. They supported several or all of these movements. In some respects protest itself became fashionable, especially amongst the young, heavily influenced by protest singers such as Bob Dylan.* ●

● *Revision tasks*

1 Using key words explain three reasons for the student movement.
2 What part did the following play in the student movement of the 1960s and early 1970s:
   a) Students for a Democratic Society
   b) Kent State University, 1970
   c) hippies?

G The Watergate scandal and its impact

1 Key events of the scandal

The Watergate scandal rocked the USA in the 1970s and was seen as the single greatest threat to the US Constitution in its history. The scandal had three phases:

- Phase 1 was June 1972 to January 1973. On 17 June 1972 five 'burglars' were arrested in the Democratic Party offices in the Watergate Building, Washington DC. They had been planting electronic devices and all five were found to have connections with CREEP, the Committee for the Re-election of the President, set up by President Nixon. Two reporters from the *Washington Post*, Carl Bernstein and Bob Woodward, pursued their own investigations and publicised the identity of the burglars and the activities of CREEP. John Mitchell was head of CREEP. He had been organising 'dirty tricks' campaigns against the Democrats and forcing corporations working for the government to make contributions to CREEP for fear of losing their government contracts.
- Phase 2, March 1973. At the trial of the Watergate burglars, in March 1973, one of them insisted that the White House was involved in a cover-up of its involvement in the break-in. Three of Nixon's top advisers resigned, but Nixon still denied all knowledge of the break-in or cover-up and appointed Archibald Cox as special prosecutor to investigate. The Senate also set up an investigation under Senator Sam Ervin.
- Phase 3, the battle for the tapes. At a televised public hearing of the Senate Committee, one of Nixon's advisers admitted discussing the break-in with the president. It also emerged that since 1971 Nixon had been secretly taping White House conversations. Archibald Cox, the special prosecutor in the Watergate case, insisted on being given the tapes but was dismissed. The new prosecutor, Leon Jaworski, also insisted on being given the tapes. In December 1973 Nixon released the tapes but there was a gap of over 18 minutes. When he released transcripts of the tapes they were heavily edited. Finally, the Supreme Court ordered Nixon to hand over the complete tapes. They revealed that he had been involved in the break-in and had repeatedly tried to hide the truth. In July 1974 Congress decided to impeach Nixon (put him on trial) but he resigned the following month.

2 Results of the scandal

Nixon was pardoned by his successor, President Ford, but 31 of his officials went to prison for various offences relating to Watergate. Congress passed a series of measures to prevent similar things happening again.

- The Privacy Act of 1974 allowed American citizens to inspect government files held on them.
- The Budget Act of the same year meant that the president had to account for all money spent.
- The Election Campaign Act limited the amount of money parties could raise for elections and banned foreign contributions.

The scandal ended Nixon's political career and destroyed his reputation. He was seen as corrupt and became known as Tricky Dicky. Watergate also led to a loss of confidence among the public in American politics and its leaders.

● *Revision tasks*

1 Make a copy of the table below showing the events of the Watergate scandal and use key words to complete each section.

	Events of the Watergate scandal
Phase 1	
Phase 2	
Phase 3	
The end of the scandal	

2 What effects did the scandal have on Nixon and on American attitudes to politics?

Revision session

The aim of this session is for you to see how you can apply your knowledge of the content of this chapter to the kind of questions you will face in the examinations.

Examination questions

The main theme of the examination questions will be on change within the USA in the period 1941 to 1980. The following questions are adapted by permission of Edexcel from the Specimen Paper 1.

a) i) What was meant by 'New Frontier'? *(3 marks)*

What is required? This is a simple test of knowledge and memory. A simple factual answer will do, although you do need to put your answer in the context of the time.

Ideas for your answer You could write about Kennedy's ideas for reduction of poverty, reform of civil rights and the economy, and his commitment to the space programme. The context could be the start of a new decade and Kennedy's youthful approach.

ii) Why did President Kennedy face problems in his attempts to improve civil rights in the years 1961–63? *(5 marks)*

What is required? This is a causation question and is asking you to identify and explain at least two causes. You need to write a paragraph for each cause and try to make a link between the causes.

Ideas for your answer
1 Your first reason could be Kennedy himself, his youth, inexperience and lack of political ability in dealing with opposition and Congress. This could easily link to the second reason.
2 Strong opposition from the southern states. Explain why they opposed civil rights legislation and their position in Congress and Kennedy's party.

iii) Why was President Johnson unable to build his 'Great Society' in the years 1963–68? *(5 marks)*

What is required? Again this is a causation question and you will need to explain at least two reasons. Write a paragraph for each reason, with a link between the two.

Ideas for your answer
1 One reason could be the impact of the Vietnam War on the economy and on attitudes to the government.
2 A second reason is the growth of opposition such as the student movement and black militancy. There is an obvious link between the war in Vietnam and student activities.
3 A third reason could be opposition from conservatives and liberals in American politics.

iv) In what ways did President Johnson improve civil rights in the years 1963–68? *(7 marks)*

What is required? This question is about change. You need to explain at least two, preferably three, important changes in the area of civil rights, as this question is worth seven marks. Write a paragraph explaining each change and how you think it improved the area of civil rights. Try to make links between each of the changes.

Ideas for your answer

1 The Civil Rights Act of 1964. This prevented discrimination in education and housing and links with Johnson's other social and economic reforms.

2 The Voting Rights Act which followed the Civil Rights Act.

3 Johnson's social and economic reforms which attacked poverty and the problems of the inner cities, such as the Medicare, Medicaid and VISTA programmes.

b) i) Describe the main features of the Watergate scandal in the USA. *(10 marks)*

What is required? This question is about key features, which means the important points or developments in the Watergate scandal. If you identify, explain and link the main developments in the scandal this will be enough for level 3 (6–8 marks). To achieve a top-level answer (9–10 marks) you will have to do more.

1 Ensure your explanation of each key feature is supported by relevant knowledge.
2 Link one feature to the next.
3 Write an introduction that explains the meaning of the question and the key features you intend to explain.
4 Write a conclusion that sums up the key features.

Ideas for your answer Draw up a table like the one below and use it as a check-list to plan your answer. One example is given for you.

Key features	Explanation	Why important and link
CREEP and dirty tricks	CREEP set up to ensure re-election of Nixon and prepared to use dirty tricks	This campaign led to the break-in which started scandal and led to the cover-up

Some key features include:

- CREEP and dirty tricks
- the cover-up and the role of television
- Senate hearings
- Nixon's resignation and the scandal's impact on politics.

Remember to write an introduction and conclusion.

ii) Why was the fear of communism so strong in the USA in the years 1945–54?
You may use the following information to help you with your answer:

- spread of communism
- Korean War 1950–53
- Hiss and Rosenberg cases
- McCarthyism. *(15 marks)*

What is required? This is a causation question. You will need to explain the four causes mentioned in the question, although you could add at least one more. If you explain in detail each cause and make links between them this would be enough for level 3 (9–12 marks). For a top-level answer you would need to ensure that you:

1 give a precise and detailed explanation of each cause
2 make clear links between each cause
3 write an introduction that explains the meaning of the question and how you will answer it
4 write a conclusion that summarises the causes and possibly identifies the most important/fundamental reason.

Ideas for your answer Draw up a table like the one below and use it as a check-list for your answer. One section has been completed for you.

Causes	Explanation	Link with next cause
Spread of communism	*Early Cold War and Soviet expansion*	*Fear in USA of communist expansion in Asia*
Korean War		
Hiss and Rosenberg cases		
McCarthyism		
Extra reason		

For your extra reason you could mention the activities of the FBI and the attitude of its director, Hoover, or the House Un-American Activities Committee, although either of these would probably go after the first two causes.

Remember to include an introduction and conclusion.

Practice questions

Now have a go at the following questions without any guidance. Remember to bear in mind how many marks each question is worth before deciding on the length of your answer.

a) **i)** What was meant by 'civil rights'? *(3 marks)*

ii) What impact did Martin Luther King have on the civil rights movement? *(5 marks)*

iii) Describe the key features of the 'Black Power' movement of the 1960s. *(5 marks)*

iv) Why was education such a key issue in the struggle for civil rights in the 1950s? *(7 marks)*

b) **i)** Describe the key features of the women's movement of the 1960s and 1970s. *(10 marks)*

ii) Why did a student movement develop in the USA in the 1960s?
You may use the following information to help you with your answer:

- hippies
- music
- President Kennedy's assassination
- the war in Vietnam. *(15 marks)*

Summary and revision plan

Below is a list of headings which you may find helpful. Use this as a check-list to make sure that you are familiar with the material featured in this chapter. Record your key words alongside each heading.

A The impact of the Second World War on the US economy and society
- ❏ The impact on the economy
- ❏ The impact on women
- ❏ Internment of Japanese-Americans
- ❏ Black Americans

B McCarthyism and the Red Scare
- ❏ Why was there a Red Scare?
- ❏ Joseph McCarthy
- ❏ The end of McCarthyism

C The growth of the civil rights movement in the 1950s
- ❏ Racism in the 1950s
- ❏ The struggle for equal education
- ❏ The Montgomery bus boycott
- ❏ Direct action gathers pace

D The civil rights movement in the 1960s
- ❏ Martin Luther King
- ❏ The Civil Rights Act and events 1964–65
- ❏ Black nationalism and black power

E The achievements of Kennedy and Johnson
- ❏ Kennedy and the 'New Frontier'
- ❏ The achievements of 'New Frontier'
- ❏ Johnson and the 'Great Society'
- ❏ Johnson and the economy

F The protest movements of the 1960s and early 1970s
- ❏ The women's movement
- ❏ Women's organisations
- ❏ The student movement
- ❏ Student activities

G The Watergate scandal and its impact
- ❏ Key events of the scandal
- ❏ Results of the scandal

Superpower Relations, 1945–90

During the Second World War the USA and the USSR had fought together as allies against Germany and Japan. Once this war was won, relations between the two 'SUPERPOWERS' quickly worsened. A new war began – it was a war of ideas. For this reason it is known as the Cold War and it lasted until the break-up of the Soviet Union in 1990.

To answer questions on superpower relations you need to be familiar with the key content and key themes of the period.

Key content You need to show that you have a good working knowledge of these areas:

A Origins of the Cold War and the partition of Germany
B Reasons for superpower rivalry
C The Truman Doctrine, the Marshall Plan and the Berlin Crisis
D NATO, the Warsaw Pact and the arms race
E The Cold War, 1949–61
F The Cuban missile crisis
G Attempts at détente and the impact of the Soviet invasion of Afghanistan
H The roles of Gorbachev and Reagan and the end of the Cold War

Key themes As with other topics you will be expected to do more than simply write out all the content you have learnt about superpower relations. The questions you face will be asking you to show your understanding of these themes from the period:

● Why did the USA and USSR become rivals after the Second World War?
● How did the rivalry develop in the period 1945–48?
● Why and with what effects did Stalin impose the Berlin blockade of 1948–49?
● What were NATO and the Warsaw Pact and how did they affect relations between the superpowers?
● How did the Hungarian Crisis of 1956 and the building of the Berlin Wall worsen relations between the two?
● What were the causes, events and main consequences of the Cuban missile crisis?
● How successful was détente in the 1970s?
● What was the impact of the Soviet invasion of Afghanistan in 1979?
● How did the policies of Reagan and Gorbachev influence superpower relations in the 1980s?
● Why did the Cold War end?

For example, look at the question below which is adapted by permission of Edexcel from the Specimen Paper for Paper 1.

a) i) Give ONE reason to explain why the leaders of the Allies met at Yalta in 1945. *(3 marks)*

> *The question is asking you to show knowledge and understanding of the topic.*

ii) Describe the key features of the Potsdam Conference. *(5 marks)*

> *You will need to explain the main decisions reached by the Allies at Potsdam.*

iii) Why was Berlin blockaded by the Soviet Union in 1948? *(5 marks)*

> *For this question you will have to explain at least two reasons why Stalin decided to blockade Berlin.*

iv) Why was the Hungarian Uprising in 1956 crushed by the Soviet Union? *(7 marks)*

> *You will need to look at reasons for the Soviet actions in 1956.*

b) i) Why was there such a major crisis between the superpowers over Cuba in 1962? *(10 marks)*

> *We will look at this question in more detail at the end of the chapter.*

ii) In what ways did relations between the USA and USSR change in the years 1979–90? You may use the following information to help you with your answer:

- 1979 invasion of Afghanistan
- 1980s USA threatens to develop 'Star Wars'
- roles of Gorbachev and Reagan
- 1986 INF treaty signed. *(15 marks)*

> *We will look at this question in more detail at the end of the chapter.*

A Origins of the Cold War and the partition of Germany

1 Conflicting ideologies: communism and capitalism

During the war the communist superpower, the USSR, had united with the capitalist superpower, the USA, to defeat fascism. However, communism and capitalism were very different economic systems, strongly opposed to one another (see pages 79–80). With Germany and Japan defeated, the reason for co-operation was gone. Differences of opinion soon began to emerge.

2 Political changes in Europe: occupation, resistance and liberation

In Europe most countries had been occupied by the German army, and run by German governors. When the Germans left, there was no government in place. The question was: who would take over?

New national leaders could possibly come from the resistance movements that had fought an undercover war against the Germans (for example, sabotaging railways, helping servicemen to escape). However, there was sometimes more than one resistance movement in a country.

- In France the main resistance movement recognised General Charles de Gaulle, head of the Free French based in London, as their leader, but there was also a communist resistance movement.
- In Greece and Yugoslavia there were also rival communist and non-communist movements. In both countries, the rival movements fought the Germans but were soon fighting each other once the Germans had gone. The superpowers had strong views as to which of the resistance groups they wished to take over. The USSR favoured the communist groups, the USA the non-communists.

Defeating the Germans had been the main aim of all of the resistance movements. However, it was clear that once the Germans had gone it would not be a simple task to form new governments to run liberated countries. Where there were rival communist and non-communist groups, outside powers might get involved to support either the communists or non-communists. By 1947 this was the cause of great tension between the superpowers.

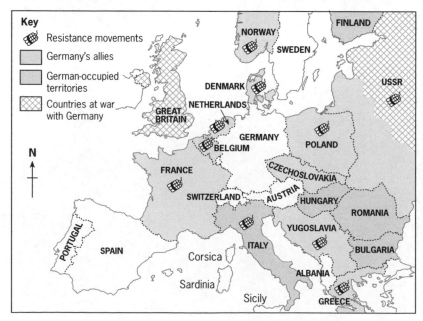

European resistance movements during the war

3 The Yalta Conference, February 1945

At the Yalta Conference the Allied leaders (Churchill, Roosevelt and Stalin) got on well together. The following points were agreed at Yalta:

* Germany would be divided into four zones. These would be run by the USA, France, Britain and the USSR.
* Germany's capital city, Berlin (which was in the Soviet zone), would also be divided into four zones.
* The countries of Eastern Europe would be allowed to hold free elections to decide how they would be governed.
* The USSR would join in the war against Japan in return for territory in Manchuria and Sakhalin Island.

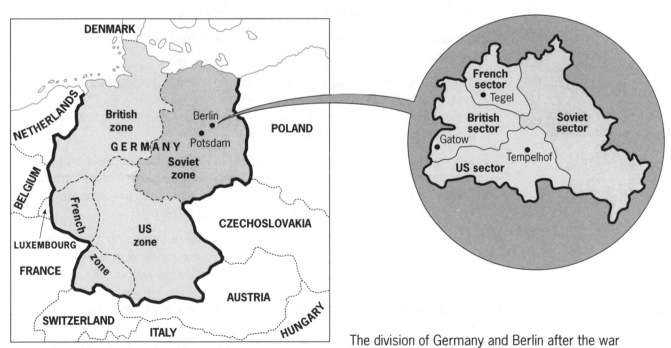

The division of Germany and Berlin after the war

4 The Potsdam Conference, July–August 1945

In April 1945 President Roosevelt died, so by the time of the Potsdam Conference there was a new US president – Harry Truman. During the conference Churchill was replaced by Clement Attlee as British prime minister. The new leaders did not get on nearly so well with Stalin as the previous two.

Potsdam continued the discussions left over from the Yalta Conference. There were two points of agreement:

* The Nazi party was to be banned and its leaders would be tried as war criminals.
* The Oder–Neisse Line (two rivers) was to form part of the future border between Poland and Germany.

However, on other issues there were disagreements. There were clear signs that Stalin did not trust the USA and Britain and that they did not trust him.

Tensions at Potsdam

1 Britain and the USA denied Stalin a naval base in the Mediterranean:

- They saw no need for Stalin to have such a base.
- Stalin saw this as evidence that his allies mistrusted him.

2 Stalin wanted to take more in reparations from Germany than Britain and the USA did:

- The USA and Britain did not wish to cripple Germany; they had seen the results of reparations after the First World War.
- Stalin was suspicious about why his allies seemed to want to protect Germany and even help it to recover.

3 Stalin had set up a communist government in Poland. Britain preferred the non-communist Polish government that had lived in exile in Britain throughout the war. Truman and Attlee were very suspicious of Stalin's motives in setting up a communist government in Poland based at Lublin.

● *Even before the end of the war, disagreements were beginning to appear among the Allies. Britain and the USA represented one political system, the USSR another – each side was suspicious about the motives of the other.* ●

● *Revision tasks*

1 Use four key words to describe two important differences between the superpowers.
2 Draw up a table like the one below on the Yalta and Potsdam Conferences and produce a key word summary to complete it.

Conference	Points agreed	Areas of disagreement
Yalta		
Potsdam		

3 List three important changes that occurred between the Yalta Conference and the Potsdam Conference.

B Reasons for superpower rivalry

To understand how and why tension built up in the years immediately after the Second World War, it is important to understand the beliefs and ideas of each of the superpowers. This helps to explain the attitude of each side towards the other.

1 The USA

What were the main political and economic features of the USA?

- It had a democratic system of government. The president and Congress of the USA were chosen in free democratic elections.
- It had a capitalist economy. Business and property were privately owned. Individuals could make profits in business or move jobs if they wished. However, they might also go bankrupt or lose their jobs.
- The USA was the world's wealthiest country, but under capitalism there were always great contrasts – some people were very rich, others very poor.
- Americans firmly believed in the freedom of the individual and in government by consent.

In the 1920s and 1930s the USA had followed a policy of isolationism (staying out of world affairs). Now, faced by communism extending into eastern Europe, the US government was prepared to help and support people and countries who wanted democratic states with capitalist economies. This was seen as simply the defence of people's freedom against a system they did not want.

The main political and economic features of the USA

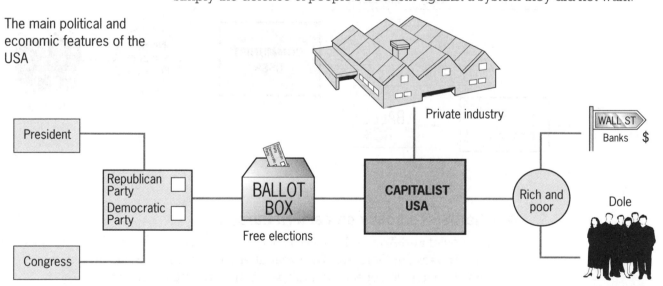

2 The attitude of Truman

Relations between the two superpowers worsened when, in 1945, Truman succeeded Roosevelt as president.

- Truman was much less willing to trust the Soviet Union than Roosevelt had been.
- He believed Stalin intended to set up buffer states in eastern Europe, under the control of the USSR.

3 The USSR

The USSR was a communist state under Stalin's dictatorship.

- People could vote in elections for the Supreme Soviet. But they could only vote for members of the Communist Party and the Supreme Soviet had no power. The USSR was governed by Stalin and committees of the Communist Party.

- In the communist system, people's lives were closely controlled. The rights of individuals were seen as less important than the good of society as a whole.
- The USSR had a planned economy. The government owned all industry and planned what every factory should produce.
- The general standard of living in the USSR was much lower than in the USA, but unemployment was rare, and there were not the extremes of wealth and poverty seen in the USA.
- Unlike the USA, the USSR had been attacked many times in the past. Germany had invaded Russia in 1914 and Hitler's invasion in 1941 had been particularly vicious. Stalin was determined that this would never happen again. In his view, the USSR could only be safe if the countries on its borders were controlled by communist governments. He believed that if he did not set up communist governments the USA would set up hostile countries on his border.

The main political and economic features of the USSR

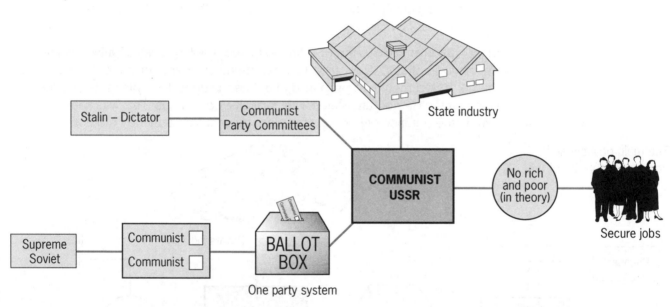

4 The USSR's policy on eastern Europe

The Soviet Red Army advanced through large areas of eastern Europe whilst driving back the Germans. One year after the war, many Soviet troops remained in much of eastern Europe, as the table below shows:

	Troops in Europe (millions)	
	1945	**1946**
USA	3.1	0.4
UK	1.3	0.5
USSR	6.0	6.0

Creating satellites

Elections were held in each east European country as promised at Yalta in 1945, but the evidence suggests that they were rigged to allow the USSR-backed communist parties to take control. In Bulgaria, Albania, Poland, Romania and Hungary, opponents of the communists had been beaten, murdered or frightened into submission. By 1948 all eastern European states had communist governments.

Yugoslavia was also under communist rule, although the communist leader Tito was not controlled by Stalin like the other communist governments. Tito had refused to submit to Stalin's control and Yugoslavia was cut off from any type of support from the USSR.

Europe was now divided – East and West. In 1946 Churchill called this division the Iron Curtain.

Stalin created the Cominform and later Comecon – a trading alliance of communist countries (see page 84) – to help him keep a tight grip on his neighbours. These countries became known as satellite countries because their governments and economies depended so heavily on the USSR.

● *Stalin was simply carrying out his policy of making sure he had friendly governments on his doorstep. However, to the British and Americans he seemed to be trying to build up a communist empire.* ●

● *Revision tasks*

1 Choose six key words to summarise the USA's system of government. Now choose six key words to summarise the USSR's system of government.
Compare the two under the headings:

USA	USSR

2 Use six to eight key words to explain why Stalin was determined to keep control of eastern Europe.

Greece and the spread of communism

C The Truman Doctrine, the Marshall Plan and the Berlin Crisis

1 Greece

You can see from the map that Greece appeared to be next in line in the spread of communism. Greek resistance against the Germans had been divided into two movements – the royalists (who wanted the return of the king) and the communists. After the war, the royalists were in charge and had restored the king with the help of British troops. However, they were under attack from the communist forces and asked the USA for help early in 1947.

Truman was already very worried about the spread of communism. Under a foreign policy initiative known as the Truman Doctrine, the USA provided Greece with arms, supplies and money, and the communists were defeated in 1949 after a civil war.

2 The Truman Doctrine

Events in Greece convinced Truman that, unless he acted, communism would continue to spread. He therefore explained his policy to the world. This became known as the Truman Doctrine:

- Truman said:

> *I believe it must be the policy of the USA to support all free peoples who are resisting attempted subjugation by armed minorities or by outside pressure.*

- The USA would not return to isolation – it would play a leading role in the world.
- The aim was to contain (stop the spread) of communism but not to push it back. This was the policy of CONTAINMENT.

Under the Truman Doctrine, the USA provided military and economic aid to Turkey as well as Greece. At this point it became clear that a 'cold war' – the term was first used by one of President Truman's advisers in 1947 – had started. The two sides believed in totally different political ideas. Each side feared the spread of the other idea. When one tried to extend its influence or support (for example, the USSR in eastern Europe), this was seen as a threat by the other side.

3 Marshall Aid, 1947

Truman believed that poverty and hardship provided a breeding ground for communism and so he wished to make Europe prosperous again. It was also important for American businesses to have someone to trade with in the future, yet Europe's economies were still in ruins after the war.

The American Secretary of State, George Marshall, therefore visited Europe and came up with a European Recovery Programme – usually known as the Marshall Plan or Marshall Aid.

This had two main aims:

- to stop the spread of communism (although Truman did not admit this at the time)
- to help the economies of Europe to recover (this would eventually provide a market for American exports).

Twelve billion dollars poured into Europe in the years 1947–51, providing vital help for the recovery of Europe. However, Marshall Aid also caused tensions:

- Only sixteen European countries accepted it – and these were all western European states.
- Stalin refused Marshall Aid for the USSR and banned the eastern European countries from accepting it.

● *Marshall Aid was a generous gesture by the USA but it was not entirely an act of kindness. Stalin saw it as an attempt by American business to dominate western Europe. If the USA was determined to 'buy' western Europe with its dollars, then he was determined to control eastern Europe with his communist allies and the Red Army.* ●

4 The Berlin blockade and airlift, 1948–49

At the end of the war the Allies divided Germany and Berlin into zones (see map on page 77). Germany's economy and government had been shattered by the war and the Allies were faced with a serious question: should they continue to occupy Germany or should they try to rebuild it?

- Britain and the USA wanted Germany to recover. They could not afford to keep feeding Germany and they felt that further punishment would not help future peace.
- The French were unsure about whether to get Germany back on its feet or to 'ram home its defeat'.
- The USSR did not want to rebuild Germany and Stalin was suspicious about why the USA and Britain did.

In 1948 the French, US and British zones merged to become West Germany. With the help of Marshall Aid, West Germany began to recover and prosper. However, in East Germany, controlled by the USSR, there was poverty and hunger. Many East Germans were leaving for the seemingly more attractive West Germany.

In Stalin's eyes it seemed the Allies were building up West Germany in order to attack him. When they introduced a new West German currency (the Deutschmark), this was the last straw.

Stalin tried to blockade Berlin. Berlin, the former capital of Germany, was in East Germany (see map on page 77). In a month Stalin closed all road and rail connections from Berlin to West Germany, hoping he could force the Western Allies out of Berlin. To many people it seemed there was a real risk of war.

The USA and Britain faced a choice:

- They could withdraw – but this would be humiliating and it might encourage Stalin to think he could invade West Germany.
- They could lift supplies into West Berlin by air. They had the planes but it would be risky – their planes might be shot down.

The Allies decided to airlift supplies. The airlift was a great success. The planes were not attacked. By May 1949 the USSR had lifted the blockade. It was a victory for the West. Relations with the USSR hit rock bottom. Co-operation in Germany in the future was very unlikely. Germany would remain divided. The Federal Republic of Germany (West Germany) was decreed in August 1949. In October 1949 the Soviet zone became the German Democratic Republic (East Germany).

● *The Berlin blockade was an extreme example of Cold War relationships. The USA and USSR held totally different ideas and neither side trusted the other. Any attempt by one side to help another country was seen as a threat to the other side.* ●

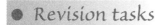

● *Revision tasks*

1 Use six key words to explain why Truman was worried about Stalin's plans.
2 Write your own definition of Marshall Aid.
3 Draw a table like the one below and use the information in this section to complete it. You should summarise the different views about the Berlin blockade using not more than five key words for each view.

Berlin blockade	Causes	Effects
US view		
USSR view		

4 How far do you feel each side was to blame for the tension after the Second World War? Decide where you would put the USA and the USSR on the scale below:

Mostly to blame ➤ Not to blame

D NATO, the Warsaw Pact and the arms race

1 Cominform, 1947

Stalin set up the Cominform – an alliance of communist countries – in 1947, probably as a response to the Marshall Plan. Its aim was to spread Stalin's communist ideas. Cominform helped Stalin tighten his hold on his communist allies because it restricted their contact with the West.

Only one communist leader, Marshal Tito of Yugoslavia, was not prepared to accept Stalin's total leadership and split with Moscow. However, Yugoslavia remained communist.

2 Comecon, 1949

This was set up by Stalin to co-ordinate the production and trade of the eastern European countries. It appeared rather like an early communist version of the European Union. However, Comecon favoured the USSR far more than any of its other members.

3 NATO (North Atlantic Treaty Organisation), 1949

This military alliance contained most of the states in western Europe as well as the USA and Canada. Its main purpose was to defend each of its members. If one member was attacked, all the others would help to defend it.

When the USSR developed its own atomic bomb in 1949, NATO seemed even more important to the defence of western Europe, since at the time no western European country had atomic weapons.

4 The Warsaw Pact, 1955

In 1955 West Germany joined NATO. The Soviet response was to set up the Warsaw Pact – a communist version of NATO. The Soviets had not forgotten the damage that Germany had done to the USSR in the Second World War.

NATO, Warsaw Pact and Comecon members

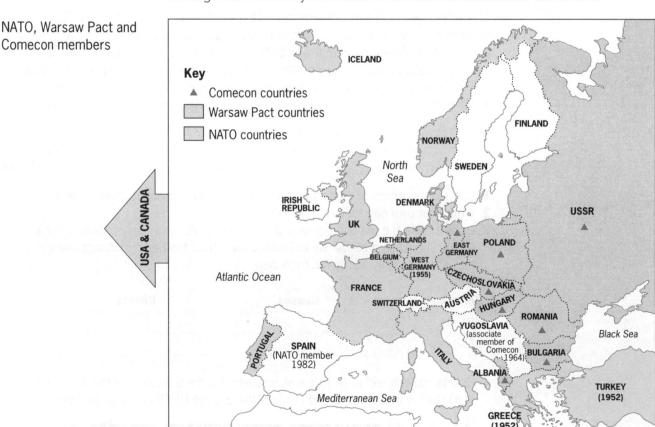

● *These alliances again demonstrated the fear and mistrust that brought about the Cold War. The Western democracies and the USSR both feared the rise of another state like Nazi Germany. However, each side saw the other as this potential threat, certainly not itself. The creation of alliances for self-defence on one side could very easily look like an alliance preparing for attack to the other side.* ●

5 The arms race

As relations between the USA and the Soviet Union worsened in the years after the Second World War, both sides began to develop their weapons so as to be able to 'outgun' their opponents. This meant:

- developing more powerful weapons
- trying to build more of each type of weapon than the other side.

Both sides developed nuclear weapons for several reasons:

- They were cheaper than conventional weapons or large armies.
- Nuclear weapons could act as a deterrent. Each side realised that in a nuclear war they would suffer appalling destruction.
- Prestige was also important. It was a test of capitalism *v.* communism.

Within four years of the USA dropping the first atomic bomb in 1945, the USSR had tested its own. In 1952 the USA tested its first hydrogen (H) bomb, followed, in 1953, by the Soviet Union. By 1957, however, the USSR appeared to have taken the lead. It tested the Intercontinental Ballistic Missile (ICBM) which was theoretically capable of carrying an H-bomb from the USSR to the USA. Within a year the USA had the same capability. In 1960 the USA launched the first nuclear-powered submarine capable of firing a Polaris missile with an atomic warhead from underwater.

The arms race was important because:

- it greatly increased tension between the two superpowers
- it became very expensive for both countries, especially in the 1960s and 1970s.

Nuclear weapons may well have prevented a third world war. Once ICBMs had been developed, it was certain that both superpowers could retaliate in the event of an attack. The enemy would not dare strike first for fear of retaliation. This idea was known as MAD – Mutually Assured Destruction.

● *The arms race certainly worsened relations between the USA and the USSR. It increased rivalry during the Cold War and led to the development of highly destructive nuclear weapons. On the other hand, it also had a positive effect. It made war less likely between the two superpowers because of the potential damage that these new weapons could cause and the fear of retaliation.* ●

● *Revision tasks*

1 Draw up a table like the one below and use the information and the map on page 84 to complete it.

Organisation	Members	Purpose	Effects on East–West relations
Cominform			

2 Use six key words to explain the arms race.
3 Write your own brief definition of the following:
   a) ICBMs
   b) H-bombs
   c) MAD.

E The Cold War, 1949–61

Relations between the superpowers deteriorated during this period. You will need to be aware of the crisis in Hungary in 1956, the U-2 incident of 1960 and the building of the Berlin Wall in 1961.

1 Khrushchev and the 'thaw'

Stalin died in 1953. There was a power struggle to succeed him as leader of the USSR. The winner was Nikita Khrushchev. Khrushchev seemed to be a less aggressive leader than Stalin and talked of peaceful coexistence (living in peace) with the West. In 1956, in a closed session at the Twentieth Congress of the Communist Party, he made a speech attacking Stalin for being a dictator.

Peaceful coexistence

The West began to see hopeful signs from the new Soviet leader.

- Khrushchev seemed to be encouraging greater freedom within the USSR and its allies.
- On a visit to Warsaw in 1956 he indicated that the Polish people should be allowed more freedom.

Up to 1956 the signs seemed very positive in terms of improving relations between East and West. Khrushchev appeared much less hostile to the West than Stalin had been. He also seemed to be willing to relax the USSR's grip on eastern Europe.

Eastern Europe

Later in 1956, events in Hungary showed a different side to Khrushchev.

- In 1956 a reforming government took power in Hungary. It announced its intention of leaving the Warsaw Pact and throwing off the influence of the USSR (see page 84).
- Khrushchev showed that he was not willing to allow this kind of change inside the Warsaw Pact. He sent Soviet troops and tanks into the Hungarian capital, Budapest. The rebellion was crushed and its leaders were killed.

● *Many historians doubt whether there was a real 'thaw' in the Cold War. Khrushchev was prepared to show a more friendly attitude to the West and was also prepared to consider reform inside the USSR. However, he was not prepared to let the USSR's iron grip on eastern Europe be threatened. This inevitably raised the tensions between the USA and the USSR.* ●

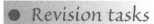 **Revision tasks**

1 Find four to six key words to summarise how Khrushchev was:
  a) different from Stalin
  b) similar to Stalin.
2 Describe Khrushchev from the point of view of the USA
  a) early in 1956
  b) towards the end of 1956.

2 Hungary, 1956

In July 1956 a reforming government led by Imre Nagy took power in Hungary after repeated rioting by students in Budapest. The new government planned to increase personal freedom and even talked of taking Hungary out of the Warsaw Pact.
The Soviet response was harsh:

- On 4 November Khrushchev sent 6000 Soviet tanks into Hungary to overthrow the rebellion and crush any further protest.

- The Soviets arrested Nagy and installed a loyal communist, Kadar, to set up a new government.
- Nagy was taken prisoner and later (in 1958) shot for his part in the rebellion.
- Soviet troops remained on Budapest streets until the crisis was over.

An estimated 3000 Hungarians were killed during the crisis and 200,000 fled to the West. The Western powers protested about the Soviet interference. However, the NATO powers did not assist or send any help to the Hungarian rebels at any point.

● *Although they were sympathetic to the Hungarian rebels, Western governments were not willing to risk a possible war with the Soviet Union over reform in Hungary. It is a feature of the Cold War that neither side intervened in the areas of the world that were of most vital interest to their opponents. They preferred to challenge each other in less direct ways.* ●

3   The U-2 incident

On 1 May 1960 another incident occurred which developed into a crisis. The Soviets shot down an American U-2 spy plane over the USSR and captured the pilot, Gary Powers. According to the Soviets, he admitted he was on a spying mission.

The American government denied that spying flights took place over Soviet territory and claimed that Gary Powers had accidentally strayed into Soviet airspace whilst on a flight to study weather conditions. The Soviets were keen to show the world that the American government was lying so they developed the film taken by Powers on his mission. It showed he had clearly been spying. This severely embarrassed the American government.

The results in terms of Cold War relations were extremely serious. Khrushchev demanded that the Americans must:

- apologise for the U-2 affair
- stop future spying flights
- punish those responsible.

Eisenhower, the American president, agreed to stop spying flights but refused to apologise. Gary Powers was sentenced to ten years in prison in the USSR but was in fact exchanged in 1962 for a Soviet agent. The incident was especially damaging for President Eisenhower:

- Not only had a US plane been shot down spying over Soviet territory, but the Americans had lied about it for all the world to see.
- The Soviets had scored a propaganda victory.

The U-2 affair showed how quickly conflict between the superpowers could develop from a single incident.

4   Berlin, 1961

Berlin had always been a source of conflict between the Soviets and the Western allies. Capitalist West Berlin – surrounded by the communist state of East Germany – continued to be a problem for East Germany and the USSR:

- The high standard of living enjoyed by the people of West Berlin contrasted sharply with that of the communist half of the city – East Berlin. It was a continual reminder to the people in East Germany of their poor living conditions.
- It was estimated that 3 million people had crossed from East to West Berlin between 1945 and 1960. Many of these people were skilled workers and it seemed that the survival of East Germany was in doubt if this escape route remained open.

In 1961 Khrushchev and the East German leadership decided to act. Without warning, on 13 August 1961, the East Germans began to build a wall surrounding West Berlin.

- At first the wall was little more than barbed wire, but by 17 August this was replaced with a stone wall.
- All movement between East and West was stopped.
- For several days Soviet and American tanks faced each other across divided Berlin streets.

The building of the Berlin Wall had some immediate effects:

- The flow of refugees was reduced to a trickle. Between 1961 and 1989, when the wall was knocked down, only 5000 people managed to escape across it.
- Western nations were given a propaganda victory, since it appeared that communist states needed to build walls to prevent their citizens from leaving.

However, it was only a propaganda victory. For it was clear that the USA and NATO were not going to try to stop the building of the wall. In reality, there was little the Western powers could do to stop it.

For the West, from the 1960s until the 1980s, the Berlin Wall became a symbol of the division between the capitalist West and communist East. US president John F. Kennedy made a historic visit to West Berlin and declared that the city was a symbol of the struggle between the forces of freedom and the communist world. For the USSR and East Germany, however, the wall was simply an economic and political necessity. The loss of so many refugees from East Germany was beginning to threaten the existence of the East German state.

● *Revision task*

1 Create a five-question quiz on the three crisis points. You can write your questions (and answers) here.

Questions
a)
b)
c)
d)
e)

Answers
a)
b)
c)
d)
e)

F The Cuban missile crisis

This was the most serious crisis between the two superpowers and almost led to armed conflict.

1 Causes of the crisis

The crisis was caused by worsening relations between the USA and Cuba.

- The USA had played an important role in Cuban affairs since the beginning of the twentieth century as the island is very near to the US mainland. In 1933 the Americans helped the Cuban military officer Fulgencio Batista to take power.
- Batista was corrupt and his government was overthrown in 1959 by Fidel Castro. Castro began appointing communists to the government and signed a trade agreement with the Soviet Union.
- In 1961 President Kennedy agreed to support a military expedition of Cuban exiles which aimed to overthrow Castro. This Bay of Pigs operation, as it became known, was a disastrous failure. It worsened relations between the USA and Cuba and drove Castro closer to the Soviet Union.
- Khrushchev, the president of the USSR, agreed to station ballistic missiles on Cuba. This was partly to defend Cuba against another US-sponsored invasion but also to test out Kennedy and try to achieve a Soviet diplomatic triumph.
- In October 1962 US spy planes identified nuclear missile sites being built on Cuba.

The location of missile sites on Cuba and the threat posed to US cities

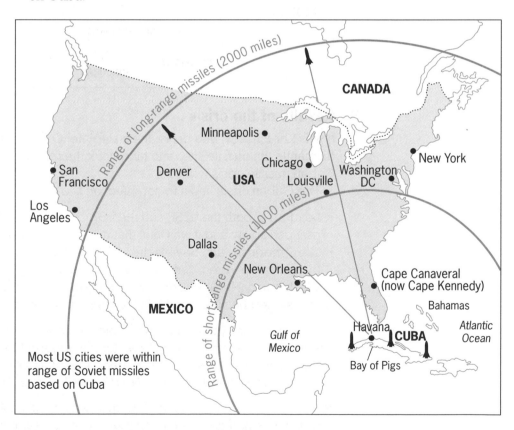

2 The events of the crisis, October 1962

President Kennedy and his closest advisers discussed what to do about the Soviet missiles in Cuba.

- Kennedy broadcast to the American people, informing them of the potential threat and what he intended to do about it.

- The Americans blockaded Cuba and began to stop any ship suspected of carrying arms and equipment.
- The Soviets and the Cuban leader Fidel Castro complained about US action to the United Nations and said it was a threat to world peace.
- President Kennedy threatened to invade Cuba and remove the missiles by force. The next ten days were tense. The world seemed to hold its breath as the USSR and USA headed towards nuclear conflict.

American blockade of Cuba, October 1962

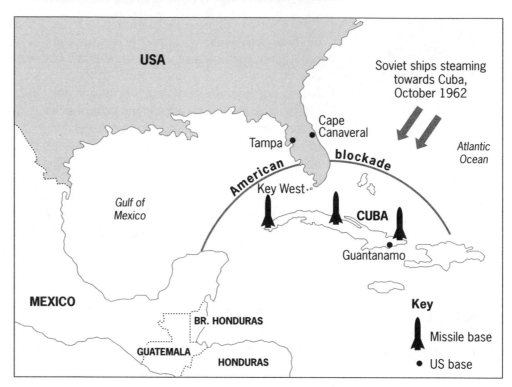

3 Results of the crisis

It was Khrushchev who broke the stalemate. On 28 October he agreed to dismantle the missile sites and take back the missiles to the Soviet Union. The Cuban missile crisis was over.

The Cuban crisis had a major effect on East–West relations:

- Leaders of both the USSR and the USA realised that nuclear war had been a real possibility and it was vital that a similar crisis should not happen again.
- The Americans and Soviets decided to set up a telephone link (hot line) so that, in future, direct communications could take place between Moscow and Washington. Nuclear arms talks also began, and in 1963 a Test Ban Treaty was signed between the USA, the USSR and Britain.

Debate over the Cuban crisis has continued ever since. President Kennedy became an instant hero in the West for his apparent tough handling of the Soviets. However, questions have been raised as to whether he made a secret deal with the Soviets to remove NATO missiles from Turkey.

● *In some ways the Cuban missile crisis was the height of Cold War tension. Never before had the world been so close to nuclear conflict as it was in October 1962. However, the crisis actually resulted in arms reductions and improved communications (if not better relations) between the USA and the USSR.* ●

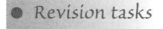

Revision tasks

1 Using eight key words list the main causes of the Cuban missile crisis.
2 List two ways in which the Cuban missile crisis made relations between the USA and the USSR worse.
3 List two ways in which the crisis made relations better.

G Attempts at détente and the impact of the Soviet invasion of Afghanistan

The Cuban missile crisis in 1962 brought the superpowers to the edge of nuclear war. In the years that followed, both the USA and USSR began to look for ways in which future conflict could be avoided. By the end of the 1960s there was a general easing of tension between the superpowers. This easing of tension became known as DÉTENTE.

1 Reasons for détente

Détente came about because a number of favourable factors came together at the same time.

- The Vietnam War had damaged the confidence of the USA. The USA was keen to find ways to avoid further conflict.
- The cost of the nuclear arms race was escalating.

The arms race was based on the policy of MAD (Mutually Assured Destruction). This meant that in theory neither side would use nuclear weapons because the other side would retaliate – both sides would be destroyed. However, there was a wish to move away from this policy for the following reasons:

- The cost of the arms race was huge.
- Stockpiles of weapons were so large that both superpowers had the capacity to destroy the earth many times over.
- The Soviets wanted ways to reduce their arms budget so that they could spend more on improving standards of living.
- The Americans also wanted to reduce expenditure on arms in order to increase spending on reducing poverty at home.

Hostility between China and the USSR, which had developed during the Khrushchev era, meant that there was no longer the simple situation of a single communist enemy facing the capitalist countries of the West.

- For the USA, détente was a way of helping further to divide the USSR from China.
- For the Chinese, détente was an opportunity to develop relations with the USA and end China's isolation. The Chinese leadership was looking for American investment to help modernise their country.

● *Détente came about in the late 1960s because several factors coincided. It was in the interests of the superpowers to have better relations.* ●

2 Key trends in the period of détente

The late 1960s saw a series of initiatives that improved relations between the communist and non-communist world.

East and West Germany
During the late 1960s, Willy Brandt, Chancellor of West Germany, worked hard to form closer ties with communist East Germany. This policy was called OSTPOLITIK. In 1972 agreements were signed between East and West Germany recognising each other's frontiers and developing trade links.

Strategic Arms Limitation Talks (SALT)
In 1969 the USA and USSR began the SALT negotiations in an effort to control the arms race. The talks lasted for three years and in 1972 SALT 1 was signed. Both sides agreed to keep the numbers of nuclear weapons and warheads within strict limits. They also agreed to begin further talks to discuss weapons systems not included in SALT 1.

Cooperation in space

Throughout the 1960s the Americans and Soviets had been arch rivals in the 'space race'. Yet in July 1975 three American astronauts and two Soviet cosmonauts docked their Apollo and Soyuz spacecraft together in orbit around the Earth. It was one of the most visible signs of détente in action and gave a further impetus to superpower co-operation.

3 The Helsinki Conference, August 1975

In August 1975, at Helsinki in Finland, 35 countries including the USSR and the USA signed the Helsinki Agreement. This was a high point for détente.

- The Western powers recognised the frontiers of eastern Europe and Soviet influence in that area.
- The Soviets agreed to allow greater freedom in the Soviet Union to Western journalists, and to give 21 days' notice before holding military manoeuvres near to a frontier.
- West Germany officially recognised East Germany.
- The Soviets agreed to buy US grain and export oil to the West.
- All countries agreed to improve human rights throughout the world.

It should be remembered that these resolutions were not always entirely put into force. For example, abuses of human rights continued in the USSR and other countries after 1975.

● *Although not all aspects of détente in this period were total successes, events such as SALT 1 and the Helsinki Agreement were important because they showed a commitment by the superpowers to work to improve relations.* ●

4 Détente between the USA and China

Relations between the USA and China began to improve at the beginning of the 1970s.

- Visits by US and Chinese table tennis teams to each other's countries in 1971–72 led to the term 'ping-pong diplomacy'.
- In October 1971 the USA dropped its support for Taiwan as the sole Chinese representative at the United Nations and accepted communist China.
- In 1972 US President Richard Nixon made a historic visit to see the ageing Chairman Mao in Beijing.
- Trade talks and improving relations followed. Contact between Western nations and China continued after the death of Mao in 1976.

In the 1980s private firms were given greater freedom in China and communism was relaxed. In 1989, however, student demonstrations aimed at increasing democracy in China were crushed by the army. Relations between China and Western nations deteriorated immediately and have yet to recover fully.

5 Afghanistan, 1979

The improving relations between the superpowers during the 1970s were once again damaged by the USSR's invasion of Afghanistan in 1979. The Soviets insisted that they had been invited into Afghanistan to restore order, but Western nations protested that it was a straightforward invasion that could not be justified. Despite world-wide protests, the invasion and occupation of Afghanistan continued.

The Soviets invaded Afghanistan for several reasons:

- They were concerned about the Muslim revolution in neighbouring Iran which could have spread to Afghanistan and Muslim areas inside the Soviet Union.

- The political situation in Afghanistan was very unstable at the end of the 1970s and the Soviets wanted to maintain their influence in the area.
- Afghanistan was close to the Middle East oil reserves of the Western powers and the ports of the Indian Ocean. The Soviets wanted to develop their interests in this area.

The invasion of Afghanistan brought a return to Cold War tensions:

- The USA did not agree to SALT 2.
- The USA boycotted the Moscow Olympics.
- The USA stopped grain shipments to the Soviet Union and increased aid to Afghan rebels.
- Relations between the USA and the USSR did not begin to improve again until Gorbachev became leader of the Soviet Union in 1985.

There were similarities between the USA's experience in Vietnam and the USSR's in Afghanistan.

- Within weeks of the invasion, Soviet troops were being killed by Mujahadin GUERRILLAS using the same tactics as those developed by the VIET CONG against American troops in the Vietnam War.
- There was protest against the war at home in the USSR.
- After a nine-year occupation, President Gorbachev agreed in 1988 at an international summit with the USA that Soviet troops would leave Afghanistan – apparently with little of anything positive to show for their long war.

Afghan resistance to Soviet forces, 1979

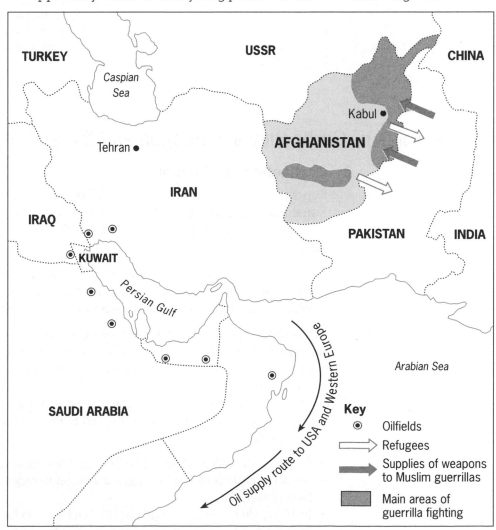

● *Revision tasks*

1 Produce your own definition of détente using two examples from this section.
2 Explain why the Helsinki Conference was important (use six to eight key words).
3 Use six to eight key words to produce a summary of why arms reduction was so successful in the 1980s.
4 Draw a table like the one below and use key words on the Soviet invasion of Afghanistan to complete each section.

Causes	
Events	
Results	

5 This final task looks back over the whole Cold War period, 1948–1980s.
   a) Copy the table below and use the information in this section to complete it. Your aim is to create a summary of the major Cold War crises of the period. One example has been done for you.
   b) When you have completed columns 1–3, give each incident a mark out of ten which in your view reflects the seriousness of the incident. Put your marks in column 4.

Incident/Date	Countries involved	Cause of tension	How serious?
Hungary 1956	Hungary USSR	New government in Hungary. Possibility that it would leave Warsaw Pact. Soviet invasion	

H The roles of Gorbachev and Reagan and the end of the Cold War

1 Gorbachev and Reagan

Superpower diplomacy during the 1980s was dominated by US President Ronald Reagan and Mikhail Gorbachev of the USSR.

Reagan was elected US president in 1980. He was not worried about standing up to the USSR.

- Reagan began to build up American defence forces and spending.
- He ordered further research into the Strategic Defense Initiative (SDI or Star Wars programme, a satellite anti-missile system that would orbit the Earth).

In the USSR, Brezhnev continued to support hard-line communist policies up until his death in 1982. Brezhnev was followed first by Andropov (who lived only a few months longer) and then by Chernenko. Neither lived long enough to make an impact.

In March 1985 Mikhail Gorbachev became leader of the Soviet Union and immediately set about reforming the old Soviet system and improving relations with the USA.

- Gorbachev realised that the USSR could not afford an arms race with the USA.
- He accepted President Reagan's invitation to meet with him in Geneva in November 1985.
- In 1987, after several meetings, Gorbachev and Reagan signed the Intermediate-range Nuclear Forces (INF) treaty, which removed all medium-range nuclear weapons from Europe.

- SALT had developed into START (STrategic Arms Reduction Talks), and on an official visit to Washington in December 1988 Gorbachev also proposed deep cuts in conventional (non-nuclear) US and Soviet forces.

The key figure in this period is Gorbachev. He firmly believed that the USSR could not continue to compete with the USA and that the USSR needed to be reformed.

Revision tasks

1 Explain how Reagan was a new kind of American leader compared to American presidents of the 1970s.
2 In what ways was Gorbachev a new kind of Soviet leader?
3 What progress did disarmament make in the 1980s?

2 The collapse of communism

As the period of renewed co-operation developed, the pace of change increased in eastern Europe. In the USSR Gorbachev had made major reforms to the Soviet system, and in neighbouring communist countries old-style communist leaders began to face opposition to their rule.

- In 1989 Gorbachev refused to provide assistance to the East German government as it faced protesters demanding increased freedom. In October, crowds in Berlin took the initiative and began taking down the Berlin Wall whilst East German guards stood by.
- Within two years Gorbachev was also swept from power. The Soviet Union began to disintegrate, the Warsaw Pact collapsed and communist governments throughout eastern Europe fell from power.
- By the beginning of the 1990s the USA was the sole world superpower – the Cold War had been won.

The collapse of communism in the USSR and its satellites

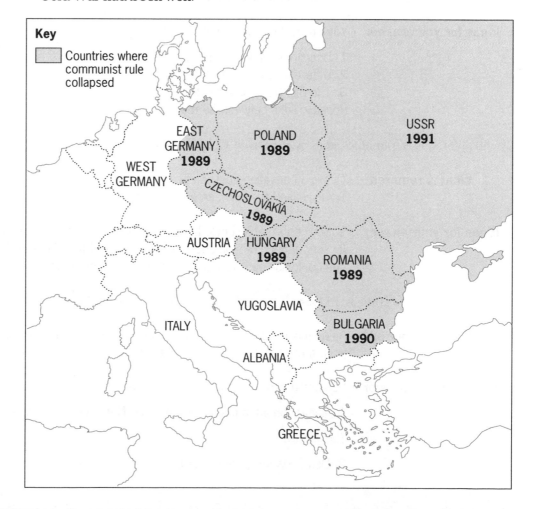

Key

▨ Countries where communist rule collapsed

EAST GERMANY **1989**

WEST GERMANY

POLAND **1989**

USSR **1991**

CZECHOSLOVAKIA **1989**

AUSTRIA

HUNGARY **1989**

ROMANIA **1989**

YUGOSLAVIA

ITALY

BULGARIA **1990**

ALBANIA

GREECE

Revision session

The aim of this session is for you to see how you can apply your knowledge of the content in this chapter to the kind of questions you will face in your examinations.

Examination questions

The most important theme that examiners ask about in questions on this topic is how and why relations between the superpowers changed at different times after 1945. For example, look at these examination questions adapted by permission of Edexcel from the Specimen Paper for Paper 1.

---

a) i) Give ONE reason to explain why the leaders of the Allies met at Yalta in 1945. *(3 marks)*

What is required? This is a simple test of knowledge and memory. A simple factual answer will do. It is only worth three marks.

Ideas for your answer You could write about the need to divide up territory after the Allied victory, the issue of whether Germany should be made to pay damages or how best to deal with war criminals.

---

ii) Describe the key features of the Potsdam Conference. *(5 marks)*

What is required? This question is asking you to identify and describe at least two important features or points about the Potsdam Conference. Identify the feature and then describe it as precisely as possible. Try to make links between the key features you describe.

Ideas for your answer You could describe two of the following key features:

1 Decisions made about Germany.
2 Differences over reparations.
3 The Big Three and the UN.
Possible links between Germany and the problem of reparations.

---

iii) Why was Berlin blockaded by the Soviet Union in 1948? *(5 marks)*

What is required? This is a causation question and you need to identify and explain at least two causes. Try to make links between each cause.

Ideas for your answer 1 Your first reason could be the success of West Berlin compared to East Berlin.
2 Your second reason could be the impact of the Marshall Plan on West Berlin.
You could link each reason to the development of West Berlin.

---

iv) Why was the Hungarian Uprising in 1956 crushed by the Soviet Union? *(7 marks)*

What is required? Again this is causation, and you need to identify and explain as precisely as possible at least three reasons for the Soviet actions. Try to make links between each reason.

Ideas for your answer You could explain the following reasons:

1 Hungarian attempts at reform under Nagy and their impact on the Soviet Union.

This led to:

2 Demands for greater freedom and far less Soviet control.

This resulted in:

3 Khrushchev's fears about the effects the Uprising would have on Soviet control of eastern Europe.

---

b) i) Why was there such a major crisis between the superpowers over Cuba in 1962?   *(10 marks)*

What is required? Another causation question. You will need to identify and explain at least three reasons for the Cuban missile crisis. If your explanation is relevant and precise this would be enough for level 3 (6–8 marks). For a top-level answer you will need to ensure that:

1 your whole answer relates to the question
2 you make links between each reason
3 you include an introduction that discusses the meaning of the question and how you will tackle it
4 you finish with a conclusion that sums up and explains the main reason for the crisis.

Ideas for your answer For your introduction, think about the following points:

- What is the question asking?
- Which causes will I discuss?

Draw up a table like the one below and use it as a check-list to plan your answer. One section has been done for you.

	Identify the cause	Explain the cause	Link with next cause
First cause	The Cuban revolution	Castro and closer relations with USSR	Cuba close to USA which feared communism
Second cause			
Third cause			

You could explain the following reasons:

1 Castro and his closer relations with the USSR. US fears of communist influence.
2 Khrushchev and the decision to build missile bases.
3 The US discovery of the missile bases and Kennedy's actions.

For your conclusion, you could cover the following points:

- What were the causes of the crisis?
- Which was the basic cause and why?

---

ii) In what ways did relations between the USA and USSR change in the years 1979–90?
You may use the following information to help you with your answer:

- 1979   invasion of Afghanistan
- 1980s   USA threatens to develop 'Star Wars'

- roles of Gorbachev and Reagan
- 1986   INF treaty signed.   *(15 marks)*

What is required?   This is a question about change. You will need to identify and explain the four main changes mentioned in the question, although you could add at least one more. If your explanation is relevant and precise this would be enough for level 3 (9–12 marks). For a top-level answer (13–15 marks) you would need to ensure that:

1 your whole answer relates to change
2 you link one paragraph (change) to the next
3 you write an introduction that explains the meaning of the question and how you will tackle it
4 you write a conclusion that sums up and possibly links the main changes.

Ideas for your answer   Copy and complete the table below and use it as a check-list to plan your answer. One section has been done for you.

	Invasion of Afghanistan	Star Wars	Reagan and Gorbachev	INF treaty	Another change?
Cause of change	Soviet invasion				
Nature of change	Poorer relations				
Scope or how much change	Major turning-point with return to Cold War tensions				

Now write your answer.

1 You need an introduction setting the scene for your answer by identifying the major areas of change.
2 For your extra change you could explain the end of the Cold War.
3 Your conclusion should sum up your main points and identify the main change.

Practice questions

Now have a go at the following questions.

a)   **i)**   Give ONE reason for the introduction of the Marshall Plan in 1947.   *(3 marks)*

      ii)   Describe the key features of the Marshall Plan.   *(5 marks)*

      iii)   Why did the Truman Doctrine of 1947 increase rivalry between the two superpowers?   *(5 marks)*

      iv)   Why was the Soviet blockade of Berlin, 1948–49, defeated by Britain and the USA?   *(7 marks)*

b)   **i)**   Why did rivalry between the USA and USSR increase in the period 1950–61?   *(10 marks)*

      ii)   Describe the key features of the Cuban missile crisis of 1962. You may use the following information to help you with your answer:

- US discovery of Soviet missile sites
- US blockade of Cuba

- reactions of USSR
- end of crisis.   *(15 marks)*

Summary and revision plan

Below is a list of headings which you may find helpful. Use this as a check-list to make sure that you are familiar with the material featured in this chapter. Record your key words alongside each heading.

A Origins of the Cold War and the partition of Germany
- ❑ Conflicting ideologies: communism and capitalism
- ❑ Political changes in Europe: occupation, resistance and liberation
- ❑ The Yalta Conference, February 1945
- ❑ The Potsdam Conference, July–August 1945

B Reasons for superpower rivalry
- ❑ The USA
- ❑ The attitude of Truman
- ❑ The USSR
- ❑ The USSR's policy on eastern Europe

C The Truman Doctrine, the Marshall Plan and the Berlin Crisis
- ❑ Greece
- ❑ The Truman Doctrine
- ❑ Marshall Aid, 1947
- ❑ The Berlin blockade and airlift, 1948–49

D NATO, the Warsaw Pact and the arms race
- ❑ Cominform, 1947
- ❑ Comecon, 1949
- ❑ NATO (North Atlantic Treaty Organisation), 1949
- ❑ The Warsaw Pact, 1955
- ❑ The arms race

E The Cold War, 1949–61
- ❑ Khrushchev and the 'thaw'
- ❑ Hungary, 1956
- ❑ The U-2 incident
- ❑ Berlin, 1961

F The Cuban missile crisis
- ❑ Causes of the crisis
- ❑ The events of the crisis, October 1962
- ❑ Results of the crisis

Continued on page 100

G Attempts at détente and the impact of the Soviet invasion of Afghanistan
- ❏ Reasons for détente
- ❏ Key trends in the period of détente
- ❏ The Helsinki Conference, August 1975
- ❏ Détente between the USA and China
- ❏ Afghanistan, 1979

H The roles of Gorbachev and Reagan and the end of the Cold War
- ❏ Gorbachev and Reagan
- ❏ The collapse of communism

Section B – Depth Studies

Exam Skills: How to succeed in Edexcel Paper 2

Format of Paper 2

You have to select questions from two Depth Studies including:

- The Russian Revolution, *c.* 1910–24
- The War to End Wars, 1914–19
- Depression and the New Deal: the USA, 1929–41
- Nazi Germany, *c.* 1930–39
- The World at War, 1938–45
- Conflict in Vietnam, *c.* 1963–75.

You could also choose:

- The End of Apartheid in South Africa, 1982–94

but we have *not* covered that option in this revision guide.

Each Depth Study question has six sources followed by four source questions.

Historical sources

In every GCSE History course, it is important to make use of *historical sources*. In Paper 2 examination questions, you will be asked to evaluate these sources.

A historical source can be virtually anything that survives from the past, such as:

- a poster or photograph
- an extract from a diary
- an extract from a textbook
- a recorded interview written down at a later date.

You have probably seen many other types of historical source in your GCSE course. Make your own list of sources.

Answering source-based questions

In this chapter we look at the particular skills required to answer source-based questions for Paper 2. One important point to remember is that you cannot demonstrate your skills in analysing sources without a good background knowledge of the period you are studying. So it is extremely important to revise for these questions.

In examinations you will come across questions such as:

- What can you learn from Source A about...?
- How could Source D be useful as evidence about...?

To answer such questions you must be able to:

- understand what a source is saying
- find in a source the relevant pieces of information to answer questions
- see the difference in a source between facts, opinions and judgements
- recognise how and why a source is or is not biased.

Making judgements

Remember there are no black and white answers to source questions. Examiners usually provide a range of sources which present different viewpoints in questions. Your task is to show that you:

- understand each source
- know the context or background of each source
- can express views on its reliability
- can look at several sources, evaluate them against each other, decide whether they fit in with your own knowledge and reach a conclusion.

You are being asked to think about the sources and to make judgements about them. In practice this means producing answers along the lines of:

- Source A is useful for . . . but it has these drawbacks . . .
- At the time the source was written . . . was happening. This might have affected the author's views about . . .

If you need help in evaluating sources then this memory aid summarises the questions you have to ask yourself:

Source: where it comes from (date/author, etc.)
Objective: why it was written (for a diary/a newspaper)
Usefulness: how useful it is to the enquiry or question you are doing
Reliability: how reliable it is for your purposes
Context: how does your background knowledge help you understand or explain the source
Example: always use examples from the source to back up what you say.

Question-specific skills

There are four different questions on each Depth Study.

a) What can you learn from Source A about . . . ?   *(4 marks)*
b) Does Source C support the evidence of Sources A and B about . . . ? Explain your answer.   *(6 marks)*
c) How useful are Sources D and E as evidence about . . . ?   *(8 marks)*
d) 'Cause x was the main reason for event y.'
    Use the sources, and your own knowledge, to explain whether you agree with this view.   *(12 marks)*

1 Comprehension of sources

What can you learn from Source A about the importance of the Battle of Britain?   *(4 marks)*

- You are expected to make inferences from the source. That means you have to read between the lines of what it says. Look for hidden meanings.
- To encourage you to do this, start your sentence with 'Source A suggests that . . .'
- Explain your inference.

2 Comparison of sources

Here you are asked to compare three sources.

Does Source C support the views of Sources A and B? *(6 marks)*

- Ensure you directly compare Source C to the other two sources.
- Look for similarities and differences. Sometimes these are quite subtle and not very obvious.
- In your conclusion judge to what extent Source C supports the other two.

You could use the following table to help you plan your answer.

Sources	Similarities	Differences
C to A		
C to B		

3 Usefulness of sources

This asks you to judge the usefulness of two sources.

How useful are Sources D and E? *(8 marks)*

You need to explain the usefulness and limitations of each source.

	Usefulness	Limitations
Content	The source is useful because of what it tells you about the event or person. It contains facts such as...	• It only provides a limited view of the event. It does not tell us... • It is not accurate because... • It is mainly opinions such as ... rather than facts.
Nature	The source is useful because it is a newspaper, poster, photograph or...	• The photograph only gives one limited view of the event. • The poster/newspaper exaggerates the event.
Who wrote it	It is written by someone whose views are worth knowing. Why?	The author is very one-sided and/or did not witness the event.
When it was written	• It was written at the time by an eyewitness. It gives the feelings, views of that time. • It was written later and the writer had the benefit of hindsight.	• It was written at the time and so does not have the benefit of hindsight. • It was written later and the author has forgotten important events...
View/attitude	• It is a very good and/or typical view of the time. • It is a good example of propaganda.	• It only gives the attitude of one person/group/party. • It does not give the attitude of...
Purpose	It reflects the purpose of the author e.g. propaganda.	It does not give a balanced view because its purpose is to win the support of the reader for...

For this type of question:

- Ensure you explain usefulness and limitations.
- Use examples from the sources to illustrate your answer.
- Judge the usefulness of each source in terms of the context in which it was produced, i.e. by what you know of that event/period.
- You must decide how useful a source is, based on **content/context** and **nature/purpose**.
- Include a conclusion that sums up the usefulness of each source and also judges their combined usefulness: for example, Sources D and E are useful because they give different views of the event.

4 Synthesis question

This is the last question and it asks you to judge an interpretation of an event using the sources and your own knowledge.

'The most important reason for the failure of the Provisional Government of Russia in 1917 was its failure to end Russian involvement in the First World War.' Use the sources, and your own knowledge, to explain whether you agree with this view.

(12 marks)

- You need an introduction that explains the interpretation and how you intend to answer the question.
- Ensure you give a balanced answer that agrees and disagrees with the interpretation.
- Use the sources and your own knowledge for both sides of your answer.
- Begin each paragraph of your answer with a sentence that agrees or disagrees with the interpretation.
- Write a conclusion that sums up your view of the interpretation and perhaps decides which was the most important reason.

It is well worth making a plan of your answer before you write it. You could use the following table.

	Supports interpretation	Disagrees with interpretation
Arguments		
Own knowledge		
Sources		

Through the next six chapters you will apply these principles to six of the most popular Depth Studies.

The Russian Revolution, *c.*1910–24

In 1910 Russia was ruled by Tsar Nicholas II and within four years had gone to war against Germany and Austria–Hungary. The war was a disaster, with defeat after defeat and economic, political and military chaos. In 1917 there were two revolutions. These were followed by three years of civil war. The Communists under Lenin emerged triumphant. Lenin introduced a series of reforms designed to modernise the country.

To answer source-based questions on Russia between 1910 and 1924, you need to be familiar with the key content and key themes of the period. This will help you to show your understanding of sources relating to this topic and help you to apply your general and question-specific source skills.

Key content   You will need to have a good working knowledge of these areas:

A Russia before the First World War: politics, society and economy
B Opposition to Tsarist rule
C The impact of the First World War on Russian government and society
D 1917: the fall of the Tsar
E The collapse of the Provisional Government
F The nature of the Bolshevik take-over; the roles of Lenin and Trotsky
G The Bolshevik dictatorship
H Opposition to the Bolsheviks and the Civil War
I War Communism and the New Economic Policy

Key themes   You will also be asked to show your understanding of some key themes:

● How important was the First World War in the fall of Tsarist rule?
● Why was there a revolution in February (March) 1917?
● How and why did the Provisional Government collapse so quickly?
● Why did the Bolsheviks successfully seize power in October (November) 1917?
● Who opposed the Bolsheviks during the Civil War of 1918–21?
● What reasons were there for the Bolshevik victory?
● How and why did Lenin change his economic policies in the period 1918–24?

Source-based questions test the following:

• your knowledge of the topic
• your understanding of sources from the period being studied
• your ability to evaluate and/or interpret the sources.

Below is an example of a source question adapted by permission of Edexcel from Paper 2, 1998.

Source A A table showing food prices and bread rations in Russia in 1917

Selected food prices, 1917 (in roubles)		
	July	**October**
Lard (1lb)	1.10	5.40
Cheese (1lb)	1.60	5.40
Cabbage (1lb)	1.60	2.20
Sausages (1lb)	1.00	6.00

Bread rations, 1917 (per day)				
	March	**April**	**Sept**	**Oct**
Manual workers	$1\frac{1}{2}$lb	$\frac{3}{4}$lb	$\frac{1}{2}$lb	$\frac{1}{4}$lb
Others	1 lb	$\frac{3}{4}$lb	$\frac{1}{2}$lb	$\frac{1}{4}$lb

a) Study Source A.
What can you learn from Source A about the situation in Russia in 1917? *(4 marks)*

You can see from this sort of question that you need to use your knowledge in order to put the source in context and interpret information from the source.

· You need to look closely at the source and interpret what it shows about the situation in Russia in 1917.
· Explain what the source shows, using information from the source but developing it further from your own knowledge and making inferences from the source.

We will look at this and other source questions in more detail at the end of this chapter.

A Russia before the First World War: politics, society and economy

1 The Tsarist system of government

The Russian monarch was known as the Tsar. He ruled as an AUTOCRAT. He believed that God had made him Tsar and that he therefore had absolute authority to rule Russia. The Tsar ruled with the support of the aristocracy (landowners), Church, army and the civil service.

2 Russian economy and society

The Russian economy was developing fast in the years before 1914, especially in the period 1908–11. Russia, however, was still far behind modern industrial powers such as Britain, Germany and the USA. There was much discontent.

• The numbers working in industry were growing fast. Between 1880 and 1900 the population of Moscow doubled. As more and more people swarmed into the big cities, conditions deteriorated rapidly. Food shortages, poor wages and terrible living conditions were commonplace.

- In 1905 more than 80 per cent of the population were peasants living in the countryside on the estates of wealthy landlords. Most were illiterate and used outdated farming methods which produced barely enough to live on.
- At the same time there was a significant minority of subject nationalities – Finns, Estonians, Poles, Latvians – who hated Russian rule and wanted independence.

3 Failures, 1906–14

In 1905 a protest by industrial workers (Bloody Sunday) turned into a full-scale revolution. The Tsar survived the revolution of 1905 but only because he promised the rebels a Duma or parliament to give them a say in government. However:

- He gave the Dumas very little power. The first and second Dumas were critical of the Tsar and only lasted a year.
- In 1906 he appointed a tough new prime minister – Peter Stolypin. Stolypin used a 'carrot and stick' approach to the problems of Russia. The carrot was land reform to win over the peasants, but this was too little too late. The stick was to come down hard on strikers, protesters and revolutionaries. Over 20,000 were exiled and over 1000 hanged by the noose known as 'Stolypin's necktie'. He was assassinated in 1911.
- In 1912 there was a downturn in the economy, causing unemployment and hunger. Strikes were commonplace. The most important strike took place at Lena goldfields in 1912 where troops opened fire on strikers.

● *Revision tasks*

1 Copy the table below and complete it using key words to explain why these groups were becoming discontented in the years before 1914.

Group	Reasons for discontent
Peasants	
Town workers	
Subject nationalities	

2 What contribution did the following make to discontent in the period 1906–14:
   a) the Dumas
   b) Stolypin
   c) the Lena goldfield strike?

B Opposition to Tsarist rule

Several opposition groups emerged at the beginning of the twentieth century.

1 The Socialist Revolutionaries

This was the largest and most violent of the groups and was supported by many peasants.

- They wanted to carve up the huge estates of the nobility and hand them over to the peasants.
- They believed in violent struggle and were responsible for the assassination of two government officials as well as the murder of a great number of the members of the Okhrana or secret police.

2 The Social Democratic Labour Party

This was a smaller party which followed the ideas of Karl Marx and believed in communism. They believed that communism would be achieved through revolution by the proletariat (town workers). In 1903 the party split itself into:

- BOLSHEVIKS – led by Lenin who believed it was the job of the party to create a revolution
- Mensheviks – who believed Russia was not ready for revolution.

Both the Socialist Revolutionaries and the Social Democratic Labour Party were illegal and many of their members were executed or sent into exile in Siberia.

3 Moderate opposition

These opposition groups did not want revolution and included:

- the Constitutional Democrats or Kadets, set up in 1905 and led by Paul Miliukov. They were mostly lawyers, teachers, doctors and civil servants. They believed in working with the constitution or laws of Russia to bring about change, especially through the Dumas.
- the Octobrists, formed in 1906. They believed in change through the October Manifesto, which the Tsar issued in 1905, creating a Duma.

● *There were major problems in Russia even before the First World War. Peasants in the countryside and workers in industry were unhappy with their way of life. Tsar Nicholas II had survived the revolution of 1905 but this had not stopped the growth of opposition, especially of revolutionary groups such as the Bolsheviks.* ●

● *Revision task*

1 Copy the following table and complete it using key words to explain the opposition groups.

Opposition group	Aims/activities
Socialist Revolutionaries	
Bolsheviks	
Mensheviks	
Kadets	
Octobrists	

C The impact of the First World War on Russian government and society

1 Rasputin

Many of the Tsar's supporters were alarmed by the influence of Rasputin over Nicholas and his wife Alexandra, before and during the war. Through the use of hypnosis, Rasputin, a monk, seemed to be able to control haemophilia, a disease that afflicted the Tsar's son, Alexis. Rasputin became unpopular because of:

- his womanising and drinking
- the control he had over the government of Russia, especially when the Tsar took command of the Russian army in 1915 and left Alexandra in control of the government. Rasputin brought about the dismissal of capable ministers and officials.

He was assassinated by a group of nobles at the end of 1916, by which time the damage had been done.

2 Military defeat

The Russian soldiers were poorly equipped, often with shortages of weapons and ammunition. They suffered a series of crushing defeats at the hands of the Germans, including Tannenburg in August 1914, and were further weakened by the long-term effects of the Brusilov offensive of 1916, which resulted in one million casualties and further hardship at home.

The Tsar took over personal command of the army in 1915. This was a mistake as he was now directly to blame for any defeats.

3 Economic chaos

The Russian economy could not cope with the increased demands of war.

- There was even greater overcrowding in the towns and cities, low wages and rising prices.
- The Russian transport system proved totally inadequate and food often failed to reach towns and cities.
- There were serious fuel shortages by the end of 1916.

4 Social misery

By the end of 1916 there was discontent throughout Russia.

- In the towns and cities there were high prices and food and fuel shortages.
- In the countryside there were too few peasants to work on the land due to conscription. Consequently they suffered from increasing food shortages.
- Conditions in the army were so bad (lack of equipment and even boots) that an increasing number of soldiers deserted.
- There was a severe winter (even by Russian standards) in 1916–17.

● *Revision tasks*

1 a) What hold did Rasputin have over the Tsar and his wife?
   b) Why was he so unpopular by 1916?
2 Copy the table below on the impact of the First World War on Russia and complete it using key words.

	Impact of First World War
Military situation	
Economic situation	
Social situation	

D 1917: the fall of the Tsar

1 The February Revolution

This is often called the March Revolution because in 1917 Russia was using a different calendar from the West. As a result, the first Russian revolution took place in February by the Russian calendar, but March for the rest of Europe. This book will use the 'Russian' dates.

The unrest began in February 1917 with a strike at the Puetilov steelworks in Petrograd.

- Unrest and strikes spread quickly and bread queues turned into riots.
- The workers began to form councils (called Soviets) and the leaders of the Duma (including Kerensky) began opposing the Tsar openly.
- By the end of February the troops had joined the rioters and the Tsar had no choice but to abdicate (give up power) on 3 March. The Tsar's regime was replaced by a provisional government.

The fall of the Tsar and the February Revolution of 1917 were due to long-term, short-term and immediate factors.

2 Long-term factors

These included:

- the growth of opposition to Tsarist rule at the beginning of the twentieth century
- discontent amongst several groups, including peasants, town workers and national minorities
- the troubled years 1906–14, especially the failure of the Dumas and Stolypin's repression.

3 Short-term factors

- The impact of the First World War.

4 Immediate factors

- The severe winter of 1916–17.
- The situation in Petrograd, including food and fuel shortages.
- Demonstrations and loss of support of the army.
- Nicholas's absence from the government while he was at the battle front.

● *The Bolsheviks later claimed that the events of February 1917 were planned by leading Bolsheviks. This was not the case. In many respects the strikes and protests were a spontaneous reaction to the disasters of the First World War and the severe winter of 1916–17.* ●

● *Revision tasks*

1 Do your own spider diagram showing the long-term, short-term and immediate causes of the February Revolution of 1917.
2 Do you agree that the First World War was the key factor in the overthrow of the Tsar? Explain your answer using evidence from this section and your own reading.

E The collapse of the Provisional Government

After the abdication of the Tsar in 1917, the Duma appointed a Provisional Government headed at first by Prince Lvov. He was replaced by Alexander Kerensky in July of that year. Kerensky had already served in the Provisional Government as Justice Minister and War Minister. He was also Deputy Chairman of the Petrograd soviet (workers' council). Many people already believed the soviets were more effective as a means of government than the Duma.

1 Conditions in 1917

The Provisional Government was faced with pressures from outside as well as its own weaknesses. Continuing the war against the Germans made the Provisional Government deeply unpopular. This was made worse by continued military failure and heavy casualties:

- Mutinies broke out in the army.
- There was a revolt at the Kronstadt naval base in July.
- Peasants were simply taking over the landowners' estates.
- Opposition was growing from parties like the Bolsheviks.
- The Petrograd soviet became more and more hostile to the government as it failed to solve Russia's economic problems (food shortages, high prices, poor working conditions and low wages).

2 Lenin and the Bolsheviks

At the time of the February Revolution, Lenin, leader of the Bolsheviks, was in exile in Germany. On his return, a month after the abdication of the Tsar, his aim was to overthrow the Provisional Government with a second revolution of the working classes.

Lenin published his views in April 1917 in the 'April Theses'. In simple terms, he said that the Bolsheviks offered 'bread, peace, land and all power to the soviets'.

3 Kerensky, the Kornilov revolt and the Bolsheviks

Alexander Kerensky began to take a grip on his opponents and Lenin was forced to leave Russia again. However, Kerensky was then challenged by the new commander of the army, General Kornilov, who wanted to impose a strict regime and crush opponents, rather like the Tsar had done.

Kerensky asked the Bolsheviks to help him to defeat Kornilov, which they did. Kerensky was now in real trouble. He had lost the support of the army and was dependent upon the Petrograd soviet (with its strong Bolshevik influence) to run Russia.

4 Mistakes made by the Provisional Government

The Provisional Government made several mistakes which weakened its position.

- It continued the war effort out of loyalty to Russia's allies and in return for supplies. The offensive of June 1917 was a disastrous failure and was followed by further German advances and more desertions from the Russian armed forces.
- Failure to end the war worsened the food shortages in the towns and cities.
- Because of its temporary nature, the Provisional Government would not carry out important reforms. For example, it failed to give land to the peasants, which increased discontent in the countryside.
- The Provisional Government allowed opposition parties, including Lenin and the Bolsheviks, to campaign in Russia. Real authority and support lay with the Petrograd soviet.

 *Revision tasks*

1 How did conditions in Russia make the task of the Provisional Government even more difficult? Use a few key words to record your answer.
2 Why did the Kornilov revolt:
  a) weaken the position of the Provisional Government
  b) strengthen the position of Lenin and the Bolsheviks?
3 Make a list of mistakes made by the Provisional Government.

F The nature of the Bolshevik take-over; the roles of Lenin and Trotsky

1 The Bolshevik Revolution

Bolshevik support increased throughout 1917.

- In September the Bolsheviks became the largest party in the Petrograd soviet. They also controlled the Military Committee of the soviet, with Leon Trotsky becoming Chairman.
- Trotsky used the Military Committee to plan the revolution.
- On 16 October Lenin returned to Russia (he had been forced into hiding abroad in July) and was now convinced that the time was right to overthrow the Provisional Government.

- On 24 and 25 October the Bolsheviks seized power. They took control of the key locations of Petrograd and Moscow, including the Post Office, bridges, State Bank and railway stations.
- Red Guards stormed the Winter Palace and arrested the ministers of the Provisional Government. Kerensky managed to escape and tried to rally loyal troops. When this failed, he fled into exile.

2 Reasons for Bolshevik success

Later Bolshevik propaganda claimed that the October Revolution was a popular revolution and that the Red Guards succeeded against strong opposition. In fact the Bolsheviks did not have the support of the majority of the Russian population. The Red Guards faced little opposition in either Petrograd or Moscow. Most of the people of these two cities seem to have taken little notice of what was happening.

Bolshevik success was due to other reasons:

- The unpopularity of the Provisional Government. Few rallied to support Kerensky and there were no massive demonstrations demanding the return of Kerensky.
- Lenin played an important role. He had spent many years organising a disciplined party dedicated to revolution. His campaigning of 1917, especially his slogan 'Peace, Land and Bread', brought more support. By October the Bolshevik Party had 800,000 members with supporters in the right places. At least half the army supported them, as did the sailors at the important naval base at Kronstadt near Petrograd. The major industrial centres, and the Petrograd and Moscow soviets especially, were also pro-Bolshevik.
- The Bolshevik Revolution is often described as a classic work of planning by Trotsky. He organised the seizure of key buildings and positions in the two major cities.

● *The success of the Bolshevik Revolution was due to a variety of factors. Lenin certainly played an important part in preparing the Bolshevik Party and winning support from the Russian people with his slogan of 'Peace, Land and Bread'. There were other important reasons. Trotsky's role was important, especially his planning and organisation before and during the revolution. The Bolsheviks also benefited from the mistakes and inexperience of the Provisional Government.* ●

● *Revision tasks*

1 Make a key word summary of the Bolshevik take-over.
2 Copy the table below on the reasons for the success of the Bolshevik Revolution and fill it in using key words to explain each reason. In the last column give a rating for the importance of each reason (using 5 as the highest), with a key word explanation of your rating.

Reason	Explanation	Rating (1–5)
Unpopularity of Provisional Government		
Kornilov revolt		
Work of Lenin		
Planning by Trotsky		

3 What links can you make between these reasons?

G The Bolshevik dictatorship

The Provisional Government was replaced by the Council of the People's Commissars under Lenin. Lenin's aims were clear. He followed the theories of the political thinker Karl Marx and wanted a DICTATORSHIP OF THE PROLETARIAT. Since the Bolsheviks saw themselves as representing the proletariat, 'dictatorship of the proletariat' came to mean dictatorship by the Bolsheviks – that is, by the Communist Party.

1 Setting up a Marxist state

Lenin was not interested in democracy. The elections which were held late in 1917 showed that the Bolsheviks did not have the support of most Russians.

- The Constituent Assembly which met in January 1918 contained twice as many Socialist Revolutionaries (SRs) as Bolsheviks and the SRs opposed Lenin.
- Bolshevik Red Guards closed down the Assembly. By July 1918 the Russian Congress of Soviets had agreed a new system of government for Russia.

The result was that Lenin effectively became a dictator, and his secret police (the Cheka) began to intimidate, imprison and murder political opponents.

The road to communism

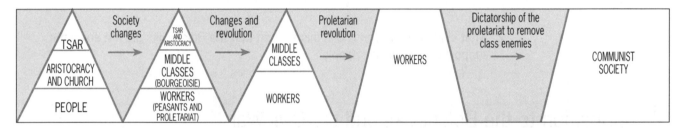

2 Negotiating peace

The Bolsheviks had always planned to pull out of the war with Germany. They agreed a ceasefire in December 1917. Trotsky was given the job of negotiating terms, but his only real achievement was to hold the Germans up until March 1918 when the Bolsheviks were forced to sign the Treaty of Brest-Litovsk.

- Russia lost vast amounts of territory (see map below).
- Russia also lost important coal and iron resources and about one-third of its population.
- Russia had to pay 300 million gold roubles in compensation.

Russian losses under the Treaty of Brest-Litovsk

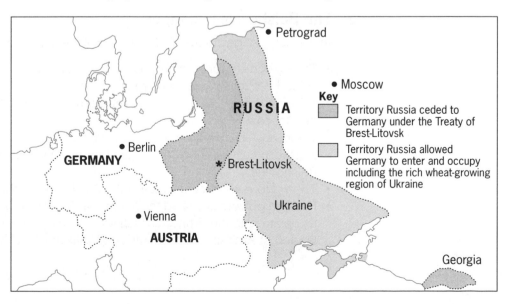

3 The state of the land and the economy

The question of land was vitally important in Russia. Farming was still by far the most important business. Lenin abolished the private ownership of land. This effectively meant that the peasants stripped the lands from landowners and the Church. In reality, the countryside was in a state of chaos in the early Bolshevik days, and no government was truly in control. The Bolsheviks were strong in the towns and cities but not in the countryside.

- There was soon a problem of food shortages because Russian money was worthless and the peasants were not being paid for their produce.
- Peasants did not trust the Bolsheviks who wanted to change the way that farming was organised from individual to collective (or co-operative) farming.

● *Revision tasks*

1 Make a key words summary of the changes brought about by the Bolsheviks after they took power. Use these headings to help you:

Government	Brest-Litovsk	Land and economy

2 What evidence can you find in this section that the Bolsheviks did not enjoy the support of the Russian people?

H Opposition to the Bolsheviks and the Civil War

1 Who made up the opposition?

The Bolsheviks did not have the support of all Russians when they seized power. By May 1918 they had more enemies still, especially after the losses of the Treaty of Brest-Litovsk.

By the summer of 1918 the Bolsheviks were faced with a range of opponents. The only thing uniting these opponents was their opposition to the Bolsheviks. These opponents were called the Whites, as opposed to the Bolshevik Reds. The Whites were made up of former Tsarists, Mensheviks, Socialist Revolutionaries and foreign powers opposed to the new regime in Russia.

2 The Bolsheviks in danger

In the early stages of the civil war the Bolsheviks faced several different threats:

- The Czech Legion (which was made up of former prisoners of war) had seized sections of the vital Trans-Siberian railway.
- Admiral Kolchak had set up a White government in Siberia and was marching on Moscow.
- General Denikin was advancing with his army from southern Russia.
- Northern Russia, led by the White General Yudenich, was opposing the Bolsheviks.
- There were also risings against the Bolsheviks in the Ukraine and Turkestan.
- Foreign powers supplied the Whites with arms and weapons and later landed troops to help the Whites as well. US, Japanese, French and British troops landed at Archangel, Murmansk and Vladivostok.

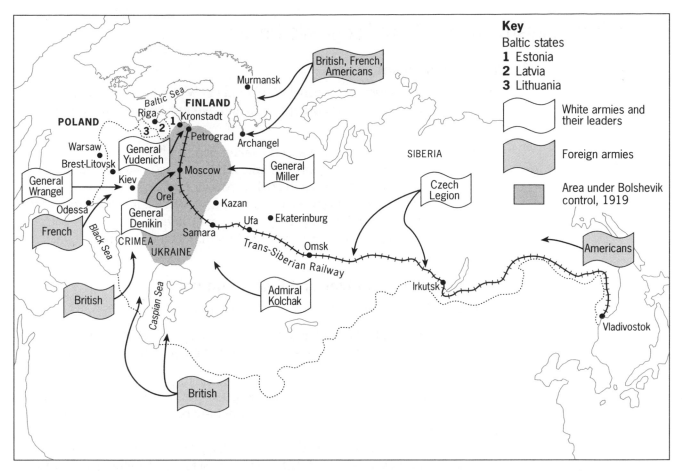

Key

Baltic states
1 Estonia
2 Latvia
3 Lithuania

White armies and their leaders

Foreign armies

Area under Bolshevik control, 1919

Bolshevik, White and foreign forces involved in the Civil War

3 Bolshevik victory

Against what seemed to be overwhelming odds, the Bolsheviks won the Civil War. The crucial year was 1919. Under Trotsky's leadership the Red Army defeated Kolchak and destroyed the Czech Legion. Denikin's advance on Moscow was stopped and by 1920 he was being pushed back. By late 1920 White forces were defeated. The strengths of the Bolsheviks (the Reds) were:

* The Reds had large, well-organised armies under the leadership of Trotsky. They also had good communications.
* They made good use of propaganda to show that the Whites were in league with foreigners and wanted to bring back the Tsar.
* The Red Army and the Cheka (secret police) kept ruthless control over the Bolshevik territories, making sure that most people obeyed Lenin's rule.
* The brutal policy of War Communism (see page 116) ensured that the troops of the Red Army and the population of the towns were fed and supplied.
* The Reds controlled the major towns so their factories and industries could be used to support the war effort.

The failings of the Whites were:

* The Whites had no aim upon which they all agreed. In some cases they disliked each other almost as much as they opposed the Reds.
* Their forces were spread across a huge area and they could not co-ordinate their attacks – they were beaten one by one.
* Their harsh treatment of people in the lands they captured led many to support the Bolsheviks against them.

● *Revision tasks*

1 Create your own key words summary of who the Whites were and why they opposed the Bolsheviks.

2 Use eight to ten key words to explain how the Bolsheviks won the Civil War.

War Communism and the New Economic Policy

1 War Communism

To defeat his opponents in the Civil War Lenin knew that he had to make sure that his armies were fed and equipped. To achieve this he introduced the policy of 'War Communism'.

- Land and industry were nationalised – taken over by the state.
- In the factories there was severe discipline (for example, strikers could be shot), and key items like food and coal were rationed.
- In the countryside peasants were forced to hand over their surplus produce (what they did not need themselves) to the government.
- Opposition was rooted out and destroyed by the Cheka (even the royal family was executed).

2 The cost of the Civil War and War Communism

By 1921 Lenin was facing a shattered and demoralised country.

- War Communism had left the industrial workers poor and restless.
- War Communism and war damage had led to famine in the countryside – millions died in 1921.

The Kronstadt mutiny of 1921 was a turning point. The Kronstadt sailors had been leading supporters of the revolution, but they revolted against War Communism in February 1921.

Although the Kronstadt revolt was destroyed by Trotsky and the Civil War was being won, it was clear in 1921 that Lenin had to do something to improve living conditions for the Russian people. His solution was the New Economic Policy (NEP).

3 The New Economic Policy (NEP)

Lenin introduced the NEP at the Party Congress in March 1921. Its measures were simple but controversial:

- Peasants could keep part of their surpluses to sell at a profit.
- Small factories were given back to private ownership.
- Small private businesses could be set up to trade at a profit.

Some communists saw the NEP as a betrayal, but Lenin saw it as a temporary measure to keep the Russian people happy and get the economy moving. All of the major industries remained in state hands, and political control (under the Cheka) remained very strict.

4 The importance of Lenin

Lenin died in January 1924. He had brought huge changes to Russia and indeed the world:

- He had led the communist revolution.
- He had established the USSR (Union of Soviet Socialist Republics).
- He had created a powerful, disciplined Communist Party by using the Cheka to purge (remove) opponents of his policies.
- The USSR had become a one-party state which was effectively a dictatorship where the Communist Party controlled industry, the army, the police, the press – in fact almost all aspects of life.

● *Lenin was very popular during his period in power. This popularity increased after his death with the 'cult of Lenin' in the USSR. Statues were erected, and streets and cities were named after him. This tended to cover up the less successful aspects of his government: the suffering caused by War Communism, the activities of the secret police, the Cheka, and Lenin's refusal to allow democracy to develop.* ●

● *Revision tasks*

1 Write your own definition of 'War Communism' by listing key words under these headings:

Government	Brest-Litovsk	Land and economy

2 Now write a definition of the NEP, using the same headings.
3 If you were a Russian being interviewed by a British newspaper after Lenin's death, how would you explain the importance of Lenin to the USSR?

Revision session

The aim of this revision session is for you to see how you can apply your knowledge of the Russian Revolution, *c.*1910–24, to answer source-based questions.

Examination questions

Below are examples of sources and source questions adapted by permission of Edexcel from the specimen papers for the new specifications.

Source A A table showing food prices and bread rations in Russia in 1917

Selected food prices, 1917 (in roubles)		
	July	**October**
Lard (1lb)	1.10	5.40
Cheese (1lb)	1.60	5.40
Cabbage (1lb)	1.60	2.20
Sausages (1lb)	1.00	6.00

Bread rations, 1917 (per day)				
	March	**April**	**Sept**	**Oct**
Manual workers	1½lb	¾lb	½lb	¼lb
Others	1 lb	¾lb	½lb	¼lb

Source B From a book by John Reed, a US journalist who was in Petrograd in September and October 1917. The book was published in 1926
Week by week, food became scarcer in Petrograd. The daily allowance of bread fell. There was one week without bread at all. There was only milk for half the babies in the city. Most people never saw it for months. People had to stand in queues for hours in the freezing rain to buy milk or tobacco.

Source C From a school textbook on the history of Russia published in 1998
The Provisional Government decided to continue the war. Nobody, including the Petrograd Soviet, wanted to be defeated by the Germans. But the war continued to go badly. More and more soldiers began to desert. Because of the war, food and fuel remained in short supply. Now the people desperately wanted the war to end.

a) Study Source A.
What can you learn from Source A about the situation in Russia in 1917?   *(4 marks)*

What is required? This question is testing your understanding of a source and your ability to interpret what it says. Try to make at least one inference from the source. In other words, read between the lines of what the source shows.

Ideas for your answer
- To encourage you to make an inference or inferences you could start at least one of your sentences with 'This source suggests that. . .' or 'This source shows that. . .'.
- One possible inference could be about the prices of foodstuffs and how this would affect the Russian people.

b) Study Sources A, B and C.

Does Source C support the evidence of Sources A and B? Explain your answer. *(6 marks)*

What is required? This question is asking you to compare the information in Source C to that of Sources A and B. A simple answer which compares the sources at their face value will only achieve level 1 (1–2 marks). An answer that makes developed statements about similarities or differences between two or three of the sources will reach level 2 (3–4 marks). For level 3 (5–6 marks) you need to:

- ensure you directly compare Source C to Source A and then Source C to Source B
- look for similarities and differences between them in information, tone and attitude
- ensure your comparisons are developed and precisely explained.

Ideas for your answer

1 Begin by explaining the information/attitude/tone of Source C. In this case Source C explains how the Provisional Government continued the war. This proved very unpopular with the armed forces and created food and fuel shortages.

2 Now compare Source C to Source A.

  a) Does Source C support Source A? Yes, because both mention food shortages. Explain this.

  b) Are there any differences? Yes, Source C goes further and mentions other reasons for discontent. Explain this.

3 Compare Source C to Source B.

  a) Does Source C support Source B? Yes, because once again both mention food shortages. Explain this.

  b) Are there any differences? Yes, Source B describes the food shortages in more detail but Source C mentions what effect the food shortages had on people's attitude to the war.

4 Now write a conclusion summing up your answer to the question, making a judgement as to how far Source C supports Sources A and B.

Source D A freeze frame from the film *October* by Sergei Eisenstein, made in the USSR in 1927. Eisenstein was a Bolshevik supporter. In this shot Lenin is shown standing on top of an armoured car during the storming of the Winter Palace. He is urging the Red Guards forward

Source E From a biography of Lenin written by a Soviet historian in the USSR in 1976

On 10 October Lenin told the Central Committee of the Bolsheviks that the time had come for the proletariat and the peasants to seize power. The Central Committee agreed to go ahead with an armed uprising. The Revolution went ahead according to Lenin's plans. The Bolshevik fighting units were highly organised and well disciplined. The Revolution showed Lenin's genius as a leader of the masses. He acted wisely and with great courage.

Source F From a school textbook about Soviet Russia published in the 1990s

Trotsky, not Lenin, planned and organised how the Bolsheviks seized power. On the night of 24 October the Bolsheviks took control of key points in Petrograd. There was little resistance; no shots were fired. Lenin arrived at the Bolshevik headquarters in disguise and when some people recognised him he hid. Trotsky had to keep him informed about how the Revolution was going.

c) Study Sources D and E.

How useful are these sources as evidence of Lenin's leadership? *(8 marks)*

What is required? A simple statement based on the content or nature of the sources will achieve no more than three marks. More developed statements which lack balance – for example, by ignoring the nature of the sources and/or their limitations, will reach level 2 (4–6 marks). To reach level 3 (7–8 marks) you need to ensure that your answer is fully balanced in the following ways:

- Explain the usefulness of both sources.
- Evaluate the **usefulness** of each source in two areas – **content/context** of the sources and their **nature/origin/purpose**.
- Analyse the **limitations** of each in the same two areas – **content/context** and **nature/origin/purpose**.

Try to finish with a conclusion summarising the usefulness of the two sources. In some cases the two sources might be useful because they have similar views of an event.

Ideas for your answer Draw a table like the one below and use key words to complete each section. Use the table to plan your answer.

	Source D	Source E
Usefulness of content		
Limitations of content		
Usefulness of nature, origin, purpose		
Limitations of nature, origin, purpose		

Examine the usefulness of each source in turn.

1 Source D is useful because its content shows Lenin leading the storming of the Winter Palace during the Bolshevik Revolution of 1917. Lenin was the leader during the Revolution. It is also useful because of its origin and nature – it is a still from a communist film called *October* made in 1927, which was giving the communist version of the October Revolution. Finally it is useful because of its purpose. It is propaganda promoting, even glorifying, the role of Lenin, and is an excellent example of the communist use of such methods. It also shows the attitude towards Lenin that was developed after his death.

2 Now discuss the limitations of Source D, first of all in terms of its content. The film is not based upon what really happened during the storming of the Winter Palace. Lenin was not there and did not lead the way. The source is also of limited use because it was made by a communist whose aim was to promote the role of Lenin and the Bolsheviks. He exaggerates Lenin's role and the nature of the assault on the palace.

3 Now you will need to do the same for Source E. A few hints:

   a) How accurate are the contents of the source?

   b) Did Lenin, himself, plan the revolution?

   c) Who wrote the textbook?

   d) What would be its purpose?

4 Now for a conclusion. In this case both sources are useful in that they support each other in their views of Lenin. In what other respects are they useful?

---

d) Study all the sources.

'The leadership of Lenin was the main reason why the Bolsheviks were able to seize power in 1917.'

Use the sources, and your own knowledge, to explain whether you agree with this view. *(12 marks)*

What is required? This question is the most important. The examiner wants you to reach a conclusion on the question using your own knowledge and by referring to most, if not all, of the sources.

Making simple points using the sources and/or your own knowledge will score no more than three marks. To reach the next level (4–7 marks) you will need to make developed statements in support of or against the view, using the sources, or your own knowledge. An answer at this level may make developed statements for and against the view but use *only* the sources or *only* your own knowledge. To reach the next level (8–10 marks) you must make developed statements for and against the view, using the sources *and* your own knowledge. To achieve the very top level (11–12 marks) you will have to do the following:

- ensure that your whole answer is focused on the question
- include an introduction that explains the question and how you intend to answer it
- give a balanced argument for and against the view
- use most if not all of the sources and your own knowledge to give this argument
- try to begin each paragraph with your argument and then back it up with your own knowledge and evidence from one or more of the sources – in other words, integrate your own knowledge and evidence from the sources
- write a conclusion that gives your final judgement on the view in the question. Make sure this is consistent with what you have already written.

Ideas for your answer Draw up a table like the one below and complete each section using key words. Use this as a plan for your eventual answer. Part of it has been completed for you.

	Supporting the view	**Against the view**
Arguments	Lenin gained support and decided timing of revolution	
Own knowledge	Slogan 'Peace, Land and Bread'	
Sources	Sources D and E	
Conclusion		

---

1 In support of the view, you will need to give a developed explanation from your own knowledge of how Lenin organised the Bolshevik Party in the years before 1917 and his activities from April to October 1917.

2 Against the view, you will need to explain from your own knowledge other important reasons for the success of the Bolsheviks. These could include:
   a) Trotsky and the planning and organisation of the revolution
   b) the mistakes of the Provisional Government
   c) the extent of discontent due to food and fuel shortages.

3 The following sources could be used against the view:
   a) Source F to back up your knowledge of Trotsky
   b) Sources A, B and C to back up the other two reasons.

4 For a conclusion, decide whether you believe Lenin was the main reason why the Bolsheviks were able to seize power. If so, give a final reason. If, on the other hand, you think it was one or more of the other reasons, then explain why.

Practice questions

Now look at the following sources and questions. Have a go at answering them without any help.

Source A
A demonstration against the government in 1913

Source B From a report by a Moscow Okhrana agent in 1912
There has never been so much tension. People can be heard speaking of the government in the sharpest tones. Many say that the shooting of the Lena workers recalls the shooting of the workers at the Winter Palace in January 1905. There have been references in the Duma to the necessity of calling a Constituent Assembly and to overthrow the present system by the united strength of the proletariat.

Source C From a modern history textbook published in 2000
Many Russian people were unhappy with the way in which their country was run. There was a tradition of revolutionary violence against the Tsars. In 1881 revolutionaries had assassinated Tsar Alexander II. The rapid industrial changes at the beginning of the twentieth century, together with the attitude of the Tsar, did much to foster the growth of opposition.

Source D A cartoon of Rasputin with the Tsar and Tsarina, 1916

Source E By the Chairman of the Military Commission of the Duma, 1916
As early as the beginning of the second year of the war desertions of soldiers at the front and on the way to the front became commonplace. The average number of deserters reached 25 per cent. I happen to know of three cases when the train was stopped because there were no passengers on it. All, with the exception of the officer in command, had run away.

Source F From a history textbook published in 1996
In August 1915, Rasputin advised Nicholas to take over command of the army. This proved to be a disaster. Nicholas was not a good leader and was not good at military tactics. Worse, as Commander-in-Chief of the army, he could be blamed for everything that went wrong.

a) Study Source A.
What can you learn from Source A about attitudes to the Tsarist government in 1913? *(4 marks)*

b) Study Sources A, B and C.
Does Source C support the views of Sources A and B about attitudes to the Tsar before the First World War? Explain your answer. *(6 marks)*

c) Study Sources D and E.
How useful are these two sources as evidence of the effects of the First World War on Russia? *(8 marks)*

d) Study all the sources.
'It was the First World War that led to the downfall of Tsar Nicholas II.'
Use the sources, and your own knowledge, to explain whether you agree with this view. *(12 marks)*

Summary and revision plan

Below is a list of headings which you may find helpful. Use this as a check-list to make sure that you are familiar with the material featured in this chapter. Record your key words alongside each heading.

A Russia before the First World War: politics, society and economy
- ❏ The Tsarist system of government
- ❏ Russian economy and society
- ❏ Failures, 1906–14

B Opposition to Tsarist rule
- ❏ The Socialist Revolutionaries
- ❏ The Social Democratic Labour Party
- ❏ Moderate opposition

C The impact of the First World War on Russian government and society
- ❏ Rasputin
- ❏ Military defeat
- ❏ Economic chaos
- ❏ Social misery

D 1917: the fall of the Tsar
- ❏ Long-term factors
- ❏ Short-term factors
- ❏ Immediate factors

E The collapse of the Provisional Government
- ❏ Conditions in 1917
- ❏ Lenin and the Bolsheviks
- ❏ Kerensky, the Kornilov revolt and the Bolsheviks
- ❏ Mistakes made by the Provisional Government

F The nature of the Bolshevik take-over; the roles of Lenin and Trotsky
- ❏ The Bolshevik Revolution
- ❏ Reasons for Bolshevik success

G The Bolshevik dictatorship
- ❏ Setting up a Marxist state
- ❏ Negotiating peace
- ❏ The state of the land and the economy

H Opposition to the Bolsheviks and the Civil War
- ❏ Who made up the opposition?
- ❏ The Bolsheviks in danger
- ❏ Bolshevik victory

I War Communism and the New Economic Policy
- ❏ War Communism
- ❏ The cost of the Civil War and War Communism
- ❏ The New Economic Policy (NEP)
- ❏ The importance of Lenin

The War to End Wars, 1914–19

In 1914 the Great Powers went to war: Austria–Hungary and Germany against Britain, France and Russia. Most people expected a quick war, possibly decided by Christmas 1914. In fact it was a long-drawn-out conflict due to the failure of Germany's Schlieffen Plan and the emergence of trench warfare.

Key content

You will need to have a good working knowledge of these areas:

A The failure of the Schlieffen Plan
B Stalemate: the experience of trench warfare
C Stalemate: the role of Haig
D The war at sea and the Gallipoli campaign
E The impact of new technology
F The collapse of Russia and US intervention
G The defeat of Germany
H The peace settlement
I German reactions to the Treaty of Versailles
J Criticisms of the Treaty of Versailles

Key themes

You will be asked to show your understanding of some key themes:

● Why did the Schlieffen Plan fail and what were the consequences for the progress of the war?
● Why was there a stalemate for four years on the Western Front?
● Has Haig been unfairly criticised for his role on the Western Front?
● What was the importance of the war at sea?
● What were the reasons for the failure of the Gallipoli campaign?
● What was the importance of US intervention in 1917?
● Why was Germany defeated in 1918?
● How was the peace settlement drawn up and what was the German reaction to it?

Source-based questions test both your knowledge of the topic and your source-evaluation skills. For example, look at the question on page 126 from the 2000 Edexcel Paper 2, adapted by permission of Edexcel.

Source D A graph showing Allied shipping losses (in thousands of tonnes) during January to September 1917, published by the British Government after the war

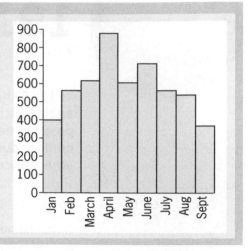

Source E An artist's impression of British planes bombing German trenches, published in the magazine *Sphere*, October 1918

c) Study Sources D and E.
How useful are Sources D and E as evidence of the use of new technology in the First World War? *(6 marks)*

This question is asking you to evaluate the usefulness of two sources based upon:

- *your knowledge of new technology in the war*
- *your understanding of source skills.*

We will look at this question in more detail at the end of this chapter.

A The failure of the Schlieffen Plan

1 What was the Schlieffen Plan?

Because of the alliance system, Germany knew it might have to fight France and Russia at the same time. It therefore developed the Schlieffen Plan to overcome the problem of fighting on two fronts:

- The German army was to sweep quickly through Belgium and defeat France in the first few weeks of war.
- This would allow the German army to move to the Eastern Front to defeat the Russians.

In 1914, Germany had approximately 1.5 million well-trained troops. Its navy had 17 Dreadnoughts (warships).

2 The failure of the Schlieffen Plan

The Schlieffen Plan was designed to give Germany a quick and decisive victory against France.

However, the plan failed for several reasons:

- The Belgian army fought very bravely and delayed the German advance at Liège.
- The British Expeditionary Force (BEF) slowed the German advance at the Battle of Mons.
- Some German troops had to be transferred from the Western Front to the Eastern Front because the Russians had mobilised their forces more quickly than expected.
- The German commander Kluck decided to turn his forces south rather than encircle Paris. This allowed the British to continue sending troops ashore, since the Channel ports were not attacked.

3 The Battles of the Marne and Ypres, 1914

At the Battle of the Marne, 6–12 September, the commander of the French army, Joffre, was able to halt the German advance and push them back. The French even transported fresh troops to the front in taxis in order to face the exhausted Germans.

Both the British and German forces now abandoned their original plans and tried to cut each other off from fresh supplies and equipment. This led to a race to the English Channel between the British Expeditionary Force and the German army. At the First Battle of Ypres, the British managed to stop the German advance but at a terrible cost. It is estimated that one British division lost nearly 11,000 of its 12,000 men.

4 Stalemate, December 1914

At the beginning of the war, the French forces also tried to carry out their plans. They planned to counter-attack into German territory. They launched Plan 17 against the Germans but their advance was also halted. It has been estimated that French casualties were 300,000 in just three months.

By December 1914, the war of movement had come to a halt. From the English Channel in the north to the Swiss border in the south, troops on both sides dug trenches in order to prevent the enemy from advancing further. The soldiers expected to be home by Christmas. But instead the war reached stalemate. No side could make the vital breakthrough.

● *The Schlieffen Plan failed due to changes in the original plan, the resistance of the Belgians and the early arrival of the BEF. The failure was a major turning-point in the war. There would be no quick victory by Christmas. Instead it would be a long-drawn-out conflict fought in a narrow area of France and Belgium known as the Western Front.* ●

● *Revision tasks*

1 Draw a table like the one below and give each of the factors listed a rating to show its importance in the failure of the Schlieffen Plan (5 means very important and 1 relatively unimportant). Use key words to explain your decision.

The factors	Rating (1–5) and reason
The BEF	
Belgian resistance	
German mistakes	
Battle of the Marne	

2 Can you make any links between these factors?
3 Why was there a stalemate by the end of 1914?

B Stalemate: the experience of trench warfare

1 Why was there a stalemate, 1914–17?

This was due to several reasons:

- The defences of both sides were very strong. Both sides dug a line of trenches stretching from the North Sea, in the north, to Switzerland in the south. These became increasingly sophisticated and by 1916 there were three or even four lines of trenches protected by thick barbed wire and machine-gun positions. The area in between, known as no-man's-land, had no cover at all for the attacking forces.
- The machine gun was an ideal weapon for defending trenches. Machine-gunners could fire up to 600 rounds a minute at attacking forces, causing very heavy casualties.
- Outdated tactics were used by both sides. These involved mass attacks across no-man's-land against heavily defended positions. Attacks were often slowed down by poor weather conditions, such as the non-stop rain in Flanders in 1917 which turned the battlefield of Ypres into a mudbath.
- New weapons failed to break the stalemate until 1918. Gas was first used by the Germans at the Second Battle of Ypres, in April 1915. It was not a war-winning weapon because it often blew in the faces of the attacking soldiers. Tanks were introduced in 1916 but were a disastrous failure at the First Battle of the Somme where most broke down. Tank tactics were not properly developed until 1918.
- Artillery was misused. Both sides used huge field guns to bombard the enemy trenches. These simply churned up no-man's-land and warned the defenders that an attack was imminent. There was a fatal gap between the artillery bombardment and the attack across no-man's-land. The defenders had time to re-man their machine-gun positions.

2 Trench warfare

Life was very unpleasant for soldiers who fought in the trenches. There were many problems.

- Boredom was the greatest problem. The front-line soldiers had certain duties to perform but otherwise there were often long periods of inactivity.
- There was danger – from gas or artillery attacks, snipers or being sent over the top to attack the enemy trenches. Some soldiers were psychologically affected by their experiences and suffered 'shell shock'.
- Poor living conditions included inadequate and often cold food rations and contaminated water supplies. Soldiers were often infested with lice and there were many rats feeding off the dead bodies in no-man's-land. They brought disease. The soldiers lived in dugouts or holes in the walls which gave little protection from the snow and rain. Some soldiers suffered from 'trench foot', rotting of the feet, due to standing in water all day long.

3 The Western Front, 1915

Some generals on the side of the Allies (Britain and France) were convinced that the Germans could be beaten back if large numbers of troops charged at enemy trenches. Through 1915, wave after wave of soldiers was sent 'over the top' – only to be mown down by enemy machine guns:

- At Neuve Chapelle, the British suffered 11,000 casualties in only three days.
- At the Battle of Loos in September 1915, 60,000 British soldiers were killed in less than two weeks.

● *Revision tasks*

1 Explain using key words **three** reasons for the stalemate on the Western Front.
2 Give four reasons why life was so unpleasant in the trenches.

C Stalemate: the role of Haig

1 Views of Haig

Sir Douglas Haig became Commander-in-Chief of the British forces on the Western Front in 1915 and was responsible for the major British offensives of 1916 and 1917. He believed in 'attrition' or constantly attacking the Germans and wearing down their resistance until they were defeated.

This tactic of all-out frequent attacks brought much criticism both at the time and later, as it resulted in very heavy casualties, especially at the First Battle of the Somme in 1916 and the Third Battle of Ypres, July 1917.

2 The Western Front, 1916

The most significant events on the Western Front in 1916 were two battles, Verdun and the Somme.

Verdun

Verdun was a heavily fortified city in the north-east of France. The Germans believed they could defeat the French army by concentrating their troops in one small area. They believed that since Verdun was seen as such an important fortress by the French people, its loss would destroy French morale and lead to France's defeat.

- On 21 February 1916 the Germans launched a bombardment of Verdun and within three days it looked as if the city was about to be captured.

- The problem of saving Verdun was given to General Pétain. He moved food, ammunition and equipment into the city and after five months the Germans stopped their attack.
- Pétain became a national hero. The cost to the French and Germans had been high. The Germans lost 281,000 men and the French 315,000.

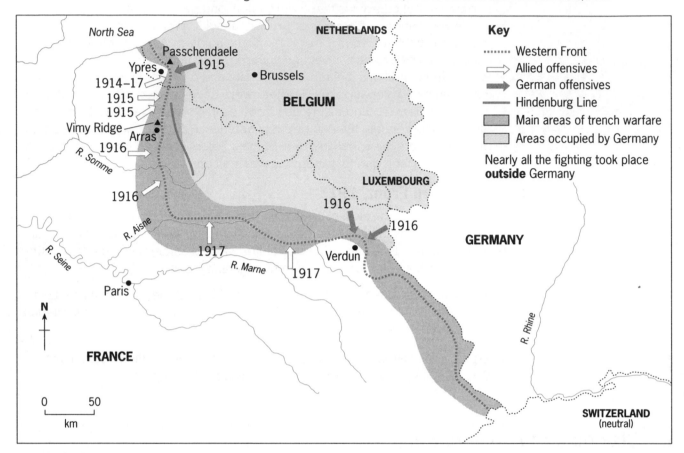

The Western Front and major offensives, 1914–17

The Somme

General Haig, the British commander, decided to launch a major attack against the Germans along the Somme river. He hoped that by using heavy artillery he would be able to weaken the German front line and so allow the British troops to advance. He also hoped to relieve the pressure on Verdun. This is what happened:

- The battle began with a five-day bombardment of the German positions along an 18-mile front.
- The German troops had prepared dugouts deep underground in order to survive the bombardment.
- On 1 July, 200,000 Allied soldiers attacked the German trenches along the Somme. British troops were ordered to walk, not run, since each man was carrying up to 66 pounds of equipment.
- In the ten minutes between the end of the bombardment and the British attack, the Germans were able to return to their trenches and machine guns.
- On the first day of the battle, the British suffered terribly: 20,000 men were killed and 40,000 were wounded.

The Battle of the Somme ended in the middle of November 1916. Only 9 miles of land had been gained by the Allies at a cost of 600,000 casualties. At the end of 1916, there was still no breakthrough on the Western Front.

3 The Western Front, 1917

The following year, 1917, was another mixed year for the Allies, particularly for the French. A new French commander, General Nivelle, launched his troops against what he thought was the weakest section of the German front line. Unfortunately, the Germans had discovered the French plans and prepared for their advance. The French suffered nearly 125,000 casualties and made no breakthrough. French morale suffered as a result.

- In early 1917 thousands of French troops mutinied and refused to obey orders.
- General Pétain restored discipline by having hundreds of mutineers shot, improving food rations and extending leave for his soldiers.

The British also had a mixed year.

- They had a major victory in June 1917 at Messines, when they blew up a hillside occupied by German troops by placing TNT explosive in tunnels dug out by engineers.
- In the summer, however, at the Third Battle of Ypres (Passchendaele), 400,000 British troops were killed or wounded in a sea of mud created by heavy rain.
- At Cambrai in November the British successfully used tanks against the Germans. But the tank advance had been so swift that the soldiers were unable to keep up, and in a counter-attack the Germans regained the lost ground.

● *Most commanders on the Western Front, including Haig, have been given a bad press. They certainly seemed to lack imagination in the tactics they used, which resulted in heavy casualties. However, in many respects this is understandable. Trench warfare, on the scale of the Western Front, was new. The defensive systems became very strong and sophisticated. Commanders often use the tactics which have been successful in previous wars.* ●

4 Conclusions on Haig

Haig is often blamed for the British failure to break through between 1915 and 1917, and for the heavy casualties brought about by sending men over the top. However, all the commanders made the same mistakes and Haig was no worse than most of the others. The Somme and Passchendaele were not total failures. In both cases they took pressure off the French and inflicted heavy casualties on the Germans. Haig was forced to fight both battles without the forces that he believed he needed.

● *Revision tasks*

1 Make a copy of the following table and using key words describe the key battles, 1916–17.

Battle	Key events
1916 Verdun	
1916 First Battle of the Somme	
1917 Nivelle offensive	
1917 Third Battle of Ypres	

2 Using key words construct arguments for and against Haig's leadership, 1915–17.

Arguments for Haig's leadership	Arguments against Haig's leadership

D The war at sea and the Gallipoli campaign

1 Background

The British and German navies were the most powerful in the world and control of the seas was an important factor in the final outcome of the war. The aim of the Royal Navy was to:

- keep shipping lanes free from German attack
- blockade German ports
- re-supply British troops in the colonies.

The German navy aimed to:

- disrupt Britain's food and munitions supplies
- protect German colonies from British attack.

2 Minor clashes

Before 1916 there were only a few clashes between the Allies and the other powers at sea.

- In 1914 German raiders bombarded Scarborough and in 1915 another group of German vessels clashed with the British near the Dogger Bank in the North Sea.
- In the Pacific region British ships were sunk at the Battles of Coronel in November 1914 and the Falkland Islands in December 1914.

3 The Battle of Jutland, May/June 1916

At the end of May 1916 Admirals Hipper and von Scheer led the German fleet into the North Sea. In a carefully worked-out plan, they aimed to destroy the British Grand Fleet by tempting the British ships into a trap. However, the British had discovered the German radio codes and were able to decode German messages.

On the evening of 31 May 1916, the two fleets had a running battle off the coast of Jutland in Denmark. The outcome of the battle was indecisive although both sides claimed victory. The losses were as follows:

Losses	Germany	Britain
Ships (sunk)	11	14
Men (killed)	2,500	6,000

German casualties were much lighter than the British, but the German fleet never set sail into the North Sea again. The British Grand Fleet had not proved its superiority, but Admiral Jellicoe claimed it had been the Germans who had fled and headed for home.

4 War against the submarine

Most of the food and raw materials that Britain needed to keep up its war effort came into Britain by ship.

In 1915 the German government announced it would attack any ships it suspected of carrying supplies to Britain.

- The most famous victim of the German U-boat (submarine) war was the large British passenger liner, *Lusitania*, sunk in 1915.
- US protests led to Germany suspending its policy of unrestricted submarine warfare against passenger liners in September 1915.

- At their peak in October 1917 the Germans had 130 U-boats. The Germans resumed unrestricted submarine warfare in February 1917.
- This tactic was so effective that at one stage Britain was reduced to six weeks' supply of grain.

The German submarine campaign had severe consequences. On 6 April 1917 the USA entered the war on the side of the Allies. The American president, Woodrow Wilson, said the German policy of unrestricted submarine warfare was a major factor in the USA's decision to declare war on Germany.

Towards the end of the war, various tactics were used by Britain against the German submarines:

- The British developed the convoy system to protect merchant ships.
- Nets and mines were used, particularly in the English Channel, to trap and destroy U-boats.
- Some Allied ships were equipped with depth charges.
- Q-boats (gunboats disguised as merchant ships) were developed to trick U-boats into attacking them.

5 The British blockade of Germany

Despite the attacks on shipping, Germany was unable to isolate Britain by using its navy or submarines. In fact, Germany was successfully blockaded by the Allies. This led to severe food shortages in Germany in 1918 and speeded up the German surrender in November of that year.

6 The Gallipoli campaign

Before the war, both the British and German governments had been trying to win the support of the Turks. Just before the outbreak of war, however, the British refused to deliver two Dreadnought battleships they had been building for the Turkish navy, but the Kaiser sent two German ships to help the Turkish navy. In October 1914 Turkey joined the war on Germany's side.

By the end of 1914, with stalemate on the Western Front and the Russians under pressure on the Eastern Front, Winston Churchill, First Lord of the Admiralty, came up with an imaginative and daring plan to shorten the war.

Churchill's plan
- Capture the Turkish capital Constantinople and force Turkey to surrender.
- Re-open a supply route to Russia.
- Encourage the neutral countries of Bulgaria, Greece and Romania to join the war on the side of the Allies.
- Surround Germany and Austria–Hungary.

What actually happened?
- In February 1915 the British naval bombardment began, but failed to open the stretch of water known as the Dardanelles. In March the fleet retreated. No advance could be made without military support.
- In April a force of British and Anzac (Australian and New Zealand Army Corps) troops landed on the Gallipoli peninsula. They were soon pinned down by Turkish machine guns.
- In August, the Allies attacked again, this time landing a force at Suvla Bay. By delaying their advance, the Allies gave the Turks the chance to regroup and no further advance was made. Many Allied soldiers died of disease.

In Britain the commanders of the Gallipoli campaign were heavily criticised. After several weeks, the decision was taken to evacuate the Gallipoli peninsula. At the end of 1915 the Allies withdrew, having suffered 200,000 casualties.

A map of the Gallipoli campaign is shown on p.134.

Gallipoli campaign

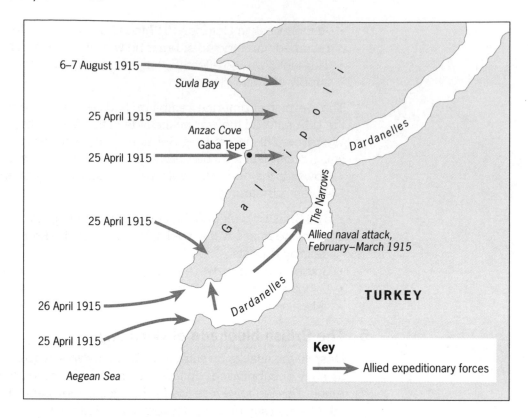

● *The importance of the war at sea has often been underestimated compared to the events on the Western Front. This is because there was no obvious British naval victory. Nevertheless, it was very important. Jutland was a long-term success for the British. The German fleet remained bottled-up in port and the British blockade seriously weakened the German war effort in 1917 and 1918.* ●

● Revision tasks

1 In your view, which side won the Battle of Jutland? Give reasons for your answer.
2 Was the U-boat campaign a major threat to Britain in the First World War? What evidence is there for this?
3 Copy the following table on the Gallipoli campaign and use key words to complete each section.

The event	What happened?
Churchill's plan	
Navy at Dardanelles	
Gallipoli landings	
Why the campaign failed	

E The impact of new technology

1 Submarines

Submarines had been developed well before the First World War but were now used in a different way. The Germans used their U-boats to try to starve Britain out of the war. They sank ships sailing to and from Britain. This affected civilians as it created serious food shortages, especially in 1917.

2 Machine guns

In 1914 many military commanders had thought the machine gun an unreliable and untested invention. However, Lloyd George was so impressed with these new weapons that by the end of the war nearly 250,000 had been manufactured for the British army.

On the battlefield the machine gun had a devastating effect. The water-cooled machine guns used by both sides could fire up to 600 rounds a minute and frequently cut down hundreds of troops before they were able to advance more than a few metres.

Source 1 Recollections from a German machine-gunner at the Somme, 1916
The officers were in front. I noticed one of them walking calmly carrying a walking stick. When we started firing we just had to load and reload. They went down in their hundreds. You didn't have to aim, we just fired into them.

3 Gas

Poison gas was used for the first time by the Germans at the Second Battle of Ypres in April 1915. It was later used by both sides in the war. There were different kinds of gas:

- Chlorine and phosgene gas destroyed the victim's lungs.
- Mustard gas was particularly horrible and destroyed flesh.

Gas attacks were widely feared. But they did not have a major impact on the outcome of the First World War. Gas was unpredictable in battle – a change in wind direction could blow the gas back to the sender – and by 1917 effective gas masks had been produced to protect soldiers on the battlefield.

Most people have regarded gas as a particularly horrific weapon. In fact, the use of poison gas in war had been banned by international agreements signed at the Hague in 1899 and 1907.

There are first-hand accounts of gas attacks. Sometimes, these accounts are full of personal detail and emotion, but they are a vital tool for the historian who is trying to find out what life at the front was really like.

Source 2 G. Chapman, *Vain Glory*
We have heaps of gassed cases. I wish those who call this a holy war could see the poor things burnt and blistered all over with great mustard-coloured, suppurating blisters, with blind eyes all sticky and glued together, always fighting for breath with voices a mere whisper saying their throats are closing and they will choke.

Source 3 Anthony Hossack, Queen Victoria Rifles
Suddenly down the road from the Yser Canal came a galloping team of horses, the riders goading on their mounts in a frenzied way; then another and another . . . Plainly something terrible was happening . . . In the northerly breeze there came a pungent nauseating smell that tickled the throat and made our eyes smart. The horses and men were still pouring down the road . . . while over the fields streamed mobs of infantry, the dusky warriors of French Africa; away went their rifles, equipment, even their tunics that they might run faster . . .

Historians must balance accounts like these against what they also know about the significance of gas in the outcome of the war. The descriptions in Sources 2 and 3 show how awful the results of a gas attack could be, but they do not prove that gas was a significant weapon in deciding the outcome of the war.

4 Tanks

The British used tanks for the first time at the Battle of the Somme in July 1916. The tanks were successful in battle but there were not enough of them to break the stalemate on the Western Front.

The first tanks were armour-plated, with cannon and machine guns, and moved at three miles per hour. These models were unreliable and often broke down. Those that were successful often advanced too quickly for supporting troops and were captured or destroyed. At the Battle of Cambrai in 1917 the British used 324 tanks with great success to begin with. But the infantry soldiers could not keep up with them and in the later stages of the battle much of the land captured by the tank crews was recaptured by the Germans.

5 Aeroplanes

One of the most important of the new weapons to be introduced in the First World War was the aeroplane. At first aeroplanes were slow and unarmed and used mainly for reconnaissance, such as taking photographs from the air behind enemy lines. The British had 63 aircraft at the beginning of the war and commanders used them to report on enemy troop movements. By late 1914 both Britain and Germany had carried out bombing raids.

In 1915 the Germans produced an aircraft (the Fokker EI) which was capable of firing a machine gun safely through a rotating propeller. The British and French soon copied the idea and 'dogfights' between rival aircraft became increasingly common over the battlefield. These fights captured the public interest, and the newspapers gave them more publicity than the fighting in the trenches.

By 1917 the British had developed the first twin-engined bomber (the Handley-Page 0/400), and by the time the war had ended both sides had developed four-engined bombers. However, their range and power were very limited, and they had little impact on the outcome of the war.

6 Balloons and Zeppelins

Small balloons were frequently used on the battlefield for observation purposes before the widespread use of aircraft. Hydrogen-filled Zeppelins were also used by the Germans for reconnaissance and bombing purposes. A small number of Zeppelins bombed London and the east coast of England during April 1915. Although the actual damage was slight, it was the first time civilians far from the front line had been attacked in this way. The effect upon civilian morale in Britain was alarming.

● *Revision tasks*

1 Draw a table like the one below and use the information in this section to complete it.

Type of weapon	When was it first used?	How was it used?	Why was it important?

2 In your opinion which of the weapons described in this section had most impact in the war? What evidence have you found here or from your own reading to support your view?

F The collapse of Russia and US intervention

The events of 1917 were to have a major impact on the course of the war.

1 The collapse of Russia

In February 1917 Tsar Nicholas II was forced to abdicate and was replaced by the Provisional Government. This government remained loyal to the Allies and continued Russian involvement in the war. Further Russian retreat and defeat contributed to the fall of the Provisional Government in October 1917. The Bolsheviks seized power and soon withdrew Russia from the war. They were forced to sign the Treaty of Brest-Litovsk with Germany in March 1918 and lost vast areas of land.

Germany was now able to transfer 1 million troops from the Eastern to the Western Front.

2 The involvement of the USA

The USA had remained neutral at the start of the war but had become increasingly annoyed by the actions of the German U-boats. In May 1915 a German submarine sank the passenger liner *Lusitania*. Over 120 Americans drowned. In April 1917 the USA declared war on Germany. This was for two main reasons:

- In February the Germans had resumed unrestricted U-boat warfare which meant sinking any ship trading with Britain. German U-boats began sinking US merchant ships.
- The US discovery of the Zimmermann Telegram. This was an attempt by Germany to form an alliance with Mexico and to encourage a Mexican invasion of the USA.

The entry of the USA had a decisive effect on the outcome of the war.

- The USA was now the most advanced industrial nation in the world and could supply the Allies with all their needs.
- US troops swelled the numbers on the Western Front. By July 1918 the Allies had a distinct numerical superiority.
- Allied morale received a boost.
- The USA's entry forced the German Commander Ludendorff to gamble on victory with a big offensive in the spring of 1918. This gamble brought an end to the stalemate and eventually led to Germany's defeat.

● *In many ways the outcome of the war was decided in April 1917. Once the USA entered the war, the balance swung towards Britain and France. The strength of US industry and the potential of the US labour force made German defeat much more likely.* ●

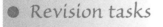

● *Revision tasks*

1 Why did Russia withdraw from the war at the end of 1917?
2 Give **two** reasons for each of the following:
   a) US entry into the war
   b) the importance of this development.

G The defeat of Germany

1 The events of 1918

The Germans knew it would take time for the USA to recruit and train an army, so they drew up plans to win a swift victory before the full impact of American entry into the war was felt on the Western Front.

By March 1918 the Russian army had been defeated. The Germans could now move a million of their own men to the Western Front. This is what happened:

- Ludendorff, the German commander, decided that since he now had many more men than the Allies, he must make an all-out attack on the Western Front before large numbers of American troops arrived in Europe.
- On 21 March 1918 the Ludendorff offensive began and the Germans advanced rapidly; they had soon moved forward 64 km along a 128-km front.
- They reached the river Marne in July and once again the French capital looked as if it might fall to the Germans.

The Allied commander, General Foch, began his counter-attack on 18 July and with the help of newly arrived American troops was able to defeat the Germans at the Second Battle of the Marne.

- In August the British, with the help of tanks, defeated the Germans at Amiens.
- More victories followed in Flanders (for example, at Ypres).

On 4 October, with the German army in full retreat, Ludendorff asked the Allies for a truce. On 11 November an ARMISTICE was signed and the First World War was over.

● *Revision tasks*

1 Use the information about the Western Front to create a timeline of key events 1914–18. Try to keep it as brief as possible. One year has been completed for you.

1914	Schlieffen Plan	Mons	Marne	Stalemate
1915				
1916				
1917				
1918				

2 First World War generals on the Western Front are usually seen as uncaring and incompetent. What evidence can you find for and against this view, either from this chapter or from other sources that you know?

2 Reasons for the German defeat

There were several reasons for Germany's defeat in 1918. These included:

- the failure of the Schlieffen Plan, which meant Germany had to fight a war on two fronts and face the stalemate in the West
- the US entry in 1917
- the impact of the British blockade on Germany
- the long-term strategic failure of Ludendorff's spring offensive in 1918
- the correct use of tanks by the Allies during the counter-offensives of July–September 1918
- the defeat of Germany's allies, Austria–Hungary and Turkey, in 1918
- discontent in Germany itself caused by war-weariness, defeat, food

shortages and a serious flu epidemic. This led to revolution at the end of October and beginning of November in 1918.

● *Revision tasks*

1 Organise the reasons for Germany's defeat under each of the following headings:

Long-term factors	Short-term factors	Immediate factors

2 Try to make links between these reasons.
3 Which do you think was the most important reason for Germany's defeat? Use key words to explain your answer.

H The peace settlement

1 The aims of the different leaders at the Paris Peace Conference

The leaders of the victorious countries met in Paris in 1919 to try to settle the issues raised by the war. The most important and influential countries at the negotiations were France, Britain and the USA. Even at the time it was clear that the different leaders had conflicting views of what a peace treaty should do. They could not all get what they wanted, so whose views would carry the most weight?

I want a treaty which will weaken Germany and keep France safe

Georges Clemenceau: Prime Minister of France

During the war France had suffered enormous damage. Large areas of land had been devastated and a lot of its factories had been destroyed. Many thousands of French people had been killed. Clemenceau was under pressure from his people to make Germany suffer.

Clemenceau was also anxious about the future. He did not want Germany to recover its strength so that it could attack France again. So his aims were clear. He wanted a harsh treaty that would punish Germany and cripple it so that it could not threaten France again.

Some historians have criticised Clemenceau's attitude, but other historians can see his point of view.

I want a just and fair peace to avoid future wars.

Woodrow Wilson: President of the USA

The USA had only been in the war for its last few months. War damage was slight. American casualties were low in comparison with those of France or Britain.

Wilson did believe that Germany was to blame for the war but he believed that the treaty with Germany should not be too harsh. His view was that if Germany was treated harshly, some day it would recover and want revenge and another war would follow. Clemenceau was quite suspicious of Wilson.

The two most important ideas Wilson put forward at the peace conference were:

- self-determination (people ruling themselves, not being ruled by a foreign power)
- international co-operation (settling disputes by all countries working together).

Wilson's views on how to achieve these aims had been published in his 'Fourteen Points' in January 1918.

The Fourteen Points

1 No secret treaties between countries.
2 Freedom of navigation upon the seas, both in times of peace and war.
3 Free trade between countries.
4 All countries to reduce their armed forces to lowest level consistent with domestic safety.
5 Overseas colonies owned by European powers to have a say in their own future.
6 All foreign troops to leave Russia. The Russian people to be allowed to decide their own future without interference.
7 Independence for Belgium.
8 France to regain Alsace–Lorraine.
9 Italy's frontier to be adjusted to take account of nationalities.
10 Self-determination for the peoples of Austria–Hungary.
11 International guarantees for the independence of the Balkan States. Serbia to have access to the sea.
12 Self-determination for the non-Turkish peoples in the Turkish empire.
13 Poland to become an independent state with access to the sea.
14 A League of Nations to be set up to settle disputes between countries by peaceful means.

● *Self-determination sounds fine in theory but in practice it would be very difficult to give the peoples of Austria–Hungary the chance to rule themselves because they were mixed and scattered across many areas. However the Austrian empire was reorganised, some people of one ethnic group were bound to end up being ruled by people from another.* ●

David Lloyd George: British Prime Minister

I want Germany punished but not so that the Germans will want revenge in the future

People in Britain were bitter towards Germany. They wanted a harsh peace treaty and Lloyd George had promised them that Germany would be punished. However, he wanted Germany to be justly punished. Like Wilson, he thought that Germany might want revenge in the future and possibly start another war. He also wanted Britain and Germany to begin trading with each other again.

Lloyd George was often in the middle ground between Clemenceau and Wilson at the peace talks. He did not agree with President Wilson about all the Fourteen Points – for example, he did not support the idea of freedom of access to the seas.

2 The terms of the Treaty of Versailles

Each of the defeated countries had to sign a separate treaty with the victorious Allies. The most important treaty was the one that dealt with Germany. This was called the Treaty of Versailles. In the end this treaty was very severe. The main terms covered these areas:

1 **G**uilt for the war
2 **A**rmed forces
3 **R**eparations
4 **G**erman territories
5 **LE**ague of Nations.

Guilt for the war

This clause was simple but harsh. Germany had to agree that it was guilty of starting the war.

Armed forces

The size of the German army worried all the Allies but especially France. The treaty therefore cut German armed forces to a level way below what they had been before the war.

- The army was limited to 100,000 men.
- Conscription was banned; soldiers had to be volunteers.
- Germany was not allowed armoured vehicles, submarines or aircraft.
- The navy could have only six battleships and 30 smaller ships.
- The Rhineland (the area on the border between Germany and France) became a 'demilitarised zone'. No German troops were allowed into that area.

Reparations

The Allies agreed (without consulting Germany, of course) that Germany had to pay compensation to France, Belgium and Britain for the damage caused by the war. These payments were called REPARATIONS. They were supposed to help the damaged countries to rebuild after the war. The exact figure (eventually set in 1921) was 132,000 million gold marks, which was an enormous amount. If these terms of the treaty had not later been changed, Germany would not have finished paying this bill until 1984.

● *Clemenceau's influence can be seen in the terms relating to the armed forces and reparations. The limits on the armed forces were clearly designed to prevent Germany attacking France again, and the demilitarisation of the Rhineland was an extra safety measure for the French against German aggression. The massive reparations figure was bound to cripple the German economy.* ●

German territories

The Allies agreed that lands and territories in Europe would be rearranged, and that Germany was going to lose out.

Germany's borders were very extensive, and the section dealing with territories was a complicated part of the treaty, as the following table and map show.

Territory	From German control to:	Other points
1 Alsace–Lorraine	France	
2 Eupen, Moresnet, Malmédy	Belgium	
3 North Schleswig	Denmark	After a vote (PLEBISCITE)
4 West Prussia and Posen	Poland	To give Poland a port
5 Danzig	League of Nations	Free city controlled by League
6 Memel	Lithuania	
7 Saar coalfields	League of Nations (coal to be given to France)	A plebiscite would be held after 15 years
8 German colonies	League of Nations	Most controlled by France and Britain under League mandates
9 Estonia, Latvia, Lithuania	Became independent states	Germany had taken these states from Russia in 1918

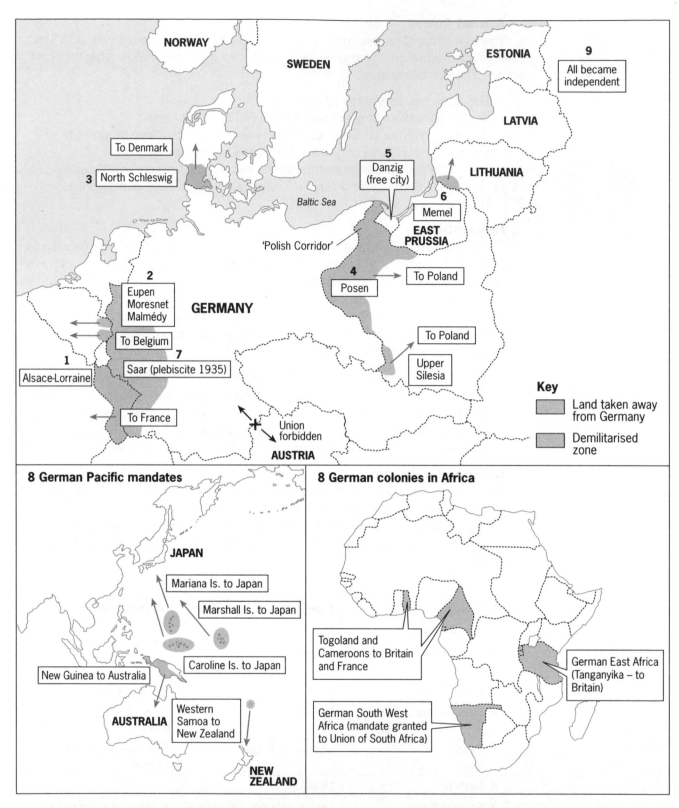

NORWAY

SWEDEN

ESTONIA

9 All became independent

LATVIA

To Denmark

3 North Schleswig

Danzig (free city) **5**

LITHUANIA

Baltic Sea

6 Memel

'Polish Corridor'

EAST PRUSSIA

2 Eupen Moresnet Malmédy

GERMANY

4 Posen → To Poland

To Belgium

1

7 Saar (plebiscite 1935)

To Poland

Upper Silesia

Alsace-Lorraine

To France

✚ Union forbidden

AUSTRIA

Key

Land taken away from Germany

Demilitarised zone

8 German Pacific mandates

JAPAN

Mariana Is. to Japan

Marshall Is. to Japan

New Guinea to Australia

Caroline Is. to Japan

AUSTRALIA

Western Samoa to New Zealand

NEW ZEALAND

8 German colonies in Africa

Togoland and Cameroons to Britain and France

German East Africa (Tanganyika – to Britain)

German South West Africa (mandate granted to Union of South Africa)

German territories lost after the Treaty of Versailles

Other conditions

1 Under the Treaty of St Germain in 1919 *Anschluss* (joining together) between Austria and Germany was forbidden. (Austria had always been a close ally of Germany and people in both countries were German-speaking.)

2 Also under the treaty of St Germain, a new country – Czechoslovakia – was created. It included parts of Austria that were German-speaking. Germans regarded both these conditions to be 'injustices' and included them in their hatred of the Treaty of Versailles.

League of Nations
Previous methods of keeping the peace had failed and so the League of Nations was set up as an international 'police force'. Germany was not invited to join the League until it had shown that it could be a peace-loving country.

● *In the treaty, the spirit of revenge and harshness seemed to have triumphed over the desire for future peace. President Wilson's influence can be seen, for example in that Estonia, Latvia and Lithuania became independent and the League of Nations was established, but his Fourteen Points did not influence the negotiations as much as he had hoped.*

Germany had been weakened and forced to accept a humiliating settlement that Germans saw as unjust. ●

● *Revision tasks*

1 Use four to six key words to describe the damage caused by the First World War.
2 Complete the following table. Summarise each leader's view in no more than five words.

Leader	Country	Views on the Peace Treaty
Clemenceau		
Wilson		
Lloyd George		

3 Where would you put each of the leaders on this scale?

Moderate treaty ➡ Harsh treaty

4 Did any state (except Germany) accept blame for the war?
5 Choose five key words to summarise the terms dealing with Germany's armed forces.
6 Explain why you think the reparations bill was so large.
7 Note three examples of territory lost by Germany.
8 Why was Germany not invited to join the League of Nations?
9 In your view which leader would have been most satisfied with the terms of the Treaty of Versailles? Explain your answer.

German reactions to the Treaty of Versailles

The reactions of Germans were horror and outrage.

1 Feelings of injustice

They felt the treaty was unjust on the following grounds:

• *They did not feel they had caused the war,* yet they were forced to sign the war guilt clause.
• *They did not even feel they had lost the war.* In 1918 Germany still had an army in the field. Many felt that Germany had not surrendered; it had simply agreed to stop fighting and seek peace. Yet they were being treated as the defeated side.
• *They felt they should have been involved in the treaty discussions.* Yet their government was not represented at the talks and they were forced to accept the treaty without any choice or even a comment.

● *Whatever ordinary Germans may have believed, the German army could not realistically have fought on in 1918. Whether they liked it or not, they had lost the war.*
Most historians agree that other German reactions were valid; for example, their point about not being consulted. However, others point out that German views would probably have been ignored in treaty negotiations. ●

2 Feelings about war guilt

The Allies had to make Germany accept war guilt in order to justify the harsh terms of the treaty. The Germans were angry at this clause. At the very least, the Germans thought that other countries should share the blame for the war.

3 Feelings about disarmament

The disarmament terms angered Germans:

- An army of 100,000 was very small for a country of Germany's size. Before the war the army had been ten times this size.
- The army was a symbol of German pride (just like Britain's navy).

When the terms of the treaty were announced, the German navy sank its own ships in the British naval base of Scapa Flow in the Orkneys.

As time went on German anger grew, particularly as none of the other countries disarmed during the 1920s, although disarmament was an aim of the League of Nations. When Hitler started to re-arm in the 1930s (secretly at first, then openly), it won him massive popular support in Germany.

4 Feelings about reparations

The war was followed by economic chaos and crippling inflation in Germany which the Germans blamed on having to pay reparations. Most people agreed that the reparations figure was far too high. It was reduced in 1929.

5 Feelings about loss of German territories

The loss of territories was deeply resented by the German people:

- Some Germans would now be living in other countries ruled by foreign governments.
- The Saar, an important industrial area, was controlled by the League of Nations, but was effectively taken over by France.
- Their colonies in Africa (which had been a great source of pride) were to be run by Britain and France.

6 Feelings about the League of Nations

Germany felt further insulted by not being invited to join the League.

7 The contrast with the Fourteen Points

The Germans said that the treaty was not in keeping with Wilson's Fourteen Points. The Allies claimed they wanted to give self-determination to the peoples of Austria–Hungary, yet the result of the treaty was that many Germans (in the Sudetenland, for example, which had become part of the new country of Czechoslovakia) were now part of a foreign country ruled by foreigners.

However, the Germans were not on strong ground in this respect. They had not previously shown much enthusiasm for the Fourteen Points. They did not pull their troops out of Russia, although the Fourteen Points demanded it. And even if Germans had ended up outside their own country, this was also true for many Poles, Russians, Romanians and Hungarians throughout eastern Europe.

● *The bitter reaction of Germans to the Treaty of Versailles is a crucial theme in the history of the 1920s and 1930s. Partly as a result of the treaty, Germany had great problems in the 1920s. Hitler used these problems and German bitterness about the treaty to gain power in Germany. He promised the Germans that he would remove the injustices of the treaty.* ●

● *Revision task*

1 Produce your own key points summary of why Germans were outraged by the terms of the Treaty of Versailles. Mention:
   a) War guilt
   b) Army
   c) Reparations
   d) German territories
   e) League of Nations
   f) The Fourteen Points.

J Criticisms of the Treaty of Versailles

The Treaty of Versailles was criticised by many people at the time and has also been criticised by historians since.

1 Views expressed at the time

People at the time criticised the treaty for many different reasons.

- Some said it was too harsh on Germany. They predicted that Germany would want revenge and there would be another war.
- Some said it was not harsh enough – that it did not punish Germany enough.
- Some said Russia should have been consulted.

The US Congress was very dissatisfied with the treaty and refused to sign it.

2 The views of historians

Historians generally agree that the Treaty of Versailles failed, because in 1939 war broke out again in Europe. They point out that it had two great weaknesses.

- Germany was punished and humiliated. Although this might have pleased people in the victorious countries at the time, it was short-sighted because when Germany did recover many of its people wanted revenge.
- The treaty created some new countries that were weak and unstable.

However, it is important to realise how difficult a job the 'victorious Allies' faced.

- The people in the victorious countries would not have accepted a fairer treaty. Clemenceau was criticised in France by those who thought that the treaty *was not harsh enough*.
- In trying to ensure self-determination they faced the real problem that ethnic groups in eastern and central Europe were so mixed up that it was impossible for each nation to rule itself.

● *There has been much criticism of the Treaty of Versailles. It was too harsh on Germany. Germany was too weak to pay the sum fixed for reparations. Yet this criticism is often made with the benefit of hindsight. We can see that less than twenty years later Germany was at war again. At the time, the conditions imposed on Germany were not as harsh as those that Germany forced on Russia in March 1918 with the Treaty of Brest-Litovsk.* ●

● *Revision tasks*

1 Use three key words to summarise why historians have criticised the Treaty of Versailles.
2 Use six key words to summarise why people at the time criticised the Treaty of Versailles.
3 In your own words say why you believe (or do not believe) that the leaders at the Peace Conference had an impossible job.

CHAPTER 8

Revision session

The aim of this session is for you to see how you can apply your knowledge of the First World War to answer some source-based questions.

Examination questions

Below are examples of source questions from the 2000 Edexcel Paper 2, adapted by permission of Edexcel.

Source A From a history textbook published in 1998
Tanks were used for the first time at the Battle of the Somme. They advanced ahead of the infantry, crushing barbed wire defences and spraying the enemy with machine-gun fire. They caused alarm among the Germans. However, these first machines moved at only walking pace and more than half of them broke down before they reached the German lines. In 1917, they were too successful! They broke through enemy lines so quickly that the infantry could not keep up with them.

Source B From an official report by a German soldier to his superior officer. The report is about the Allied offensive of 1918
The enemy made use of tanks in large numbers. Our men were unnerved. Tanks broke through our front lines causing a panic. When we were able to locate our anti-tank guns we quickly knocked out the tanks, but the damage was done and solely due to the success of the tanks. We have suffered enormous losses.

Source C From an official report by a British officer to his superiors, summer 1918
Of the 38 tanks that went into action all need overhauling; the crews are completely exhausted. The pulses of one crew were taken immediately after they got out of their tank. The beats averaged 130 per minute – twice as fast as they should have been. In some cases where infantry were carried in the tank, they fainted after forty-five minutes. It is clear that the tank is not a war-winning weapon.

a) Study Source A.
What can you learn from Source A about the use of tanks in the First World War?   *(4 marks)*

What is required?   This question is testing your understanding of a source and your ability to interpret what it says. Try to make at least one inference from the source. In other words, read between the lines of what the source says.

Ideas for your answer   • To encourage you to make an inference or inferences you could start at least one sentence with 'This source suggests that . . .' or 'This source shows that . . .'.
• One possible inference could be that tanks were brought into use at the Somme in 1916 before they had been properly developed and were not used properly in 1916 and 1917.

b) Study Sources A, B and C.

Does Source C support the evidence of Sources A and B about the use of tanks on the Western Front during the First World War? Explain your answer. *(6 marks)*

What is required? This question is asking you to compare the information in Source C to that in Sources A and B. A simple answer which compares the sources at their face value will only achieve level 1 (1–2 marks). An answer that makes developed statements about similarities or differences between two or three of the sources will reach level 2 (3–4 marks). For level 3 (5–6 marks), you need to:

- ensure you directly compare Source C to Source A and Source C to Source B, in other words, all three sources
- look for similarities and differences between them in information, tone and attitude
- ensure your comparisons are developed and precisely explained.

Ideas for your answer
1 Begin by explaining the information/attitude/tone of Source C. It is clearly opposed to tanks and does not believe they will be a war-winning weapon.
2 Now compare Source C to Source A.
   a) Does Source C support the views of Source A? Yes, because Source A says the tanks failed at the Somme in 1916 and again in 1917.
   b) Are there any differences? Yes, because in Source A it does mention that the tanks were successful, if too successful. They broke through enemy lines.
3 Compare Source C to Source B.
   a) Does Source C support the evidence of Source B? At first it seems to, as Source B says the Germans used anti-tank guns to knock out the tanks.
   b) Are there any differences? Yes, because unlike Source C, the writer of Source B believes that tanks were a war-winning weapon.
4 Now write a conclusion summing up your answer to the question and giving a judgement as to how far C supports A and B.

Source D A graph showing Allied shipping losses (in thousands of tonnes) during January to September 1917, published by the British Government after the war

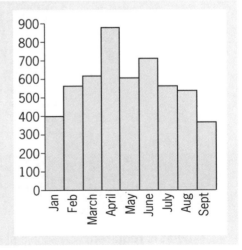

Source E An artist's impression of British planes bombing German trenches, published in the magazine *Sphere*, October 1918

Source F From a popular US song, written in 1917
Over there, over there,
Send the word, send the word over there,
That the Yanks are coming, the Yanks are coming,
The drums rum-tumming everywhere.
So prepare, say a prayer,
Send the word, send the word to beware.
We'll be over, we're coming over,
And we won't come back till it's over, over there.

c) Study Sources D and E.
How useful are Sources D and E as evidence of the use of new technology in the First World War?

(8 marks)

What is required? A simple statement on the content or nature of the sources will achieve no more than three marks. More developed statements that lack balance, for example, by ignoring the nature of the sources and/or their limitations, will reach level 2 (4–6 marks). To reach level 3 (7–8 marks) you need to ensure that your answer is fully balanced in the following ways:

- Explain the usefulness of both sources.
- Evaluate the **usefulness** of each source in two areas – **content/context** of the source and **nature/origin/purpose**.
- Analyse the **limitations** of each source in the same two areas – **content/context** and **nature/origin/purpose**.

Include a conclusion that summarises the usefulness of each source. In some cases the two sources might be useful because they give similar views of an event.

Ideas for your answer   Draw a table like the one below and use key words to complete each section. This is a good way of planning your answer.
Examine the usefulness of each source in turn.

	Source D	Source E
Usefulness of content and context		
Limitations of content and context		
Usefulness of nature, origin and purpose		
Limitations of nature, origin and purpose		

1 Source D is useful because of its content. It gives us the Allied shipping losses in 1917 and highlights the dramatic losses of April.
2 Now the limitations of the content of Source D: it only reveals the losses for the nine months of 1917 which may produce a distorted view of the war as a whole. There is no mention of what caused these losses.
3 Now you will need to do the same for Source E. A few hints: How useful are the contents of the source? What view do you get of the Allied use of planes? What are its limitations, bearing in mind it is an artist's impression?
4 For your conclusion you could explain that they are useful because they show the impact of new technology in two very different areas of the war. In what other respects are they useful?

d) Study all the sources.
'It was the entry of the USA into the war which brought about the surrender of Germany in 1918.'
Use the sources, and your own knowledge, to explain whether you agree with this view.   *(12 marks)*

What is required?   This question is the most important because it is worth twelve marks. The examiner wants you to reach a conclusion on the question using your own knowledge and by referring to most, if not all, of the sources.
   Low-level answers (1–3 marks) will make simple points using the sources and/or your own knowledge. The next level of answer (4–7 marks) will make developed statements in support of *or* against the view using the sources and/or your own knowledge. To reach level 3 (8–10 marks) you must make developed statements for *and* against the view using the sources and your own knowledge. To achieve the very top level (11–12 marks) you will have to do the following:

* ensure that your whole answer is focused on the question
* include an introduction that explains the view expressed in the question and how you intend to answer it
* give a balanced argument for and against the view
* use most, if not all, of the sources and your own knowledge to give this argument
* begin each paragraph with your argument and then back it up with your own knowledge and evidence from one or more of the sources – in other words, integrate your arguments, your own knowledge and evidence from the sources
* write a conclusion that gives a final judgement on the view in the question. Make sure this is consistent with what you have already written.

Ideas for your answer   Draw a table like the one below and complete each section with key words. Use this as a plan for your eventual answer. Part of it has been completed for you.

	Supporting the view	Against the view
Arguments		Proper use of tank in 1918
Own knowledge		Explanation of use of tank in July to August 1918
Sources		Source B
Conclusion		

1 In support of the view you need to give a developed explanation from your own knowledge of the importance of the US entry into the war and its impact on Germany.
2 You can use Source F to support the view.
3 Against the view you need to explain other reasons for the German surrender, such as the impact of the British blockade, the use of tanks and the failure of Ludendorff's offensive of 1918.
4 You can use Sources A, B and E against the view.
5 For a conclusion, decide whether the entry of the USA was responsible for the German surrender or whether there were additional reasons.

Practice questions

Now look at the following sources and questions adapted by permission of Edexcel from the Specimen Paper for Paper 2. Have a go at answering the questions without any help.

Source A From a school textbook about the First World War published in 1989
The French expected an attack to take place between Metz and Switzerland. They had heavily fortified this area. As a result, the Germans drew up the Schlieffen Plan. By this, France was to be invaded from the North through Belgium where France's border defences were weak. The Germans thought their plan would allow them to surround Paris and quickly capture it. The main French forces would then soon surrender.

Source B From a school textbook about twentieth-century world history
At the beginning of the war the British sent over their Expeditionary Force of 100,000 men. This force slowed the Germans at Mons. There were further problems for the Germans following the speed of the Russian mobilisation. Moltke, the German Chief of Staff, decided to send some of the forces which were attacking France to support the German armies fighting the Russians.

Source C A map showing the Schlieffen Plan after it was put into operation

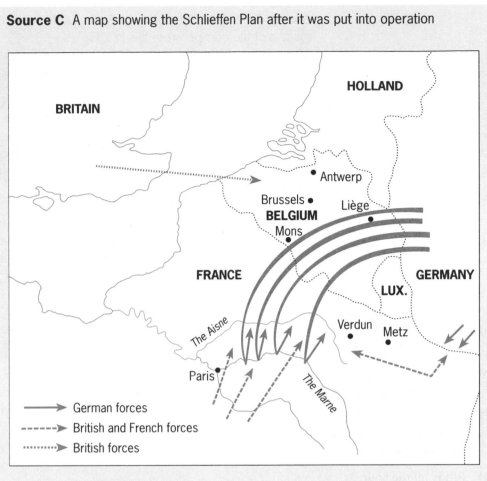

Source D A photograph showing German infantry advancing across open fields, August 1914

Source E From the memoirs of a British soldier who fought in France in the early months of the war. He wrote this in 1938

My units went into action near Mons against the Germans on 23 August. We were attacked by waves of German infantry advancing over open fields. Such tactics amazed us, and after the first shock of men slowly and helplessly falling down as they were hit, we experienced a great sense of power and pleasure.

Source F From the official history of a German regiment which fought in the early weeks of the First World War. It was included in a British history book about the war and was published in 1930

In order to march fast, the field kitchen had to be left behind, and there was no issue of bread for four days. The troops had to look for food in an area which had no supplies. It is not surprising that when the Marne was reached, the men were tired out – some men had only one piece of bread, one cup of soup, one cup of coffee and a raw turnip in a period of forty-eight hours.

a) Study Source A.
 What can you learn about the aims of the Schlieffen Plan from Source A? *(4 marks)*

b) Study Sources A, B and C.
 Does Source C support the evidence of Sources A and B? Explain your answer. *(6 marks)*

c) Study Sources D and E.
 How useful are these sources as evidence about why the Germans were unable to capture Paris in the early weeks of the war? *(8 marks)*

d) Study all the sources.
 'The Schlieffen Plan failed because the German High Command made too many mistakes in August and September 1914.'
 Use these sources, and your own knowledge, to explain whether you agree with this view. *(12 marks)*

Summary and revision plan

Below is a list of headings which you may find helpful. Use this as a check-list to make sure you are familiar with the material featured in this chapter. Record your key words alongside each heading.

A The failure of the Schlieffen Plan
- ❏ What was the Schlieffen Plan?
- ❏ The failure of the Schlieffen Plan
- ❏ The Battles of the Marne and Ypres, 1914
- ❏ Stalemate, December 1914

B Stalemate: the experience of trench warfare
- ❏ Why was there a stalemate, 1914–17?
- ❏ Trench warfare
- ❏ The Western Front, 1915

C Stalemate: the role of Haig
- ❏ Views of Haig
- ❏ The Western Front, 1916
- ❏ The Western Front, 1917
- ❏ Conclusions on Haig

D The war at sea and the Gallipoli campaign
- ❏ Background
- ❏ Minor clashes
- ❏ The Battle of Jutland, May/June 1916
- ❏ War against the submarine
- ❏ The British blockade of Germany
- ❏ The Gallipoli campaign

E The impact of new technology
- ❏ Submarines
- ❏ Machine guns
- ❏ Gas
- ❏ Tanks
- ❏ Aeroplanes
- ❏ Balloons and Zeppelins

F The collapse of Russia and US intervention
- ❏ The collapse of Russia
- ❏ The involvement of the USA

G The defeat of Germany
- ❏ The events of 1918
- ❏ Reasons for the German defeat

Continued on page 154

H The peace settlement
- ❑ The aims of the different leaders at the Paris Peace Conference
- ❑ The terms of the Treaty of Versailles

I German reactions to the Treaty of Versailles
- ❑ Feelings of injustice
- ❑ Feelings about war guilt
- ❑ Feelings about disarmament
- ❑ Feelings about reparations
- ❑ Feelings about loss of German territories
- ❑ Feelings about the League of Nations
- ❑ The contrast with the Fourteen Points

J Criticisms of the Treaty of Versailles
- ❑ Views expressed at the time
- ❑ The views of historians

Depression and the New Deal: the USA, 1929–41

CHAPTER 9

In the 1920s the US economy led the world, and many of its citizens enjoyed boom conditions. The Wall Street Crash of 1929 brought depression and unemployment. In 1932 Roosevelt was elected president and introduced a programme of reforms known as the New Deal. How successful were they in solving the economic and social problems of the USA?

<table>
<tr><td>

Key content

</td><td>

You will need to have a good working knowledge of these areas:

A The USA in the 1920s
B Causes and consequences of the Wall Street Crash
C Government reaction and attempts at recovery, 1929–32
D The nature of the New Deal; policies to deal with agriculture, industry, unemployment and welfare
E Opposition to the New Deal
F The extent of the recovery and the successes of the New Deal

</td></tr>
<tr><td>

Key themes

</td><td>

You will be asked to show your understanding of some key themes:

● Why did the US economy collapse in 1929?
● What was the economic and social impact of this collapse?
● Was Hoover unfairly blamed for the lack of government intervention?
● What were the main features of the New Deal?
● How effective was the New Deal in solving the economic and social problems of the USA?
● Who opposed the New Deal and for what reasons?
● How far had the USA recovered from the Great Depression by 1941?

</td></tr>
</table>

Source-based questions test both your knowledge of the topic and your source-evaluation skills. For example, look at this question adapted from the 2001 Edexcel Paper 2 by permission of Edexcel.

Source A A graph showing changing share prices in the 1920s

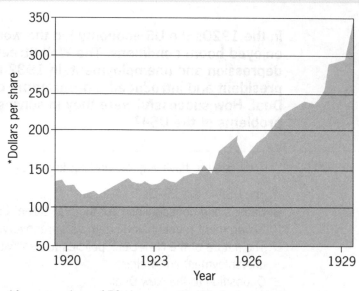

*Average prices of 50 shares on the US stock market

Share prices, 1920–29

a) Study Source A.
   What can you learn from Source A about share prices in the USA in the 1920s? *(4 marks)*

This question is asking you to:

· interpret the source
· make inferences from the source based upon your knowledge of the USA in the 1920s.

We will look at this question in more detail at the end of this chapter.

A The USA in the 1920s

1 Background: the USA up to 1920

The USA's industry and farming had grown steadily since the 1860s.

- The country had huge resources (coal, iron, timber, oil).
- It had a growing population, many of them immigrants willing to work hard.
- Railways, mining and manufacturing were all strong.

In the early years of the First World War, US businesses profited from the war in Europe.

- American industries supplied arms and equipment.
- American firms were able to take over much of the export business of the European powers while they were caught up in the fighting.

The First World War made the USA wealthy and confident. Americans felt they were doing well. It also made them ISOLATIONIST. They did not want to be dragged into Europe's wars.

2 Republican policies

Through the 1920s Republican presidents were in power, and they implemented Republican policies. President Harding believed in what he called 'normalcy': letting the USA get back to normal life as it had been before the war. His key policies were:

- isolation – the USA was not to get involved in foreign disputes
- tariffs (for example, the Fordney-McCumber tariff) – these were placed on foreign goods to make them expensive in the USA so that people would buy American goods instead
- low taxes – these helped businesses to grow, and left workers with money to spend.

When Harding died suddenly in 1923, Vice-President Coolidge became president. Coolidge followed the same policies as Harding.

3 The boom period

In the 1920s the profits of many American companies rose enormously. More goods were produced more quickly and more cheaply because of new mass-production techniques.

The biggest boom came in the industries making consumer goods – goods for ordinary families to buy. Sales of household goods such as vacuum cleaners and washing machines boosted the electrical industry.

The single most important industry was the motor industry – cars were becoming increasingly common and by 1930 there were 30 million of them on the roads. A healthy car industry helped to create further jobs in related areas, such as car parts and road-building.

The figures in Source 1 on page 158 seem to support this image of a boom in the USA during the 1920s.

Advertising, credit and hire purchase all made it easy to spend money. Wages for many Americans did rise, and there was a feeling of confidence. An example of such confidence is shown in Source 2.

As well as buying goods, Americans wanted a share of some of the profits that companies were making. To do this, they bought and sold shares in companies.

> **Source 1** US government statistics (1929) on economic performance in the 1920s
>
> | Production of cars | 1926 | 4.3 million |
> |---|---|---|
> | | 1929 | 5.3 million |
> | Number of cars registered | 1920 | 8.1 million |
> | | 1929 | 23.0 million |
> | Value of radios sold (in US dollars) | 1922 | 60.0 million |
> | | 1929 | 824.5 million |

> **Source 2** President Hoover in a speech in 1928
>
> *We in America are nearer to the final victory over poverty than ever before in the history of any land.*

4 US farmers

US farmers had a difficult time in the 1920s. This was due to several reasons.

- After the First World War many European countries began to produce their own food again and US exports dropped, as did prices.
- During the First World War there was an increased demand for food exports from the USA. Many farmers took out mortgages to buy extra land to meet the demand. When demand and food prices fell in the 1920s, farmers made smaller profits. Many could no longer afford the repayments on the mortgages. By 1924, 600,000 farmers had suffered bankruptcies.
- Demand for cotton and wool fell because of competition from synthetic fibres such as rayon.
- PROHIBITION, introduced in 1919, greatly reduced the demand for barley and grapes.

5 Weaknesses in the US economy

There were worrying weaknesses in the US economy during this period.

- Some major industries did not grow in the 1920s (for example, coal, textiles).
- Farmers had produced too much food and prices were very low.
- Many ordinary Americans did not share in the boom. Black Americans in particular suffered from discrimination, getting the worst jobs.
- Some industries were struggling against foreign competition.
- Other industries could not export goods because of TARIFFS in other countries. Often these tariffs were simply a reaction to American tariffs.

Source 3 shows some of the differences in earnings.

> **Source 3** US social survey of wages in 1929
>
> *Average wages per month of American workers (in US dollars)*
>
> | Farmers in South Carolina | 129 |
> |---|---|
> | Town workers in South Carolina | 412 |
> | Town workers in New York | 881 |
> | Fruit farmers in California | 1246 |

Trusts were another problem. These huge companies dominated the business world. They worked together to keep wages down and to keep prices high, to ensure the largest profits possible. The Republican policy of non-interference (*laissez-faire*) gave them the freedom to operate in this way. However, the combination of low wages and high prices actually stopped many people from buying goods, and this stored up problems for the future.

● *Revision tasks*

1 Use four to six key words to explain US industrial growth in the 1920s.
2 Copy the table below and complete it to show the main features of the US economy in the 1920s.

Signs of 'boom' or prosperity	Signs of weakness

B Causes and consequences of the Wall Street Crash

1 Causes of the Crash

Historians can identify long-term and short-term causes of the Crash. The longer-term causes were the weaknesses in the US economy (see page 158):

- overproduction in agriculture – driving prices down
- overproduction of consumer goods – driving prices down
- inequality – the rich were very rich while the poor were very poor
- foreign competition – reducing demand for American goods.

Short-term causes related to shares. Many ordinary Americans bought shares in companies. Normally this is good for business. However, in the USA in the 1920s the rush to buy shares caused problems:

- Many people bought and sold shares to make quick profits instead of keeping their money invested in the same businesses for some time. They were speculators, not investors.
- Companies were forced by shareholders to pay out profits to shareholders rather than re-investing them.
- Americans borrowed money on credit to buy their shares.

These kinds of share dealings depended on confidence that share prices would continue to rise. Once people started worrying about the long-term weaknesses in the American economy, disaster struck. In September 1929 the prices of shares began to edge down – slowly to start with – but people soon began to realise that the shares they owned were worth less than the loans they had used to buy them in the first place. All of a sudden, everyone tried to get rid of their shares, selling them for less and less. The worst day was 'Black Tuesday', 29 October 1929. As a result, share prices collapsed.

Source 4 Share prices, 1928–29 (from the *Wall Street Journal*)

Company	Share values in cents		
	3 Sept 1928	3 Sept 1929	13 Nov 1929
New York Central	256	256	160
Union Carbide and Carbon	413	137	59
Electric Bond and Share	203	186	50

2 Effects of the Crash

The effects of the Crash were disastrous:

- Many individuals were bankrupt – they could not pay back the loans they had used to buy their (now worthless) shares.
- Some homeowners lost their homes as they could not pay their mortgages.
- Even some who had savings lost their money when banks collapsed.
- Many farmers suffered a similar fate as banks tried to get back their loans.

The confidence of individuals was shattered. Many faced unemployment, and those in work faced reduced hours and wages. They tightened their belts and stopped spending.

Big institutions also suffered:

- About 11,000 banks stopped trading between 1929 and 1933.
- At the same time demand for goods of all types fell.
- As a result, production levels fell and so did wages and the number of jobs.

Unemployment rose dramatically as shown in the diagram:

Unemployment in the USA, 1929–36

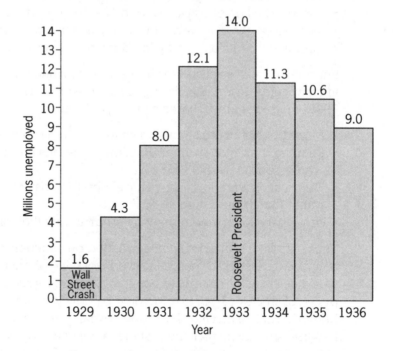

● *There was no one cause of the Wall Street Crash. It was the result of over-speculation, overproduction and the US government policy of* PROTECTIONISM *(tariffs on imports). Its effects were devastating not just for the USA but for most of the world which had become dependent on American trade and loans.* ●

C Government reaction and attempts at recovery, 1929–32

1 President Hoover's actions

Hoover eventually had to take action to deal with the effects of the Depression.

* He reduced taxes, but this mainly helped the wealthy.
* He tried to help farmers with the Federal Farming Board, which purchased surplus crops in an attempt to keep up prices. This was not enough. The farmers wanted help paying their mortgages. Despite the aid, they still could not afford to pay off their loans and bankruptcies continued.
* The Federal Home Loan Bank Act, passed in July 1932, was designed to stimulate home-building and increase home ownership. To do this Hoover set up twelve regional banks with a fund of $125 million to help fund discounted home loans.

2 Was Hoover unfairly blamed?

Most Americans blamed President Hoover for the Crash.

> **Source 5** Slogan of protesting farmers in Iowa
> *'In Hoover we trusted, now we are busted!'*

This was not wholly fair since there were larger forces at work than Hoover's policies. However, people blamed Hoover partly because of what he *did not do* as much as for what he did.

* Hoover insisted that the situation was not too serious, and that 'prosperity is just around the corner'. This unfounded optimism upset many Americans.
* Hoover believed in 'rugged individualism' and showed little sympathy for poor, starving Americans living in shanty towns called 'Hoovervilles'.
* He refused to provide federal aid for the unemployed or support a programme of public works to provide jobs for them.

3 Resentment among the people

With wages falling and unemployment rising, resentment grew among the people. Hoover became very unpopular in 1932 when he ordered the US army to disperse the Bonus Marchers. These were veterans who had fought in the First World War. They had marched to Washington demanding early payment of a monetary bonus due to be paid to them in 1945. They wanted it paid early to offset the effects of the Depression. They even built a 'Hooverville' or shanty town on the edge of Washington DC. When the army tried to clear the Bonus Marchers, many were injured and one was killed.

● *Revision tasks*

1 'Hoover deserved all the criticism he got.' Make a copy of the table below and use key words to complete each section.

Criticisms of Hoover	Defence of Hoover

2 Using a few key words explain the 'Bonus Marchers'.

D The nature of the New Deal; policies to deal with agriculture, industry, unemployment and welfare

1 Roosevelt becomes President

Franklin D. Roosevelt was well educated and a talented, passionate politician. He had complete faith in his ideas for bringing the USA out of the Depression. During the presidential election campaign in 1932, his key phrase was his offer of a 'New Deal' for the American people. He won the election by a large margin.

Due to the banking crisis and high level of unemployment, Roosevelt was determined to act quickly. From 9 March to 16 June 1933 (the 'Hundred Days') he managed to get the US Congress to pass a huge amount of legislation. This is summarised in the table below.

Hundred Days Legislation 9 March–16 June 1933		
Legislation	**Problem**	**Action**
Emergency Banking Act and Securities Exchange Act	Americans had little confidence in the banks and might withdraw all their savings – this would lead to collapse.	Government declared a 'bank holiday' and closed all banks. When, eight days later, these banks were re-opened, the government restored confidence in the banking system by officially backing 5000 banks to reassure American people their money was safe. The Securities Exchange Act was set up to regulate the stock market to make sure that the speculation which caused the 1929 Crash could not happen again.
Federal Emergency Relief Administration (FERA)	Poverty and unemployment	500 million dollars allocated to help relieve suffering of poor (food, clothing, etc.). Seed and equipment for farmers, schemes to create jobs.
Civilian Conservation Corps (CCC)	Unemployment among young men	Men aged 18–25 given six months' work. Had to send most of their pay home to parents/wives. About 300,000 joined in 1933; by 1940 there were 2 million.
Public Works Administration (PWA) (became Works Progress Administration in 1935)	Unemployment	Paid for public works projects (for example, schools, roads, hospitals) and used unemployed workers.
Agricultural Adjustment Administration (AAA)	Rural poverty, unemployment and low crop prices	Advised farmers on marketing and farming techniques and helped solve problem of overproduction by US government buying up produce. Farmers became more organised but wealthy farmers gained most.
National Industrial Recovery Act (NIRA)	General economic condition of USA	Set up NRA (National Recovery Administration) which set standards on working practices (hours, child labour). This helped create more jobs. Employers in the scheme displayed the Eagle symbol of government approval and the government encouraged people to use these firms. Over 2 million employers joined the scheme.
Tennessee Valley Authority (TVA)	Agricultural overproduction and regular flooding had ruined livelihoods of farm workers in Tennessee Valley. No alternative jobs in industry. Area covered parts of six states and was too big for any one state to deal with.	Huge public works projects: dams, irrigation, canals and water transport. Hydroelectric power created thousands of jobs. Farmers given loans and training in soil conservation. New housing built.

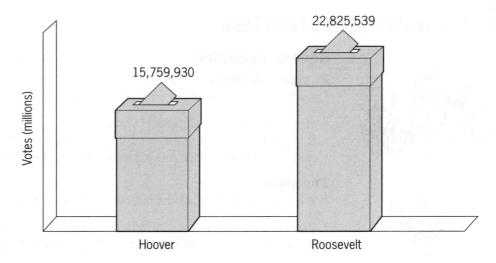

US Presidential election result, November 1932

2 New Deal legislation

As well as passing new legislation in his first hundred days of office, in later years Roosevelt updated some laws and created further legislation where it was needed.

- In 1935 the Works Progress Administration (WPA) replaced the Public Works Administration (PWA). It extended the range of work provided, from building work to the Federal Theatre Project which gave work to unemployed artists and writers.
- The National Labor Relations Act or Wagner Act (1935) forced employers to recognise trade unions after the National Recovery Administration (NRA) was declared illegal by American courts. This law meant that workers kept the protection which the NRA had given them.
- The Social Security Act (1935) provided federal aid for the elderly and set up an unemployment insurance scheme. However, the provisions were still far less comprehensive than those in Germany or Britain.

● *The 'New Deal' was a range of measures introduced by Roosevelt to deal with the problems of unemployment and poverty. Some were designed to provide immediate solutions. Others were trying to put in place schemes that would provide work and relief over a long period of time.* ●

● *Revision tasks*

1 Using a few key words explain why Roosevelt won the presidential election of 1932.

2 Make a copy of the table below. Give the full title of the measures listed and use a few key words to explain what each did.

Measure	Full title	What it did
PWA		
NRA		
AAA		
CCC		
FERA		

E Opposition to the New Deal

1 General opposition

Business leaders

They were unhappy about various aspects of the New Deal:

- regulations on working conditions
- the growth of trade unions and their increasing power
- huge cost of the welfare programmes (which came from taxes paid by Americans).

The states

They were concerned about the New Deal because:

- measures like the TVA cut right across the rights of individual states
- some states feared that the federal government was becoming too powerful.

Politicians

Some politicians opposed the New Deal:

- Republicans (not surprisingly) bitterly opposed the Democrat Roosevelt
- even some conservative Democrats opposed him
- some radicals in the USA like Huey Long (see below) believed the New Deal did not go far enough.

2 The Supreme Court

The Supreme Court clashed with Roosevelt.

- Its judges (mainly old, Republican judges) ruled that several of the New Deal measures were illegal.
- Matters came to a head in 1937 when Roosevelt wanted to reorganise the Court and appoint six new judges to alter the political balance of the Court in favour of the Democrats. This plan failed, but afterwards Supreme Court opposition was lessened.

3 Huey Long

Some opponents felt that Roosevelt was not doing enough. Senator Huey Long of Louisiana wanted Roosevelt to adopt more socialist policies. He claimed that there should have been a major redistribution of wealth in the USA and he began to develop his own plan. His 'Share the Wealth' scheme wanted the federal government to guarantee every family in the USA a minimum annual income of $5000. To pay for this, Long planned to tax wealthy people. By 1935, Long had about 27,000 'Share the Wealth' clubs and support from 7.5 million people.

● *In many respects Roosevelt could not win. If he brought in too much change he faced opposition from state governments and the Supreme Court. If he did too little he faced criticism from those who wanted more extreme measures.* ●

● *Revision task*

1 Make a copy of the table below and use key words to explain why these people/groups opposed the New Deal.

Group/people	Reason for opposition to New Deal
Business leaders	
The states	
Politicians	
The Supreme Court	
Huey Long	

F The extent of the recovery and the successes of the New Deal

1 Roosevelt and the voters

The most obvious success of Roosevelt in this period was that he won re-election in 1936, 1940 and 1944 – the only president ever to serve four terms of office. Roosevelt was the first president to talk regularly to the people; his weekly 'fireside chats' on the radio were listened to by 60 million Americans. However, most historians agree that the New Deal had mixed results.

2 Assessing the New Deal

Weaknesses

- When Roosevelt cut back his programmes in 1937 unemployment rose dramatically.
- He never fully conquered unemployment in the 1930s; unemployment was only solved by the USA's entry into the Second World War in 1941.
- The USA's trade (and the world's trade) did not recover.
- He failed to convince even his own supporters of the need to change the organisation of the Supreme Court to stop it opposing his reforms.
- Black Americans gained relatively little from the New Deal.

Successes

- In the USA the Depression did not lead to extreme movements such as communism or fascism taking hold. Roosevelt restored the American people's faith in democracy.
- Many millions of jobs were created and vital relief (food, shelter, clothing) was supplied to the poor.
- Agriculture and industry benefited from efficient infrastructure (roads, services).

● *Roosevelt is often judged on the effects of his measures on the numbers out of work. Those who criticise the New Deal point to the millions still unemployed at the end of the 1930s. They ignore the scale of the problem he faced in 1933 and the psychological effects his policies had on the morale of many American people.* ●

● *Revision tasks*

1 Draw up your own balance sheet like the one below, summarising the successes and failures of the New Deal in a few key words.

Successes of the New Deal	Failures of the New Deal

2 Overall, do you think the New Deal was successful in solving the social and economic problems of the USA 1933–41? Use a few key words to record your opinion.

Revision session

The aim of this revision session is for you to see how you can apply your knowledge of the USA, 1929–41, to answer source-based questions.

Examination questions

Below are examples of source questions from the 2001 Edexcel Paper 2, adapted by permission of Edexcel.

Source A A graph showing changing share prices in the 1920s
Share prices, 1920–29

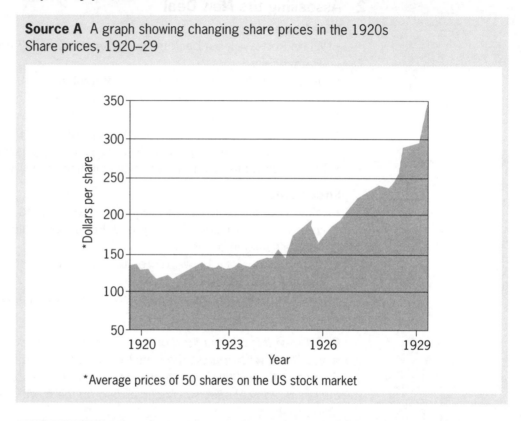

*Average prices of 50 shares on the US stock market

Source B From a history book about the USA in the 1920s, written in 1938
Stock market madness reached its high point that year (1929). Everyone was playing the market. On my last day in New York I went to get my hair cut. As he removed the sheet, the hairdresser said softly, 'Buy Standard Gas. I've doubled what I invested and it'll double again.'

Source C From a speech by a US banker in early 1929
Shares look dangerously high to me. This kind of trading has been going on too long and although prices have slipped a bit recently, they might easily slip a good deal more. Business is none too good. I'd wait awhile and see.'

a) Study Source A.

What can you learn from Source A about share prices in the USA in the 1920s? *(4 marks)*

What is required? This question is testing your understanding of a source and your ability to interpret what it says. Try to make at least one inference from the source. In other words read between the lines of what the source says.

Ideas for your answer
- To encourage you to make an inference or inferences you could start at least one sentence with 'This source suggests that...' or 'This source shows that...'.
- One possible inference could be that share prices had been rising in the 1920s but the rise was very dramatic in 1928–29.

b) Study Sources A, B and C.

Does Source C support the evidence of Sources A and B about the Stock Market in the USA in the 1920s? Explain your answer. *(6 marks)*

What is required? This question is asking you to compare the information in Source C to that in Sources A and B. A simple answer which compares the sources at their face value will only achieve level 1 (1–2 marks). An answer that makes developed statements about similarities or differences between two or three of the sources will reach level 2 (3–4 marks). For level 3 (5–6 marks) you need to:

- ensure you directly compare Source C to Source A and Source C to Source B, in other words all three sources
- look for similarities and differences between them in information, tone and attitude
- ensure your comparisons are developed and precisely explained.

Ideas for your answer
1. Begin by explaining the information/attitude/tone of Source C. A US banker is warning of the dangers of a dramatic rise in share prices in 1929.
2. Now compare Source C to Source A.
   a) Does Source C support the views of Source A? Yes, because the graph in Source A shows the dramatic rise in share prices in 1928–29.
   b) Are there any differences? Yes, because Source A makes no comment on this rise and gives no warning of the potential dangers.
3. Compare Source C to Source B.
   a) Does Source C support the evidence of Source B? Yes, because Source B refers to the dramatic rise in the share price of Standard Gas.
   b) Are there any differences? Yes, again Source B gives no warning and seems more optimistic than Source C.
4. Now write a conclusion summing up your answer to the question, and make a judgement as to how far Source C supports the evidence of Sources A and B.

Source D From an interview in 1970 with an American who was a high-school student in 1929

Everybody talks of the Crash of 1929. In small towns out West, we did not know there was a Crash. What did the Stock Market mean to us? Not a damn thing. If you were in Cut Bank, Montana, who owned stocks and shares? The farmer was a ping pong ball in a very tough game.

Source E A photograph of unemployed people queuing for free food in New York in 1930

Source F From a history textbook about the Depression and New Deal in the USA, first published in 1997

The Depression was well on its way before the Wall Street Crash happened. There had, of course, been speculation in the 1920s. But there were other, more serious, economic problems such as overproduction and a fall in demand for goods such as cars.

c) Study Sources D and E.

How useful are these two sources as evidence about the effects of the Wall Street Crash on the USA?

(8 marks)

What is required? A simple statement on the content or nature of the sources will achieve no more than three marks. More developed statements which lack balance, for example, by ignoring the nature of the sources and/or their limitations, will reach level 2 (4–6 marks). To reach level 3 you need to ensure that your answer is fully balanced in the following ways:

- Explain the usefulness of both sources.
- Evaluate the **usefulness** of each source in two areas – **content/context** of the source and **nature/origin/purpose**.
- Analyse the **limitations** of each source in the same two areas – **content/context** and **nature/origin/purpose**.

Include a conclusion that summarises the usefulness of each source. In some cases the two sources might be useful because they give similar views of an event.

Ideas for your answer

Draw a table like the one below and use key words to complete each section. This is a good way of planning your answer.

Examine the usefulness of each source in turn.

	Source D	Source E
Usefulness of content and context		
Limitations of content and context		
Usefulness of nature, origin and purpose		
Limitations of nature, origin and purpose		

1 Source D is useful because of its content. It gives us the reactions of an American in the West who is not affected by the Crash. It is also useful because of its nature/origin/purpose. It is the view of someone who experienced the Crash and provides an unusual reaction to the events of 1929.

2 Now the limitations of Source D: it is the view of only one American in the West who did not own shares. Its purpose seems to be to play down the importance of the Stock Market collapse and gain sympathy instead for the plight of farmers.

3 Now you will need to do the same for Source E. A few hints: How useful are the contents of the source? What view do you get of the effects of the Depression? What are its limitations, bearing in mind it is a photograph?

4 Now a conclusion: these two sources are useful because they give two very different views of the effects of the Depression. In what other respects are they useful?

d) Study all the sources.

'The main reason for the Wall Street Crash was that many people had gambled unwisely on the Stock Market in the 1920s.'

Use the sources, and your own knowledge, to explain whether you agree with this view. *(12 marks)*

What is required?

This question is the most important because it is worth twelve marks. The examiner wants you to reach a conclusion on the question using your own knowledge and by referring to most, if not all, of the sources.

Low-level answers (1–3 marks) will make simple points using the sources and/or your own knowledge. The next level of answer (4–7 marks) will make developed statements in support of *or* against the view using the sources and/or your own knowledge. To reach level 3 (8–10 marks) you must make developed statements for *and* against the view using the sources and your own knowledge. To achieve the very top level (11–12 marks) you will have to do the following:

- ensure that your whole answer is focused on the question
- include an introduction that explains the view expressed in the question and how you intend to answer it
- give a balanced argument for and against the view
- use most, if not all, of the sources and your own knowledge to give this argument
- begin each paragraph with your argument and then back it up with your own knowledge and evidence from one or more of the sources – in other words integrate your arguments, own knowledge and evidence from the sources
- write a conclusion that gives a final judgement on the view in the question. Make sure this is consistent with what you have already written.

Ideas for your answer

Draw up a table like the one below and complete each section with key words. Use this as a plan for your eventual answer. Part of it has been completed for you.

	Supporting the view	Against the view
Arguments	There was far too much speculation in the 1920s	
Own knowledge	Borrowing money on credit	
Sources	Source A	
Conclusion		

1 In support of the view you will need to give a developed explanation from your own knowledge of the American mania for buying shares in the 1920s and its effects on the American financial market.
2 You can use Sources A, B and C in support of the view.
3 Against the view you need to explain from your own knowledge other reasons for the Crash such as the problems of the American economy in the 1920s, especially overproduction and the problems facing farming.
4 You can use Sources D and F to argue against the view.
5 For a conclusion decide whether the Stock Market was the main reason for the Crash.

Practice questions

Now look at the following sources and questions. Have a go at answering them without any guidance or help.

Source A A cartoon of 1933 showing Roosevelt 'priming the pump' of the American economy ('priming the pump' means 'getting it started').

Source B A historian writing in 1963
The New Deal certainly did not get the country out of the Depression. As late as 1941 there were still six million unemployed and it was really not until the war that the army of the jobless finally disappeared.

Source C Thomas L. Stokes, a junior member of the government, 1940
They were exciting, exhilarating days. It was one of the most joyous periods of my life. We came alive. We were eager. We were infected with a real spirit of adventure, for something concrete and constructive was finally being done about the chaos which confronted the nation.

Source D Black people queuing for government relief in 1937

Source E Robin Langton, a black American who was a child during the Depression years, was interviewed in 1970
Roosevelt caught the mood of the black community. You did not look on him as being white, black, blue or green. He was President Roosevelt. The WPA and other projects introduced black people to handicrafts and trades. It gave black Americans a chance to have an office to work out of with a typewriter. It made us feel that there was something we could do.

a) Study Source A.
What can you learn from Source A about the effects of Roosevelt's New Deal? *(4 marks)*

b) Study Sources A, B and C.
Does Source C support the evidence of Sources A and B about attitudes to the New Deal? Explain your answer.
(6 marks)

c) Study Sources D and E.
How useful are these two sources as evidence of the effects of the New Deal? *(8 marks)*

d) Study all the sources.
According to Source A, Roosevelt's New Deal was a waste of taxpayers' money.
Use the sources, and your own knowledge, to explain whether you agree with this view. *(12 marks)*

Summary and revision plan

Below is a list of headings which you may find helpful. Use this as a check-list to make sure you are familiar with the material featured in this chapter. Record your key words alongside each heading.

A The USA in the 1920s
- ❏ Background: the USA up to 1920
- ❏ Republican policies
- ❏ The boom period
- ❏ US farmers
- ❏ Weaknesses in the US economy

B Causes and consequences of the Wall Street Crash
- ❏ Causes of the Crash
- ❏ Effects of the Crash

C Government reaction and attempts at recovery, 1929–32
- ❏ President Hoover's actions
- ❏ Was Hoover unfairly blamed?
- ❏ Resentment among the people

D The nature of the New Deal; policies to deal with agriculture, industry, unemployment and welfare
- ❏ Roosevelt becomes President
- ❏ New Deal legislation

E Opposition to the New Deal
- ❏ General opposition
- ❏ The Supreme Court
- ❏ Huey Long

F The extent of the recovery and the successes of the New Deal
- ❏ Roosevelt and the voters
- ❏ Assessing the New Deal

CHAPTER 10

Nazi Germany, c.1930–39

In 1918 Germany was defeated in the First World War. The country was in chaos. There were attempts at revolution. In the 1920s Germany recovered but the Depression caused enormous problems, which allowed Hitler and the Nazi party to gain power. From 1933 to 1945 Hitler ruled Germany with disastrous consequences for both Germany and the wider world.

Key content

You will need to have a good working knowledge of these areas:

A Hitler, Nazism and Nazi beliefs
B The Nazi rise to power: the role of Hitler
C The creation of the totalitarian state: the elimination of the opposition
D The Nazi state: propaganda and religion
E The Nazi state: education, youth movements and culture
F Racism, the persecution of the Jews and opposition to Nazi rule
G The social impact of Nazism

Key themes

You will also be asked to demonstrate your understanding of some key themes:

- What was the impact of the Great Depression on Germany in the period 1929–32?
- How did Hitler exploit the Depression to gain support for the Nazi Party?
- What were the political events of 1932–33 that brought Hitler to power?
- How did Hitler remove key opponents and set up a dictatorship in the period 1933–34?
- How was propaganda used to ensure support for the Nazi government?
- How did the Nazis seek to control the young through education and the youth movements?
- What were the Nazis' racial views and how were the Jews persecuted?
- How did the position of women change during the period of Nazi rule?

Source-based questions test your knowledge of the topic together with your source-evaluation skills. For example, look at this question adapted by permission of Edexcel from the Specimen Paper for Paper 2.

Source D A poster issued by the Nazis in 1937. The caption on the poster reads 'Mother and Child'

Source E Joseph Goebbels, a leading Nazi, writing in 1929

The mission of women is to be beautiful and to bring children into the world. The female bird pretties herself for her mate and hatches eggs for him. In exchange, the male takes care of gathering the food and stands guard and fights off the enemy.

c) Study Sources D and E.
How useful are these two sources as evidence about Nazi policy towards women? *(8 marks)*

This question is asking you to show that:

· *you understand the information in the sources and the idea of how useful a source is*
· *you know the context of the sources in order to evaluate their usefulness.*

We will look at this and other source questions in more detail at the end of this chapter.

A Hitler, Nazism and Nazi beliefs

1 The setting up of the Nazi Party

Hitler served in the German army during the First World War and was awarded medals for bravery. He was wounded on several occasions, including in 1918 when he was temporarily blinded by gas. He was in hospital recovering from these wounds when he heard of the Armistice. Hitler was very upset and, like many others, was convinced that the German army could have won the war but had been 'stabbed in the back' by the politicians.

After the war he joined the German Workers' Party and by 1921 had become its leader. Hitler reorganised the party:

- He renamed it the National Socialist German Workers' Party (Nazis).
- He gave it its own emblem, the swastika.
- He recruited ex-soldiers as members of his own private army, known as the stormtroopers, SA or brownshirts. They were used to protect his meetings and attack those of his opponents, especially the communists.

2 Nazi beliefs

- The Nazis believed that the state was more important than the individual. All Germans had to be prepared to sacrifice their own personal freedom for the good of Germany as a whole. Women were to be housewives and mothers, and men were to be soldiers and workers.
- Hitler and the Nazis believed in the notion of the master race. The Germans were the *Herrenvolk* or master race. All other races were inferior or *Untermenschen* (subhuman). At the very bottom of the racial pyramid were Jews, black people, Slavs and Gypsies. If Germany was to be great again, these people would have to be removed from Germany. Anti-Semitism (persecution of the Jews) was a strong element in Nazism but was not new to Germany.
- Hitler believed that Germany had been 'betrayed' in 1918. He refused to accept the Treaty of Versailles and promised to ignore its terms if and when he achieved power. He was determined to make Germany great again.

3 The Munich Putsch

In November 1923 Hitler and the Nazis tried to seize control of the Bavarian government. The plan was to capture Munich and from there march on Berlin. Hitler was convinced people would join him in overthrowing the Weimar government (see page 176), which was facing many political and economic problems and was seen as a failure by many Germans.

- On 8 November, at a political meeting in a Munich beer hall, Hitler forced at gunpoint Kahr, head of the Bavarian government, and Lossow, commander of the army in Bavaria, to join him.
- The Nazi plan soon began to go wrong. The next day Bavarian police opened fire on Nazi stormtroopers in Munich and sixteen Nazis were killed.
- Ludendorff (the former First World War general who was now a Nazi supporter) and Hitler were arrested and charged with high treason.

However, it was clear that Hitler's views had some support in Germany.

- Hitler received the minimum sentence. Many Nazi supporters also received light sentences.
- Hitler served his sentence in the comfortable Landsberg Fortress and spent his time writing his memoirs.

- The memoirs were later published as *Mein Kampf* (*My Struggle*). In this book, Hitler outlined his view of German history and his views on Germany's rightful place in the world.

● *Revision task*

1 Copy the table below and use the evidence and information in this section to complete it using key words.

Hitler and the growth of the Nazi Party		
Early Nazi Party	**Nazi beliefs**	**The Munich Putsch**

B The Nazi rise to power: the role of Hitler

1 The Weimar Republic, 1919–29

This had been set up after the First World War but had faced several problems in its first five years, including:

- having to sign the Treaty of Versailles in 1919, which was unpopular with many Germans
- attacks from extremists on both left and right including the Spartacists (a communist group) and the Nazis
- the French occupation of the German industrial region of the Ruhr in 1923, in retaliation for the failure of the German government to pay reparations
- massive hyperinflation which brought ruin and misery to many Germans, who blamed the Weimar Republic.

The Republic did recover in the period 1924–29, mainly under the guidance of the foreign secretary, Gustav Stresemann. He organised loans from the USA which stabilised the German currency and helped industrial expansion. Stresemann also improved relations with other countries and Germany was allowed to join the League of Nations.

2 The effects of the Depression on Germany

The recovery of the German economy was fragile. It depended heavily on American loans. In 1929 disaster struck with the Wall Street Crash:

- Many American banks were forced to recall their loans. German companies were unable to pay.
- German businesses began to close. Millions lost their jobs.

Between 1928 and 1930 German unemployment rose from 2.5 to 4 million. This provided an opportunity for extremist groups such as the Communists and Nazis.

- As unemployment rose, more and more people felt let down by the Weimar government and began to support extremist parties.
- In the 1930 election the communists increased their number of seats in the REICHSTAG from 54 to 77.
- Nazi support increased from 12 seats in 1928 to 107 in 1930. The Nazis were now the second largest political party in the Reichstag.

● *Revision task*

1 What factors changed the prospects for the Nazis between the beginning and the end of the 1920s? Use four to six key words for your answer.

3   How the Depression helped Hitler

The Depression helped Hitler in several ways:

* It caused a period of chaos in Germany.
* No government could take control of the situation and solve Germany's terrible economic problems.
* Unemployment was the big issue. By January 1932 it stood at 6 million. Hitler promised to get these people back to work. Through clever campaigning and his brilliant speaking skills, Hitler gained support in many parts of German society, including the support of wealthy and powerful industrialists.

Hitler toured Germany by aeroplane and car, and spoke in many towns and cities. He found a valuable ally in Alfred Hugenberg, leader of the German National People's Party (DNVP). Hugenberg was the millionaire owner of 53 German newspapers and, in 1929, he bought a large cinema chain. He helped to pay Hitler's expenses and allowed Hitler to spread Nazi propaganda.

4   The appeal of the Nazis

The Nazis won more and more support for several reasons.

* The German people were looking for a scapegoat for Germany's problems. The Nazis gave them scapegoats, including the Weimar politicians and the Jews.
* The Weimar Republic was seen as weak. Because of voting by PROPORTIONAL REPRESENTATION, no one party could achieve a majority in the Reichstag. Germany was ruled by weak coalitions that were unable to tackle the serious problems brought about by the Wall Street Crash. From 1930, chancellors began to rely on President von Hindenburg's power to issue decrees, rather than on trying to pass laws.
* Many wealthy Germans, especially industrialists and bankers, feared a Communist government and poured money and support into the Nazi Party.
* The Nazis put themselves forward as the party of discipline and order. The stormtroopers paraded through the streets of Germany in their uniforms. They seemed to be just what Germany needed in a time of crisis. They were also used to attack and beat up opponents, especially communists.

In 1930 the Nazis won 107 seats, and by July 1932 they had become the largest single party in the Reichstag, with 230 seats.

5   The events of 1932–33

In the 1932 presidential election, Hitler stood against the ageing President Hindenburg for the position of president.

* In his speeches, Hitler blamed the 'November criminals' (those who had signed the Treaty of Versailles) and Jews for the problems Germany was facing.
* He promised to build a better Germany, and many people believed him.

Hitler did not win, but he only lost to Hindenburg on a second vote. The Nazis felt they were close to success.

The 1932 general election campaign was very violent. Nazis and communists fought each other in street battles and nearly 100 people were killed.

The Nazis became the largest party in the Reichstag and Hitler demanded to be made Chancellor. However, Hindenburg was suspicious of Hitler and refused. Instead, he appointed Franz von Papen, a conservative politician with no party base in the Reichstag, as Chancellor.

Fresh Reichstag elections, November 1932

To achieve his aims Papen needed to increase his support in the Reichstag and so he called another election in November 1932. The Nazis lost seats in this election, but they still remained the largest party. Papen did not get the increased support he needed.

Hitler becomes Chancellor

It was becoming increasingly clear that President Hindenburg could not continue to work with a Chancellor who did not have support in the Reichstag. He simply could not pass any of the measures he wanted.

- Hindenburg and Papen decided to make Hitler Chancellor.
- They believed they would be able to control him once he was in power.
- On 30 January 1933 Hitler became German Chancellor and Papen Vice-Chancellor.

As soon as he was appointed, Hitler tried to find a way of increasing the number of Nazis in his government. He persuaded Hindenburg to dissolve the Reichstag and hold another general election.

● *Hitler's success in coming to power in January 1933 was due to a variety of factors. These included favourable circumstances such as the weaknesses of the Weimar Republic and the impact of the Depression of 1929. Nevertheless, Hitler must be given some credit. He took advantage of these circumstances to increase the support and appeal of the Nazi Party during the period 1929–33.* ●

● Revision tasks

1 Explain the reasons why Hitler was able to become Chancellor of Germany in January 1933. To help you, copy and complete the summary table below and explain each reason using key words.

How Hitler became Chancellor of Germany in 1933	
Long-term causes	**Short-term causes**

2 Now try to make links between at least two of your reasons.
3 Which do you think was the most important/fundamental reason? Explain your answer.

C The creation of the totalitarian state: the elimination of the opposition

During this period Hitler removed the major opposition to his government.

1 The Reichstag fire

During the election campaign, on the night of 27 February 1933, the Reichstag was burnt to the ground. A communist, Marinus van der Lubbe, was arrested for the crime. Hitler and the Nazis were able to exploit the fire for their own purposes.

- They quickly put the blame on the Communist Party.
- Hitler persuaded President Hindenburg to pass an emergency law restricting personal liberty.
- Using the law, thousands of communist supporters were thrown into prison.

Despite increasing their share of the vote in the election, the Nazis still did not have an overall majority in the Reichstag. They were forced to join together with the 52 nationalist members to create a government.

Election results, 1932–33

Presidential election result, 1932	
Candidate	**No of votes**
Hindenburg	19 million
Hitler (Nazi)	13 million
Thälmann (communist)	4 million

General election results, July 1932	
Moderate parties	**No of seats**
Social Democrats	133
Centre Party	75
Extremists	
Communists (left wing)	89
Nazis (right wing)	230
Nationalists	40

General election results, November 1932	
Moderate parties	**No of seats**
Social Democrats	121
Centre Party	70
Extremists	
Communists (left wing)	100
Nazis (right wing)	196
Nationalists	51

General election results, March 1933	
Moderate parties	**No of seats**
Social Democrats	120
Centre Party	73
Extremists	
Communists (left wing)	81
Nazis (right wing)	288
Nationalists	52

2 The Enabling Act, March 1933

Hitler still did not have enough support to have complete control of Germany. An Enabling Act would give him the right to pass laws for the next four years without having to obtain the support of members in the Reichstag. However, to pass an Enabling Act Hitler needed to obtain the votes of two-thirds of Reichstag members, but he only had the support of just over a half. This is what happened:

- Hitler ordered his SA (stormtroopers) to continue intimidating the opposition.
- The 81 communist members of the Reichstag were expelled.
- In an atmosphere heavy with violence and threats, the Enabling Act was passed by 441 to 94.
- Hitler was given the power to rule for four years without consulting the Reichstag.

In July 1933 Hitler increased his grip on power even further. Using the powers of the Enabling Act, he outlawed all other parties and Germany became a one-party state. The democratic Weimar Republic had been destroyed and Germany had become a dictatorship.

3 Removing other opposition

Within a few months of the passing of the Enabling Act Hitler had removed other opposition.

- He closed down state parliaments. They were reorganised to ensure a Nazi majority in each one.
- In May 1933 trade union officials were arrested and trade unions banned.
- In the same month the offices of the Social Democratic Party were occupied and the party banned. In July Hitler passed a law banning all other parties.

4 The Night of the Long Knives

Once he had gained power, Hitler's priority was to rid himself of possible rivals. Ernst Röhm, leader of the SA (stormtroopers), had played a major role in helping Hitler achieve power. However:

- The SA was seen by the German army as a rival. The army would not support Hitler unless the SA was disbanded.
- Some members of the SA looked to Hitler to follow a socialist programme of reform. Hitler was opposed to this, since he knew he would lose the support of wealthy industrialists.
- Röhm was a threat to Hitler's dominance of the Nazi party.

Hitler made a deal with the generals of the German army. They promised to support him as commander-in-chief of the armed forces if the SA was disbanded, and if he started a programme of rearmament. On 30 June 1934 SS assassination squads murdered Hitler's potential SA rivals (including Röhm). The SS had been set up as the personal bodyguards of Hitler and other Nazi leaders. They were originally themselves part of the SA but by this time were a separate force, which acted as the Nazi Party's internal police force. It has been estimated that up to 400 people were killed in the 'Night of the Long Knives'.

Just over one month later, President Hindenburg died. Hitler thereafter combined the posts of Chancellor and President and also became commander-in-chief of the armed forces. From this point onwards soldiers swore personal allegiance to Hitler who officially became known as *der Führer* (the leader).

5 The police state

Hitler ensured that he controlled people through terror, using the police state.

- The Gestapo or secret police was used to search out opponents of the regime.
- The courts were placed under Nazi control. New Nazi People's Courts replaced the old independent courts.
- Concentration camps were set up to house opponents of the Nazi government. They were harsh, brutal places and many inmates died.

● *Hitler was not a dictator in January 1933. Within eighteen months he was. He removed opposition to his government including the communists and other leading parties. The Enabling Act gave him the power to make laws without the Reichstag. Strangely, one of the most serious threats came from within the Nazi Party, from Röhm and the SA. This threat was removed on the Night of the Long Knives.* ●

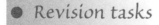

● Revision tasks

1 Make a copy of the following table and using key words explain how each of the following threatened Hitler's position and how the threat was removed.

	Why a threat?	How removed?
Communists		
Reichstag		
Röhm and the SA		

2 What position did Hitler take when Hindenburg died?
3 What part did the following play in the police state:
   a) the Gestapo
   b) concentration camps?

D The Nazi state: propaganda and religion

Hitler also wanted to control the minds of German people, what they thought, through propaganda.

1 Propaganda

Nazis believed in complete loyalty and obedience. One of the major tools for achieving this was propaganda. Hitler made Joseph Goebbels Minister of Enlightenment and Propaganda. Goebbels' job was to spread Nazi ideas and encourage all Germans to be loyal to Hitler. Goebbels (a former journalist) used his new powers to control all information that reached the German people in the following ways:

- All newspapers were censored by the government and only allowed to print stories favourable to the Nazis.
- Radio was also controlled by the government. Cheap radios were manufactured so that most Germans could afford one. Goebbels made sure that all radio plays, stories and news items were favourable to the Nazis.
- The Nazis took control of the German film industry. German films of the 1930s often showed great German heroes defeating their enemies. Cartoons were used to show Jews as weak and devious.
- Goebbels organised mass rallies. The most spectacular was held each August in Nuremberg. At the rallies hundreds of thousands of Nazi supporters listened to choirs, sang songs and watched sporting events and firework displays.
- The Nazis used sporting events to spread their propaganda. The 1936 Berlin Olympics was used by the Nazis to suggest the superiority of the 'Aryan race'. ('Aryan' was the Nazi term for non-Jewish Germans.)

2 Victims of propaganda

The main aim of propaganda was to provide the German people with a Nazi view of events. However, another aim was to target certain groups inside and outside Germany. These included:

- anyone who supported the terms of the Treaty of Versailles
- foreigners who criticised Hitler and the Nazis
- communists and socialists
- democrats and liberals
- Jews.

3 Religion

The greatest threat to Hitler was religion – a belief even stronger than Nazism. In 1933 the Catholic Church in Germany signed an agreement (Concordat) with Hitler. The two sides agreed not to interfere with each other.

The Nazis closed down a number of church organisations and set up their own 'church', called the Reich Church. It was not Christian and banned followers from using the Bible, crosses and religious symbols.

Many Christians, however, refused to accept Nazi ideas and some, like Dietrich Bonhoeffer, a Protestant minister, died for their beliefs. Another opponent was Pastor Martin Niemöller who set up an alternative Protestant Church to the official Reich Church. Niemöller spent the years 1937–45 in a concentration camp.

● *Revision tasks*

1 Make a list of Nazi methods of propaganda.
2 Who were the main victims of propaganda?
3 Using four to six key words describe Nazi policies towards the Church.

E The Nazi state: education, youth movements and culture

The Nazis were determined to control the minds of the young, to ensure that they followed Nazi beliefs.

1 Education

This was carefully controlled by the Nazi state.

- All teachers were forced to become members of the Nazi Party.
- Textbooks were rewritten to pass on the Nazi message.
- History was used to glorify German heroes and teach how Germany had been 'betrayed' at the end of the First World War.
- New subjects, such as 'race studies', were introduced to stress the Nazi message.
- Girls were trained to be housewives and mothers, with appropriate lessons in domestic science and biology.
- Boys were encouraged to study science, foreign languages and mathematics and were prepared for work and military service.
- Sport was encouraged for both boys and girls, because it would increase the fitness of mothers and soldiers.

2 Youth movements

The Nazis also wanted to control the minds of the young in their leisure time through the youth movements. Boys joined at the age of six and stayed until they were eighteen, when they went into the Labour Service for six months and were then conscripted into the army. Girls joined at the age of ten and stayed until the age of twenty-one.

These youth movements became very popular, with millions of members by 1939. They encouraged outdoor activities such as camping and hiking, but their main purpose was to emphasise Nazi ideals and prepare boys and girls for their future roles in German society.

3 Culture

This was also used by the Nazis to put across their ideas.

- Artists had little or no freedom of expression. Paintings showed Nazi ideals including the role of women as mothers, the perfect Aryan and German greatness.
- Films were carefully censored. All scripts were checked by the Propaganda Ministry. Films were used to put across racial views and ideas and to stir up hatred against Jews and communists.
- Sport was used to show the superiority of the Aryan race and Nazi regime. When the Olympic Games were held in Berlin in 1936, Germany won the most gold medals. However, Hitler was furious when the black American Jesse Owens won four gold medals.

● *Hitler wanted to create the 'Thousand Year Reich'. Fear created by the police state and the removal of opposition were not enough. The German people had to be converted to his ideas. This would be achieved through skilful use of propaganda, culture and education.* ●

● Revision task

1 Make a copy of the following table showing Nazi methods of control and use key words to complete each section.

Method of control	Nazi policies
Education	
Youth movements	
Art/films	
Sport	

F Racism, the persecution of the Jews and opposition to Nazi rule

The Nazis believed in the superiority of the Aryan race (non-Jewish Germans). They persecuted members of other races, and many minority groups such as Gypsies, homosexuals and mentally and physically disabled people. They persecuted any group that they thought challenged Nazi ideas.

1 The treatment of minorities

The persecution of such minorities varied.

- Homosexuals were a threat to Nazi ideas about family life. Thousands of homosexuals were sent to concentration camps.
- The mentally ill or disabled were a threat to Nazi ideas about Germans being a perfect master race. In families where there were hereditary illnesses, sterilisation was enforced. Over 300,000 men and women were compulsorily sterilised between 1934 and 1945.
- In 1939 the Nazis began a secret euthanasia ('mercy killing') programme for the mentally and physically disabled. By 1944, 200,000 people had been murdered by gas or lethal injection.
- Gypsies were thought to be an inferior people. Five out of six Gypsies living in Germany in 1939 were killed by the Nazis.

2 The treatment of the Jews

Persecution

In 1933 the Nazis organised a boycott of all Jewish businesses, doctors, dentists, etc. Jewish shops were marked with the star of David and the word *Jude* (Jew).

In education, Jewish children were intimidated at school and Germans were taught that Jews were unclean and responsible for Germany's defeat in the First World War.

In 1935 the Nuremberg Laws were introduced in Germany. Under these laws:

- Jews could no longer be German citizens.
- Marriages between Jews and Aryans were forbidden.

Kristallnacht

It is not clear how much most Germans knew about the persecution. However, in 1938 an event occurred that left nobody in any doubt.

In November 1938 a Polish Jew, Herschel Grynszpan, shot a German diplomat in Paris. Hitler ordered an immediate attack on Jews and their property in Germany. Between 9 and 10 November, thousands of Jewish businesses were attacked and 200 synagogues burnt down. This was called *Kristallnacht*, 'the night of broken glass'.

Violence against Jews in Germany increased. Himmler, head of the SS, began to expand the building of concentration camps.

The 'Final Solution'

At the beginning of 1942, when the Second World War was at its height, the Nazis finalised their plans for the extermination of all Jews in Europe. This policy of genocide became known as the 'Final Solution'.

- New extermination camps were built and older camps were updated.
- Between 1942 and 1945, 4.5 million Jews were gassed in death camps such as Auschwitz, Treblinka, Chelmno and Sobibor.
- In total, the Nazis murdered over 6 million Jews.

3 Opposition to the Nazis

Many Germans thought Hitler was a fine leader and genuinely supported him. Even among those who did not, many were unwilling to put their lives at risk. The Gestapo could arrest people merely on suspicion of opposing the government. People were encouraged to inform on others. Many people were imprisoned and executed without trial. Given this use of terror, together with the brainwashing techniques used by Goebbels and the youth groups, it is understandable why there was so little opposition.

However, there was some:

- Many people, including Jews, left Germany and fled to other countries. These included famous scientists, artists, writers and musicians who criticised the Nazi regime.
- Some church leaders such as Galen, the Catholic Bishop of Münster, and the Lutheran Pastor Niemöller spoke out against Hitler. Niemöller was arrested in 1937 and spent the next eight years in concentration camps.

● *Racism, particularly the persecution of the Jews, was not new to Germany. Anti-Semitism had been widespread in Europe long before Hitler came to power. What was new was the systematic way in which the Nazis denied the Jews in Germany their rights, particularly with the introduction of the Nuremberg Laws of 1935 and culminating in the 'Final Solution'.* ●

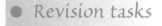

● *Revision tasks*

1 Make a copy of the following table and complete it using key words.

Minority group	Why Nazis persecuted them	How they were persecuted
Jews		
Mentally disabled		
Gypsies		
Homosexuals		

2 Why was there so little opposition to Nazi rule? Use key words to record your answer.

G The social impact of Nazism

By 1934 the Nazi Party completely dominated life in Germany. All government officials and civil servants had to be party members and promotion was only possible through loyalty.

1 Changes in everyday life

For ordinary Germans there were major changes in everyday life. Hitler, as promised, removed unemployment by a variety of methods:

- The Nazis introduced Labour Service as a means of reducing unemployment. This involved six months' work for very low pay at the age of eighteen. The Labour Service built the *Autobahns* (motorways).
- In 1935 Hitler introduced conscription. Most men went into the army after they had completed Labour Service.
- Rearmament began in 1935 and led to more jobs in industries such as munitions and engineering.
- More dubious methods included sending opponents of the Nazi government to concentration camps and reducing the number of women in the workforce.

By 1938 unemployment, which had reached 6 million by 1933, had virtually disappeared. Many of the jobs created, however, were temporary.

2 The role of women

The position of women in society changed under the Nazi government. The Nazis had traditional views about women. They believed that their role was to raise children and run the household, and that they should not seek careers as they were taking the jobs of men.

- In 1933 the Law for the Reduction of Unemployment was passed. It tried to cut unemployment (and increase Germany's birthrate) by providing loans to help young couples to marry, provided the wife left her job.
- Instead of going to work, women were asked to stick to the 'three Ks' – *Kinder, Küche, Kirche* (children, kitchen, church).
- Women doctors, teachers and civil servants were forced to leave their jobs.
- Women were encouraged to keep healthy and wear their hair in a bun or plaits. They were discouraged from wearing trousers and make-up.

Many women accepted these new policies. However, some, who had seen women's rights progress during the 1920s, criticised Nazi policies. In any case, the Nazis were forced to employ more and more women in industry as rearmament gathered pace in the late 1930s.

Revision session

The aim of this revision session is for you to see how you can apply your knowledge of Nazi Germany, 1930–39, to answer source-based questions.

Examination questions

Below are examples of sources and source questions adapted from the Specimen Paper for Paper 2 by permission of Edexcel.

Source A From the Nazi Law for the Reduction of Unemployment, 1933
People of German nationality who marry can be granted a marriage loan of 1000 Reichsmarks. The conditions are as follows:

  (i) *that the future wife has spent at least six months in employment;*
  (ii) *that the future wife gives up her job;*
  (iii) *that the future wife promises not to take up employment so long as her future husband earns more than 125 Reichsmarks a month.*

Source B An extract about the role of women in Germany taken from a textbook about Germany, 1918–45. The book was written by a British historian in the 1990s
German women in the 1920s had several rights and freedoms which women in many other countries did not have. They had the right to vote; many could earn the same pay as men for the same job and they were employed in many professions. Under Nazi rule, however, they lost these gains.

Source C From a timetable for a girls' school in Nazi Germany in the 1930s

Girls' school timetable						
Periods	**Monday**	**Tuesday**	**Wednesday**	**Thursday**	**Friday**	**Saturday**
8.00–8.45	German	German	German	German	German	German
8.50–9.35	Geography	History	Singing	Geography	History	Singing
9.40–10.25	Race studies	Race studies	Race studies	Race studies	Race studies	Race studies
10.25–11.00	Break with Sports and special announcements					
11.00–12.05	Domestic Science with Mathematics					
12.10–12.55	Eugenics [the science of breeding] or Health Biology					
2.00–6.00	Sport					

---

a) Study Source A.
  What can you learn from Source A about Nazi attitudes towards the role of women in Germany? *(4 marks)*

What is required? This question is testing your understanding of a source and your ability to interpret what it says. Try to make at least one inference from the source. In other words, read between the lines of what the source says.

Ideas for your answer
  • To encourage you to make an inference or inferences you could start at least one of your sentences with 'This source suggests that...' or 'This source shows that...'
  • One possible inference could be about Nazi attitudes to women and work.

---

b) Study Sources A, B and C.
Do Sources B and C support the evidence of Source A? Explain your answer.
(6 marks)

What is required?

This question is asking you to compare the information in Sources B and C to that of Source A. A simple answer which compares the sources at their face value will only achieve level 1 (1–2 marks). An answer that makes developed statements about similarities *or* differences between two or three of the sources will reach level 2 (3–4 marks). For level 3 you need to:

- ensure you directly compare Source B to Source A and then Source C to Source A – in other words refer to all three sources
- look for similarities and differences between them in information, tone and attitude
- ensure your comparisons are developed and precisely explained.

Ideas for your answer

1 Begin by explaining the information/attitude/tone of Source A. Source A shows the Nazi attitude towards women and employment. Wives were not to do work outside the home but were to carry out their role as mothers and housewives. This would also provide more jobs for men.

2 Now compare Source B to Source A.
   a) Does Source B support Source A? Yes, because it describes how the role of women changed under the Nazis. How did their role change?
   b) Are there any differences? Source A concentrates on women and employment. What other issues are addressed in Source B?

3 Compare Source C to Source A.
   a) Does Source C support the evidence of Source A? Yes, because it shows how girls are being prepared for their future role as housewives. How?
   b) Are there any differences? Only that Source A is about women and employment and Source B the education of girls.

4 Now write a conclusion summing up your answer to the question and making a judgement as to how far Sources B and C support Source A.

Source D A poster issued by the Nazis in 1937. The caption on the poster reads 'Mother and Child'

Source E Joseph Goebbels, a leading Nazi, writing in 1929
The mission of women is to be beautiful and to bring children into the world. The female bird pretties herself for her mate and hatches eggs for him. In exchange, the male takes care of gathering the food and stands guard and fights off the enemy.

Source F From a speech by Adolf Hitler to the National Socialist Women's Movement, September 1934
If the man's world is the state, then the woman's world is her husband, her family, her children and her home. It is not correct for women to interfere in the world of men.

c) Study Sources D and E.
How useful are these two sources as evidence about Nazi policy towards women? *(8 marks)*

What is required? A simple statement on the content or nature of the sources will achieve no more than three marks. More developed statements which lack balance, for example by ignoring the nature of the sources and/or their limitations, will reach level 2 (4–6 marks). To reach level 3 you need to ensure that your answer is fully balanced in the following ways:

- Explain the usefulness of both sources.
- Evaluate the **usefulness** of each source in two areas – **content/context** of the sources and their **nature/origin/purpose**.
- Analyse the **limitations** of each source in the same two areas – **content/context** and **nature/origin/purpose**.

Include a conclusion that summarises the usefulness of the two sources. In some cases the two sources might be useful because they give similar views of an event.

Ideas for your answer Copy the table below and use key words to complete each section. This is a good way of planning your answer.
Examine the usefulness of each source in turn.

	Source D	Source E
Usefulness of content and context		
Limitations of content and context		
Usefulness of nature, origin and purpose		
Limitations of nature, origin and purpose		

1 Source D is useful because its content shows the image that the Nazis had of women. What was this image? It is also useful because of its nature/origin/purpose. In this case it is a very good example of Nazi propaganda, which is trying to do what?

2 Now look at the limitations of D. In content it only provides one image of women as mothers. It is also limited in its nature/origin/purpose as it is a poster with the purpose of doing what? It exaggerates the role of women. How?

3 Now you will need to do the same for Source E. A few hints: How useful are the contents of the source? How important is the writer of the source? What was his purpose? Does this limit its usefulness?

4 Now a conclusion: in this case both sources are useful because they support each other in their views of the role of women. In what other respects are they useful?

d) Study all the sources.
'The Nazi regime turned women into second-class citizens.'
Use these sources, and your own knowledge, to explain whether you agree with this view. *(12 marks)*

What is required?

This question is the most important. The examiner wants you to reach a conclusion on the question using your own knowledge and by referring to most, if not all, of the sources.

Low-level answers (1–3 marks) will make simple points using the sources and/or your own knowledge. The next level of answer (4–7 marks) will make developed statements in support of *or* against the view using the sources and/or your own knowledge. To reach the next level (8–10 marks) you must make developed statements for *and* against the view using the sources and your own knowledge. To achieve the very top level (11–12 marks) you will have to do the following:

- ensure that your whole answer is focused on the question
- include an introduction that explains the question and how you intend to answer it
- give a balanced argument for and against the view
- use most, if not all, of the sources and your own knowledge to give this argument
- begin each paragraph with your argument and then back it up with your own knowledge and evidence from one or more of the sources – in other words, integrate your own knowledge with evidence from the sources
- write a conclusion that gives a final judgement on the view in the question. Make sure this is consistent with what you have already written.

Ideas for your answer

Copy the table below and use key words to complete each section. Use this as a plan for your eventual answer. Part of it has been completed for you.

	Supporting the view	**Against the view**
Arguments	Married women were denied employment outside the home	
Own knowledge	Women had to give up careers as civil servants and teachers	
Sources	Source A	
Conclusion		

1 In support of the view you will need to give a developed explanation from your own knowledge of Nazi policies encouraging women to be mothers and housewives.
2 All the sources seem to reflect the limitations on the role of women, so you could use all of them in support of the view.
3 Against the view you need to explain from your own knowledge how Nazi policies also put women on a pedestal and made them an important part of society.
4 Sources D and E seem to glorify the position of women, so you could use these to argue against the view.
5 For a conclusion decide whether you believe the Nazis did make women second-class citizens.

Practice questions

Now look at the following sources and questions adapted by permission of Edexcel from the 2000 Paper 2. Have a go at answering them without any help.

Source A From a history textbook, published in 1998
In schools, pupils were taught the Nazi version of history and biology. In history pupils were taught that the German army was 'stabbed in the back' in 1918. In biology they were taught that the Jews were racially inferior. Physical education was considered very important. It prepared the boys for war and it prepared the girls for the responsibilities of motherhood.

Source B From a Nazi-controlled newspaper, 1939
All subjects – German language, History, Geography, Chemistry and Mathematics – must concentrate on military subjects: the glorification of military service and German heroes and leaders. Chemistry will develop a knowledge of chemical warfare while Mathematics will help the young to understand artillery and range-finding.

Source C A decree issued by the Nazi Ministry of the Interior, 1934
The main task of the school is the education of young people in the service of the nation and state in the National Socialist spirit. At the beginning of every lesson the teacher goes to the front of the class and greets it by raising his right arm and says 'Heil Hitler'. The class returns his salute.

Source D A poster for the Hitler Youth published in the 1930s. The caption in the poster reads 'Youth serves the Führer. All 10-year-olds join the Hitler Youth.'

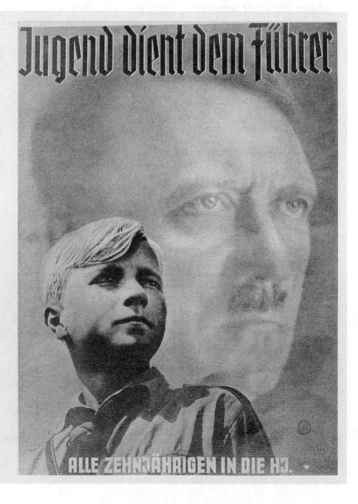

Source E A table showing the growth in the membership of the Hitler Youth during the years 1932–39. The figures were produced by the Nazi Party

Year	Total membership	Total population (aged 10–18 years)
1932	107,956	
1933	2,292,041	7,529,000
1934	3,577,565	7,682,000
1935	3,943,303	8,172,000
1936	5,437,601	8,656,000
1937	5,879,955	9,060,000
1938	7,031,226	9,109,000
1939	7,287,470	8,870,000

Source F From a speech by Hitler, on 23 March 1933
In relation to the political cleansing of our public life, the government will begin a systematic campaign to restore the nation's morals. The whole education system, theatre, film, literature, press and broadcasting will be used to do this. They will all be used to help preserve the old values which are at the heart of what it means to be German.

a) Study Source A.
What can you learn from Source A about Nazi attitudes towards education? *(4 marks)*

b) Study Sources A, B and C.
Does Source C support the evidence of Sources A and B about the purpose of education in Nazi Germany? Explain your answer. *(6 marks)*

c) Study Sources D and E.
How useful are Sources D and E as evidence about the importance of the Hitler Youth? *(8 marks)*

d) Study all the sources.
'Hitler kept control of Germany because he controlled the minds of young people.'
Use the sources, and your own knowledge, to explain whether you agree with this view. *(12 marks)*

Summary and revision plan

Below is a list of headings which you may find helpful. Use this as a check-list to make sure you are familiar with the material featured in this chapter. Record your key words alongside each heading.

A Hitler, Nazism and Nazi beliefs
- ❑ The setting up of the Nazi Party
- ❑ Nazi beliefs
- ❑ The Munich Putsch

B The Nazi rise to power: the role of Hitler
- ❑ The Weimar Republic, 1919–29
- ❑ The effects of the Depression on Germany
- ❑ How the Depression helped Hitler
- ❑ The appeal of the Nazis
- ❑ The events of 1932–33

C The creation of the totalitarian state: the elimination of the opposition
- ❑ The Reichstag fire
- ❑ The Enabling Act, March 1933
- ❑ Removing other opposition
- ❑ The Night of the Long Knives
- ❑ The police state

D The Nazi state: propaganda and religion
- ❑ Propaganda
- ❑ Victims of propaganda
- ❑ Religion

E The Nazi state: education, youth movements and culture
- ❑ Education
- ❑ Youth movements
- ❑ Culture

F Racism, the persecution of the Jews and opposition to Nazi rule
- ❑ The treatment of minorities
- ❑ The treatment of the Jews
- ❑ Opposition to the Nazis

G The social impact of Nazism
- ❑ Changes in everyday life
- ❑ The role of women

The World at War, 1938–45

In the 1930s Britain and France followed a policy of APPEASEMENT to try to keep the peace. This failed and in September 1939 Hitler's armies invaded Poland. Using BLITZKRIEG, the Germans were very successful during the first two years of the war. Eventually, however, the strength of the Grand Alliance of Britain, the USA and the Soviet Union proved too much and Germany was defeated in early 1945.

In the Far East, Japanese ambitions led to the attack on the USA at Pearl Harbor in December 1941. US economic and military strength proved decisive in this conflict, which ended with the dropping of atomic bombs on Hiroshima and Nagasaki in 1945.

Key content

You will need to have a good working knowledge of these areas:

A Appeasement, 1938–39, and the role of Chamberlain
B The outbreak of the Second World War
C Reasons for early German success
D The fall of France and the survival of Britain
E Operation Barbarossa and the Eastern Front
F The causes of the outbreak of war in the Pacific
G Reasons for the defeat of Germany
H Reasons for the defeat of Japan

Key themes

You will be asked to show your understanding of some key themes:

● Why did appeasement fail to prevent war?
● What caused the outbreak of war in September 1939?
● How far was early German success due to blitzkrieg?
● Why was Britain able to survive alone, 1940–41?
● Why did blitzkrieg fail in Russia in 1941?
● What motives were there for the Japanese attack on Pearl Harbor in December 1941?
● Was German defeat in 1945 inevitable?
● How far was the Japanese surrender of 1945 due to the use of atomic bombs?

Source-based questions test both your knowledge of the topic and your source-evaluation skills. For example, look at this question adapted from the Specimen Paper for Paper 2, by permission of Edexcel.

Source A A map showing the German invasion of the Soviet Union

Source B From a school textbook about the history of the Soviet Union in the twentieth century, published in Britain in 1991

The Nazi–Soviet pact was fragile and likely to break down when it suited either of the parties. There is no evidence that Stalin was preparing a war against Germany. It seems more likely that Hitler's long-term hatred of Bolshevism and wish to gain LEBENSRAUM (living space) played the key role in his decision to attack the Soviet Union.

Source C From a book about international relations, published in Britain in 1997

On 22 June 1941, Germany made a surprise attack on the Soviet Union. Operation Barbarossa was a three-pronged attack on the cities of Leningrad, Moscow and Stalingrad. The plan would lead to the destruction of the Soviet Union and would give Germany access to the wheatfields of the Ukraine and the oilfields of the Caucasus. Germany would also gain living space.

b) Study Sources A, B and C.
Does Source C support the evidence of Sources A and B? Explain your answer.   *(6 marks)*

This question is asking you to compare the evidence of three sources based upon:

· your knowledge of Operation Barbarossa
· your understanding of source skills, especially cross-referencing.

We will look at this question in more detail at the end of this chapter.

A Appeasement, 1938–39, and the role of Chamberlain

1 Hitler and German expansion, 1933–37

After Hitler took power in Germany in 1933 he began a policy that reversed the terms of the Treaty of Versailles and encouraged German expansion. In 1935 he reintroduced conscription, leading to a peacetime army of over 500,000 men. In the following year he ordered his troops to reoccupy the Rhineland.

2 The policy of appeasement

In 1937 Neville Chamberlain became prime minister of Great Britain and was determined to avoid war at almost any cost. Together with France, he was prepared to give way to Hitler and make concessions in order to prevent armed conflict. This policy became known as appeasement and was carried out for several reasons:

- Many British people still felt guilty about the Treaty of Versailles and felt that Hitler's claims were justified.
- Chamberlain believed that Hitler had only limited aims. Once these were satisfied, Chamberlain thought the threat of war would disappear.
- The majority of people in Britain and France did not want a repeat of the First World War.
- Britain and France were not strong enough militarily to be able to fight Germany, certainly not in 1938.
- There seemed no alternative to appeasement. The USA refused to become involved in European affairs and the League of Nations was seen as a failure.

● *This was the beginning of the controversial policy of appeasement. Britain and France certainly did not want war. They felt that they were not strong enough to go to war. They were prepared to give Hitler what he wanted. However, at the same time Britain and France began to re-arm.* ●

3 The events of 1938–39

Appeasement was needed on several occasions during this period.

- In March 1938 German troops entered Austria and set up the *Anschluss* or union of the two countries. This had been forbidden by the Treaty of Versailles. France and Britain did nothing, believing that most Austrians wanted the union.
- Hitler now demanded a part of Czechoslovakia known as the Sudetenland. It was on the border with Germany and was inhabited by 3 million Germans who wanted self-government and to join with Germany. In September Hitler threatened to invade Czechoslovakia on 1 October 1938, if he did not get his way. Chamberlain twice flew to Germany to try to appease Hitler. He failed on each occasion as Hitler stepped up his demands. Eventually Hitler agreed to attend a conference to discuss the future of Czechoslovakia.
- The Munich Conference, 29–30 September 1938, prevented war. Britain and France agreed that Czechoslovakia should hand over the Sudetenland to Hitler. The Czechs were not allowed to attend the Conference. Chamberlain returned from Munich as a great hero because he had prevented war. He also got Hitler to sign an agreement promising not to go to war and to respect the independence of the rest of Czechoslovakia.
- In March 1939 German troops marched into the rest of Czechoslovakia. Appeasement had failed.

4 Criticisms of appeasement

There were few critics at the time apart from Winston Churchill. Nevertheless, the policy has been criticised for several reasons:

- Hitler's aims were not limited and he saw appeasement as a sign of weakness on the part of Britain and France. The more they gave way, the more he wanted.
- It was morally wrong. This was especially the case with Czechoslovakia – what right did Britain and France have to give away part of another country?
- It did not work. Hitler occupied Czechoslovakia and moved on to Poland.
- It merely delayed a war with Germany that had become inevitable. Hitler was not ready for war in 1938 and could well have been defeated at that time. The Czechs were left defenceless by the loss of the Sudetenland which included their border defences against Germany.

● *Appeasement had allowed Hitler's aggressive diplomacy to triumph again. The Western powers had shown that they were unwilling to support the terms of the Versailles Treaty. By 1938 it also seemed that the League of Nations was completely irrelevant.* ●

● *Revision tasks*

1 Using five key words for each, explain:
   a) the meaning of appeasement
   b) why it was carried out.
2 Do your own timeline for the events of 1938–39.
3 Copy the table below and use the information in this section to complete it. Try to think of at least four entries for each column.

Criticisms of appeasement	Defence of appeasement

B The outbreak of the Second World War

On 1 September 1939 German troops invaded Poland. In response, Britain and France declared war on Germany on 3 September. This was the outbreak of the Second World War. It was the result of long-term and short-term factors.

1 Long-term factors

- In many respects the Second World War was caused by the peace settlement after the First World War. This created discontent in Germany and encouraged support for Hitler and the Nazis.
- The Great Depression caused by the Wall Street Crash of 1929 destroyed support for democracy in countries such as Germany and helped Hitler's rise to power.
- Hitler was determined to overthrow the terms of the Treaty of Versailles. He also wanted to create *lebensraum* or 'living space' for the German people by expanding eastwards into Poland, Czechoslovakia and the USSR.
- The success of Hitler's policies between 1933 and 1937 encouraged him to seek further expansion in 1938–39.
- Hitler saw the policy of appeasement as a sign of weakness.

2 Poland

Hitler turned his attention to Poland in March 1939. He demanded a road and railway link between Germany and East Prussia through the Polish Corridor. Poland refused and was supported by an alliance with Britain and France that guaranteed the Poles their support in the event of a German invasion.

3 The Nazi–Soviet Pact, August 1939

The key country was the Soviet Union due to its geographical location on the eastern border of Poland. Britain and France reluctantly opened talks with the Soviet leader, Stalin, but these dragged on for too long. In the meantime, the unthinkable happened. Hitler, who hated Stalin and the Soviet Union (and the feeling was mutual), agreed in August to a Nazi–Soviet Non-Aggression Pact. In secret, Stalin promised neutrality in the event of a German invasion of Poland. In return he was promised the eastern part of Poland (two-thirds of the country). Poland's fate was now sealed.

On 1 September 1939, after Poland had again refused to give way over the Polish Corridor, Germany invaded. Two days later Britain and France declared war on Germany.

● *Revision tasks*

1 What did Hitler demand from the Poles in 1939?

2 Why was the Soviet Union the key to the Polish situation? Use key words to record your answer.

3 Using a few key words explain the Nazi–Soviet Pact of August 1939.

4 Draw up a summary table like the one below and use key words to explain each of these causes of the Second World War. In the final column give each a rating out of five (with five being very important) as a cause of the Second World War. Use key words to explain your rating.

Cause	Explanation	Rating (1–5) and reason
Treaty of Versailles		
Depression		
Hitler's aims and policies		
The failure of appeasement 1938–39		
Poland 1939		

C Reasons for early German success

1 German success, September 1939–May 1940

Hitler's armies were very successful during this period. A map of the German advance in May 1940 can be seen on the following page.

- The German armies invaded Poland on 1 September 1939 and the Polish government surrendered within a few weeks.
- This was followed by a period known as the 'phoney war'. Neither side, on the Western front, did anything. France and Britain awaited a German attack but made few preparations to deal with the new German tactics known as blitzkrieg (lightning war).
- In April 1940 German forces invaded and overran Denmark. At the same time, using airborne troops and troop carriers, the Germans invaded Norway. The Norwegians were defeated despite efforts by the British to save them. Two British expeditions sent to Norway failed miserably and had to be hastily evacuated.
- In May 1940 German armies invaded Belgium and the Netherlands. Neither country could prevent German success. In mid-May the Germans invaded France. The French had based their defences on the Maginot Line which was a series of fortifications along the border of France and Germany. This defence system, however, did not include the heavily wooded area of the Ardennes. The French were convinced that it was unsuitable for German tanks and blitzkrieg tactics. Hitler's armies chose this weak point as their point of attack and quickly broke through the Ardennes and crossed the river Meuse. Within a week the German armies had reached the Channel coast and split the French and British armies.

German advance through Belgium and France, May 1940

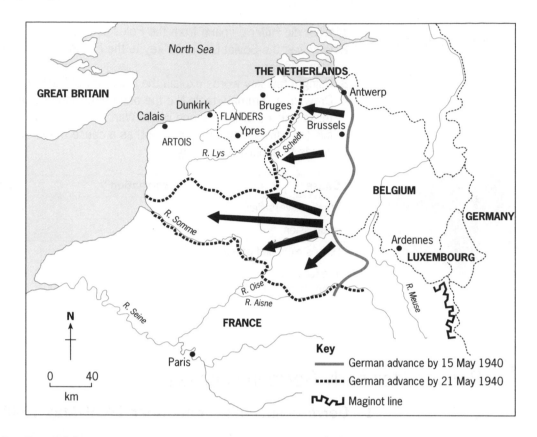

2 Dunkirk

British and French troops retreated to Dunkirk where they awaited either evacuation or capture. For reasons that are not quite clear, Hitler ordered the advancing German troops to stop. This gave the Allies a breathing space in which to carry out an evacuation. Between 26 May and 4 June 198,000 British and 140,000 French and Belgian troops were evacuated by a fleet of large and small boats.

Dunkirk was celebrated in Britain as a great achievement:

* The RAF outfought the Luftwaffe (the German air force) over the beaches of Dunkirk.
* It was a great success for the British navy.
* Many troops were rescued to fight another day.
* The 'Dunkirk spirit' was born. Winston Churchill, the prime minister, made the British people determined to fight against Hitler.

However, in many respects it was a disaster:

* Around 300,000 troops were left behind and forced to surrender.
* Most of the army's equipment had to be abandoned.
* France was left to fight alone and soon surrendered.

● *Revision tasks*

1 Construct your own timeline to show German successes 1939–40 using the following guideline. Use key words to explain German success.

* September 1939 Poland
* Winter 1939–40 Phoney war
* April 1940 Denmark and Norway
* May 1940 Belgium, the Netherlands and France
* May–June 1940 Dunkirk

2 Was Dunkirk a success for the British? Use a few key words to explain your answer.

3 Reasons for German success

German success was due to a number of reasons:

- The scale of German rearmament – the Germans had begun rearming in 1933, before Britain and France. By 1939 Germany had a fully trained army of 4 million.
- Polish weaknesses – the Poles had a large frontier with Germany to defend and tried to use outdated tactics and weapons, especially the cavalry: soldiers on horseback were no match for German tanks and armoured vehicles. The Poles also received no help from France or Britain.
- Belgium, the Netherlands, Denmark and Norway had small armies that could not withstand rapid German attacks.
- British mistakes – Britain made little preparation against German blitzkrieg tactics during the so-called 'phoney war'. In addition, it sent poorly equipped expeditions to Norway lacking in air power and protection.
- French mistakes and weaknesses – the French expected a long-drawn-out conflict like that of the First World War. Their whole strategy was defensive, based on the Maginot Line. This handed Hitler the initiative in 1940. The Maginot Line ended at the Belgian border, because Belgium was neutral, and did not include the Ardennes.
- Hitler was determined to avoid the stalemate of the First World War. Blitzkrieg involved sudden attacks using massed tank formations, dive-bombers and paratroopers. The Allied armies were taken by surprise by the speed and strength of the German attack.
- The Germans had also developed new weapons. Their tanks were more mobile than those used by their enemies and the Stuka dive-bomber was very effective in Poland.
- Hitler was prepared to use bold plans, such as the attack through the Ardennes which totally split the Allied armies.

● *Early German success was certainly due to blitzkrieg. These new tactics surprised and confused the enemy. It was not the only reason. The weakness of the opposition played into German hands. The Poles depended heavily on their cavalry which was no match for the German tanks and armoured vehicles. The French misused their tanks and, together with the British, remained on the defensive during the winter of 1939–40.* ●

● *Revision tasks*

1 Copy the table below, adding under the appropriate heading each of the reasons for German success.

German strengths	Allied weaknesses

2 Using a few key words explain what you think was the most important reason for German success, 1939–40.

D The fall of France and the survival of Britain

1 The fall of France

The remaining French armies were unable to withstand the speed and strength of the German attacks. The French government surrendered to Germany on 22 June 1940. Hitler accepted the surrender at exactly the same spot near Compiègne where the Germans had signed the Armistice in November 1918.

All of northern and western France was occupied by Germany. The remainder was governed from Vichy by a new French government headed by Marshal Pétain.

2 The survival of Britain

Britain stood alone against Germany from 1940 to 1941. The British were able to survive for several reasons:

- The leadership of Churchill. Winston Churchill replaced Chamberlain as prime minister in May 1940. He immediately brought a new urgency to the war effort. He helped to create the 'Dunkirk spirit', turning a defeat into an apparent success for the British. He insisted that Britain would never surrender and built up the confidence and morale of the British people through his speeches and 'bulldog' approach.
- Churchill also cultivated close relations with the USA and its president, Roosevelt. Although the USA remained neutral, Roosevelt was prepared to supply Britain with the needs of war, through an agreement called Lend Lease. These supplies proved vital during this difficult period.

3 The Battle of Britain

Britain would not have survived without the RAF and its success in the Battle of Britain. Hitler planned to attack Britain but he first needed to destroy the RAF and gain control of the skies over Britain. The first attacks by the German Luftwaffe were on shipping in the English Channel and the ports on the south coast. These were followed by bombing raids on radar stations and then airfields. Finally, from mid-August, came the attacks on Fighter Command. By the first week in September the Luftwaffe were getting the upper hand as the RAF ran out of reserves of pilots and planes. Fortunately Hitler diverted the Luftwaffe to attacks on London. When daylight raids were renewed on 15 September, the RAF regained the initiative.

The RAF was successful for several reasons:

- German mistakes – Hitler made the mistake of diverting the Luftwaffe from attacks on the RAF to bombing London.
- German weaknesses – the German bombers were often not escorted by fighter planes. They became easy targets for the RAF fighters.
- The British had superior fighter planes – the Spitfire and the Hurricane.
- Since the mid-1930s the British had devised an early warning system using radar which meant they knew when and where the Germans would attack. RAF fighter planes were in the air and ready when the German bombers and fighters appeared.

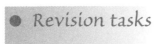 Revision tasks

1 Draw a spider diagram to summarise the parts played by Churchill and the USA in British survival.
2 Do you think the British victory in the Battle of Britain was due more to German weaknesses than to RAF strengths? Use key words to answer this question.

4 The Blitz

Hitler now decided to try to bomb Britain out of the war. Such tactics had worked against the Netherlands and Poland. This night bombing of British cities became known as the Blitz. In London, 13,000 were killed in 1940. Coventry suffered a heavy raid in November 1940, which destroyed the centre of the city and killed 500 people. The Germans used incendiary bombs which burst into flames when they hit the ground. They also used high-explosive bombs weighing up to 450 kg. The Blitz did not succeed in forcing Britain out of the war.

- In many respects it had the opposite effect. It built up the morale of the British people who became even more determined to fight on.
- The government had already introduced a whole series of civil defence measures including the blackout, air-raid shelters, evacuation and anti-aircraft guns.
- The Luftwaffe did not have the heavy bombers necessary to inflict major damage on Britain.
- In June 1941 Hitler diverted the Luftwaffe to the invasion of the Soviet Union.

● *Churchill and the spirit of the British people are rightly praised for Britain's survival alone against Germany between 1940 and 1941. Yet Britain's survival was also due to favourable circumstances, such as Hitler's decision not to use tanks at Dunkirk, Roosevelt's willingness to agree to 'Lend Lease' and, most important of all, Hitler's decision to invade the Soviet Union in June 1941.* ●

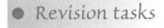
● *Revision tasks*

1 Do a balance sheet for the Blitz, like the one below, listing the successes and failures of this tactic from the German point of view.

Successes	Failures

2 What do you think was the most important reason for Britain's survival in 1940–41? Use key words for your answer.

E Operation Barbarossa and the Eastern Front

1 The German invasion of the Soviet Union

On 22 June 1941 Germany invaded the Soviet Union in an operation codenamed Operation Barbarossa. Hitler's ultimate aim was to smash the USSR and carve out an empire for his 'master race', the Germans. At first the German invasion, a three-pronged attack using blitzkrieg tactics, was a great success. Despite many warnings, Stalin had not prepared for the German invasion. The German troops were confident and experienced in this style of attack due to their successes over the previous two years. The Red Army had been seriously weakened by Stalin's purges of its military leaders in the later 1930s.

In the first three months of the campaign, the Germans destroyed the USSR's entire air and tank forces and the Red Army suffered 4 million casualties. By September 1941 Leningrad was under siege. In the south, German forces had control of the Ukraine and had reached as far as the Crimea. In the centre of the Soviet Union, the Germans almost reached the capital, Moscow, and Stalin seriously considered surrendering.

German advance through the USSR, 1941–42

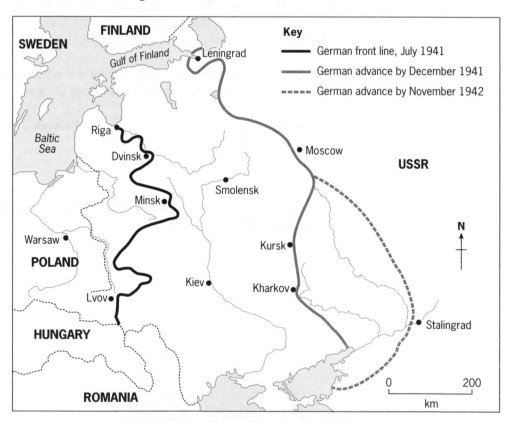

Ultimately the German invasion failed to achieve its targets of capturing Moscow and Leningrad and smashing the Red Army. Late in 1941 the German advance was halted by the Soviet winter.

The German attack failed for several reasons:

- Blitzkrieg did not work in a country as large as the Soviet Union with its poor road networks.
- Hitler delayed the invasion until June 1941. Between April and June he had diverted German troops to the Balkans to help his Italian ally, Mussolini. This delay meant the invasion of the USSR was not completed before the onset of winter.
- Soviet tactics slowed down the German advance. The Red Army carried out a 'scorched earth' policy, making it impossible for German forces to find food in the territory they occupied.
- The German troops could not cope with the winter conditions in the USSR where temperatures fell way below zero. They had inadequate clothing and the petrol in their vehicles froze.
- Hitler's tactics contributed to the failure. His three-pronged attack weakened the German advance. A single thrust might well have succeeded.

2 Soviet recovery and Stalingrad

The Eastern Front proved a nightmare for the German army. The vastness of the country, the extremes of temperature and the reserves available to the Red Army slowly turned the tide in Stalin's favour. In February 1943 the German Sixth Army was surrounded at Stalingrad and forced to surrender. Germany was defeated on the Eastern Front for several reasons:

- It was partly because of the strengths of the Red Army. The officers in the Red Army were given greater freedom and independence to act than those in the German army. Stalin banned Communist Party officials from interfering with military decisions. The Red Army copied the tactics of the Germans and created its own specialist tank armies and air forces. Harsh discipline was used. This was known as the 'not a step back' policy. The army was ordered to fight to the death for every bit of Soviet soil.
- Hitler made mistakes. He refused to allow the Sixth Army to retreat from Stalingrad when it became obvious that it was being surrounded.
- The geography of the USSR, including its size and climate. This favoured the Red Army which was used to the conditions.

● *The German invasion of the Soviet Union proved to be a major turning point in the war. Blitzkrieg failed for the first time due to the size of the USSR and the effects of the severe Soviet winter.* ●

● *Revision tasks*

1 Give what you believe are the two most important reasons for the following:
   a) early German success
   b) failure of the Germans to achieve their objectives in 1941
   c) eventual German failure on the Eastern Front.
   Use key words to explain your choice of reasons.
2 What were the following:
   a) Operation Barbarossa
   b) 'scorched earth' policy
   c) 'not a step back' policy?

F The causes of the outbreak of war in the Pacific

On 7 December 1941 Japanese forces launched a surprise air attack on the US naval base of Pearl Harbor. The following day the USA declared war on Japan.

1 Reasons for the Japanese attack

The Japanese wanted to create an empire in the Far East to boost their failing economy, which had suffered badly as a result of the Great Depression, and also to acquire much-needed raw materials such as rubber and oil. The main obstacle to such expansion came from the USA. Japanese expansion had begun in 1931 when they had invaded the Chinese province of Manchuria. In July 1937 the Japanese army invaded northern China. Shanghai and other Chinese cities were bombed into submission. Britain and the USA gave large loans to the Chinese government to help in its fight against the Japanese. Japan began to demand that Britain and other Western countries stop supporting China and co-operate with Japan in establishing a 'new order' in the Far East. This new order was called the 'Greater East Asia Co-prosperity Sphere' – in effect, a Japanese empire.

The USA refused to co-operate and in July 1941 cut off all supplies of oil in protest against Japanese actions in China.

2 Pearl Harbor

The attack on the US naval base of Pearl Harbor in Hawaii was an attempt by the Japanese to knock the USA out of the war before it had even entered it. The Japanese government believed that it would have to fight the USA sooner or later and decided to attack whilst the USA was unprepared. The attack involved a Japanese fleet sailing more than 4800 kilometres across the Pacific. From its aircraft carriers at 440 kilometres north of Hawaii, the Japanese navy launched waves of attacking planes to bomb its target. US intelligence failed to detect the Japanese force, which achieved complete surprise. Some historians believe that President Roosevelt may have known of the attack and delayed warning Pearl Harbor because he wanted an excuse to go to war with the Japanese.

The Japanese attack was not as successful as it could have been. The main aim was to destroy the US aircraft carriers, but they were at sea at the time of the attack.

3 Early Japanese success, 1941–42

The Japanese forces were very successful during this period. They quickly overran much of South-East Asia and the South-West Pacific. All of Indochina, Malaya and Indonesia were occupied, as were the Philippines and New Guinea. This success was due to several reasons.

- These countries were not well defended. France and the Netherlands, which had colonies in the Far East, had already been defeated by Germany and could offer no opposition.
- Britain was preoccupied with survival against Hitler and had inadequate air and naval forces in the region. British defences in Singapore faced the sea but the Japanese invaded overland.
- The Japanese enjoyed air and sea control through their use of aircraft carriers.
- Japanese troops were used to the tactics needed to succeed in the jungles of Burma and Malaya.
- Britain and the USA were taken by surprise by the speed of the Japanese advance.

● *Revision tasks*

1 Do a timeline showing the build-up to the Japanese attack on Pearl Harbor. Your timeline should begin with the Great Depression of 1929 and end with Pearl Harbor.

2 Was Pearl Harbor a success for the Japanese? Use key words to record your answer.

3 Make a copy of the following table and list the reasons for Japanese success 1941–42 in the appropriate columns. Try to think of at last three entries for each column.

Japanese strengths	Allied weaknesses

G Reasons for the defeat of Germany

1 Long-term factors

There were many long-term factors that contributed to Germany's eventual defeat.

- The failure of German U-boats to win the Battle of the Atlantic. The Germans had hoped to sink so many Allied ships that Britain would be starved out of the war. The U-boats were very successful between 1940 and 1943, mainly as a result of the effective use of wolf-pack tactics to attack the British convoys, which lacked effective air and naval escorts. Only in 1943 did the Allies gain the upper hand in the Battle of the Atlantic as more and more U-boats were sunk. By the end of the war more than 90 per cent of U-boats had been sunk. This was due to air cover provided by long-range flying boats (a type of seaplane) and the use of the Portuguese islands of the Azores in the mid-Atlantic to provide refuelling for Allied aircraft. Naval escorts were improved and the Allies broke the German Enigma code, allowing them to anticipate U-boat attacks.

- Hitler's decision to attack the USSR in June 1941 and declare war on the USA in December of the same year meant Germany was now fighting the two most powerful countries in the world. The Soviet Union had a vast population that could be used in the war effort and the USA the strongest economy. By 1943, US war production was in full swing, producing four times as much each month as Germany.

- Allied bombing of Germany weakened its war effort. By 1943, bomber raids involving 1000 aircraft at a time were organised, using incendiaries and heavy explosives. This caused only limited damage to German industry: 90 per cent of German industry was still working at full capacity in 1945. However, it had a devastating impact on German cities. Berlin, Hamburg and Dresden, to name but a few, were almost completely destroyed.

- Hitler over-committed German armed forces. In 1941 German troops were sent to North Africa to bolster the Italian campaign against the British. Although German forces were at first successful, they were defeated at El Alamein in October 1942 and driven out of North Africa the following year. The invasion of the Soviet Union overstretched German economic and military resources. The failure of the invasion, the subsequent defeat at Stalingrad and retreat further drained German reserves and badly affected morale.

● *Revision tasks*

1 Copy the table below and use key words to explain how each long-term factor contributed to German defeat. Then give each factor a rating for its overall importance (using 5 as the most important).

Factor	Explanation	Importance (1–5)
Battle of the Atlantic		
Over-commitment of German forces		
Allied bombings		
Involvement of USA and USSR		

2 Which do you think was the most important long-term factor? Give an explanation for your answer.

2 The Allied invasion of Normandy

D-Day landings, June 1944

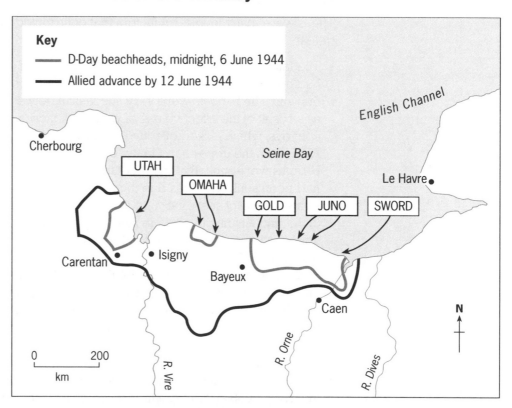

Key
—— D-Day beachheads, midnight, 6 June 1944
—— Allied advance by 12 June 1944

English Channel

Cherbourg

Seine Bay

UTAH

OMAHA

Le Havre

GOLD   JUNO   SWORD

Carentan   • Isigny

Bayeux

Caen   N

0   200
km

R. Vire

R. Orne

R. Dives

On 6 June 1944 Allied forces landed on the beaches of Normandy in France and began the campaign to liberate western Europe from German occupation. The British and Canadian forces landed on beaches codenamed Sword, Juno and Gold and the US forces landed at Omaha and Utah. The Allies were quickly able to establish a beachhead and, although pinned down in Normandy for almost a month, they eventually broke out and reached Paris within six weeks. The success of D-Day was due to a combination of factors:

- The Allies had prepared very thoroughly for the invasion. Churchill delayed the assault until he felt the time was right. Allied troops were trained in landing tactics and new devices were developed to assist the landings. These included artificial piers and harbours and an oil pipeline across the Channel.
- The Germans did not know where the landings would take place. Indeed, Allied bombing of the Calais area convinced Hitler that this was to be the

location. Even on the day of the invasion, he thought the landings in
Normandy were a decoy and was slow to send reinforcements.
- The Allies had control of the air over the Channel and northern France. Ten
thousand Allied planes escorted the invasion fleet and had also prepared the
way by bombing communications to Normandy and carrying paratroopers
behind German lines. The invasion fleet was the biggest ever assembled.
- Hitler refused to allow Field Marshal Rommel to take control of the Panzer
(tank) divisions in Normandy. This weakened the German army when it tried
to counter-attack the Allies after they had landed.

3 Allied advances, 1944–45

It took a further eleven months after D-Day to defeat the Germans. This delay
was due to the following factors:

- The Americans decided to advance slowly on a broad front rather than make
a concentrated strike at Germany, which might overstretch supply lines and
risk Allied forces being cut off by a German counter-attack. The British did
attempt to speed up the advance through the Arnhem operation of
September 1944. Airborne troops were landed behind the German lines in
the Netherlands in an attempt to outflank the German defences. The plan
failed because the land troops were unable to link up with the paratroopers.
- Hitler took a final gamble on victory in December 1944, in an attack known as
the Battle of the Bulge. He tried to repeat the success of the Ardennes
operation of 1940 but this time against the Americans. American troops were
taken by surprise and the Germans only narrowly failed to achieve a
breakthrough. It took the Americans nearly two months to recover the area
they had lost in the offensive.

In March 1945 Allied troops finally crossed the Rhine and moved into Germany.
By this time Germany was on its knees, having been bombed around the clock
and starved by the Allied naval blockade. The surrender was signed in
northern Germany on 8 May 1945.

Although the Allied landings in Normandy and subsequent advance played
an important role in the defeat of Germany, the crucial area was probably the
Eastern Front. It was in the Soviet Union that the German army had 90 per cent
of its casualties.

● *Revision tasks*

1 Copy the table below and fill it in using key words to explain the events of
1944–45.

Event	Explanation
Preparations for D-Day	
D-Day landings	
Allied advance	
Why the Allied advance slowed down	
Importance of Eastern Front	

2 Do you agree that the most important reason for German defeat was the events on
the Eastern Front?

H Reasons for the defeat of Japan

Japan was defeated in 1945 for a number of long-term and short-term reasons.

1 Battle of Midway Island, June 1942

This proved to be the turning-point in the war in the Far East. The Japanese tried to occupy Midway Island in June 1942. US intelligence was able to break the Japanese military code and intercept its fleet on the way to Midway. Four Japanese aircraft carriers were sunk. This swung the balance of military power in the Pacific to the USA.

2 Long-term reasons for Japan's defeat

- The Japanese had greatly overstretched their economic and military resources due to their conquests of 1941–42. They could not possibly hold on to such a wide area.
- The defeat at Midway meant they lost naval and air power in the Pacific, which was vital to control their conquests.
- Japan faced the most powerful nation in the world. US manpower, oil and war production made all the difference.
- In South-East Asia, the British held up the Japanese advance in the jungles of Burma and began to train their troops in jungle warfare. Raids were sent behind enemy lines to cut the Japanese supply routes. In 1944 Allied troops began to recapture the areas occupied by the Japanese.

The war in the Pacific and the Far East, 1941–45

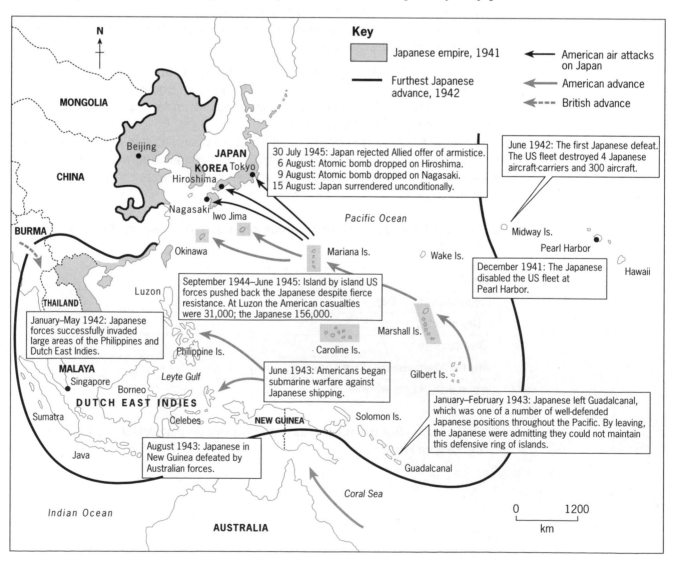

Key

Japanese empire, 1941

Furthest Japanese advance, 1942

American air attacks on Japan

American advance

British advance

30 July 1945: Japan rejected Allied offer of armistice.
6 August: Atomic bomb dropped on Hiroshima.
9 August: Atomic bomb dropped on Nagasaki.
15 August: Japan surrendered unconditionally.

June 1942: The first Japanese defeat. The US fleet destroyed 4 Japanese aircraft-carriers and 300 aircraft.

December 1941: The Japanese disabled the US fleet at Pearl Harbor.

September 1944–June 1945: Island by island US forces pushed back the Japanese despite fierce resistance. At Luzon the American casualties were 31,000; the Japanese 156,000.

January–May 1942: Japanese forces successfully invaded large areas of the Philippines and Dutch East Indies.

June 1943: Americans began submarine warfare against Japanese shipping.

January–February 1943: Japanese left Guadalcanal, which was one of a number of well-defended Japanese positions throughout the Pacific. By leaving, the Japanese were admitting they could not maintain this defensive ring of islands.

August 1943: Japanese in New Guinea defeated by Australian forces.

- US progress in the Pacific was slow. They adopted island-hopping tactics in an attempt to get closer to the Japanese mainland. They left Japanese units isolated on islands without supplies. The Japanese refused to surrender and the Americans suffered horrific casualties capturing islands such as Okinawa and Iwo Jima.
- By summer 1945, almost all Japanese conquests in the Pacific had been recaptured. US planes were bombing Japanese cities, causing considerable damage and many casualties.

3 The use of the atomic bomb

On 6 and 9 August 1945 atomic bombs were dropped on the Japanese cities of Hiroshima and Nagasaki. Within a week the Japanese government had surrendered. There was and still is great controversy over the decision to use such a weapon. The new US president, Harry S. Truman, used the bomb for several reasons:

- His chiefs of staff estimated that there would be as many as 500,000 casualties if they invaded the Japanese mainland. Using the bomb would shorten the war and prevent further Allied casualties.
- Some believe it was a warning to the Soviet Union which was expanding too quickly in eastern Europe.
- One motive could have been revenge for the Japanese attack on Pearl Harbor.

There has been much criticism of Truman's decision.

- One view is that the Japanese were about to surrender in any case. There is some truth in this, although it seemed unlikely that they would accept unconditional surrender.
- The effects of the bombs were devastating at the time and later for the civilians of the two Japanese cities. At Hiroshima at least 75,000 died instantly and tens of thousands more died from radiation poisoning in the years that followed.
- It was also argued that Truman should have used the bomb on an uninhabited island in order to demonstrate to the Japanese its effects and persuade them to surrender.

● *The greatest controversy is not over why Japan was defeated but how this was achieved. The debate goes on over the use of atomic weapons. On the one side is the view that Japan was ready to surrender and the bombs were unnecessary. On the other hand is the argument that many more Allied soldiers would have been killed in any invasion of Japan.* ●

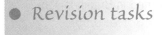
● *Revision tasks*

1 Make a list of all the reasons for the defeat of Japan in 1945. Now prioritise your list. In other words, put the reasons in order of importance with the most important at the top. Next to each reason explain your decision using key words.
2 Make your own balance sheet, like the one below, of arguments for and against the use of the atomic bomb in 1945.

For the atomic bomb	Against the atomic bomb

3 Do you believe Truman was right to use the atomic bomb? Explain your answer using key words.

Revision session

The aim of this revision session is for you to see how you can apply your knowledge of the World at War, 1938–45, to answer source-based questions.

Examination questions

Below are examples of source questions from the Specimen Paper for Paper 2, adapted by permission of Edexcel.

Source A A map showing the German invasion of the Soviet Union

Source B From a school textbook about the history of the Soviet Union in the twentieth century, published in Britain in 1991
The Nazi–Soviet pact was fragile and likely to break down when it suited either of the parties. There is no evidence that Stalin was preparing a war against Germany. It seems more likely that Hitler's long-term hatred of Bolshevism and wish to gain lebensraum (living space) played the key role in his decision to attack the Soviet Union.

Source C From a book about international relations, published in Britain in 1997
On 22 June 1941, Germany made a surprise attack on the Soviet Union. Operation Barbarossa was a three-pronged attack on the cities of Leningrad, Moscow and Stalingrad. The plan would lead to the destruction of the Soviet Union and would give Germany access to the wheatfields of the Ukraine and the oilfields of the Caucasus. Germany would also gain living space.

210

© IT IS ILLEGAL TO PHOTOCOPY THIS PAGE

a) Study Source A.

What can you learn from this source about the aims of the German invasion of the Soviet Union? *(4 marks)*

What is required? This question is testing your understanding of a source and your ability to interpret what it says. Try to make at least one inference from the source. In other words, read between the lines of what the source says.

Ideas for your answer
- To encourage you to make an inference or inferences you could start at least one sentence with 'This source suggests that...' or 'This source shows that...'.
- One possible inference could be that the Germans wanted to capture Soviet resources, such as...

b) Study Sources A, B and C.

Does Source C support the evidence of Sources A and B? Explain your answer. *(6 marks)*

What is required? This question is asking you to compare the information in Source C to that in Sources A and B. A simple answer that compares the sources at their face value will only achieve level 1 (1–2 marks). An answer that makes developed statements about similarities *or* differences between two or three of the sources will reach level 2 (3–4 marks). For level 3 (5–6 marks) you need to:

- ensure you directly compare Source C to Source A and Source C to Source B, in other words, refer to all three sources
- look for similarities and differences between them in information, tone and attitude
- ensure your comparisons are developed and precisely explained.

Ideas for your answer
1. Begin by explaining the information/attitude/tone of Source C. It clearly outlines Germany's motives which include gaining Soviet resources and living space, and the destruction of the USSR.
2. Now compare Source C to Source A.
   a) Does Source C support the views of Source A? Yes, because Source A shows the initial German targets as being Soviet resources.
   b) Are there any differences? Yes, because there is no mention in Source A of living space and the destruction of the Soviet Union.
3. Compare Source C to Source B.
   a) Does Source C support the evidence of Source B? Yes, because Source B mentions Hitler's desire for living space.
   b) Are there any differences? Yes. Source B does not mention resources but does state Hitler's long-term hatred of Bolshevism.
4. Now write a conclusion summing up your answer to the question, and giving a judgement as to how far C supports A and B.

> **Source D** From the diary of General Halder, August 1941. Halder was one of the German commanders leading the German invasion
>
> *We have underestimated the Russian giant. At the start of the war, we reckoned that we would face about 200 enemy divisions. Now we have already counted 360. Time favours the Russians. They are near their own resources and we are moving farther away from ours. Our troops are spread out over an immense line and are subjected to the enemy's constant attacks.*

Source E A photograph showing Soviet troops in action against the Germans in 1941

(A similar photo was used in the actual specimen examination paper)

Source F From Stalin's radio broadcast to the Soviet people at the time of the German invasion, June 1941

The enemy is cruel. They are out to seize our lands, our grain and oil. They are out to restore the role of landlords, to turn our people into slaves of Germany. If we are forced to retreat, the enemy must not be left a single engine, a single pound of grain or a gallon of fuel. All valuable property including grain and fuel that cannot be withdrawn must be destroyed without fail. In areas occupied by the enemy, guerrillas must be formed, sabotage groups must be organised to combat the enemy by blowing up bridges and roads.

c) Study Sources D and E.

How useful are these two sources as evidence of the problems faced by the German armies in the Soviet Union? *(8 marks)*

What is required? A simple statement on the content or nature of the sources will achieve no more than three marks. More developed statements which lack balance, for example by ignoring the nature of the sources and/or their limitations, will reach level 2 (4–6 marks). To reach level 3 (7–8 marks) you need to ensure that your answer is fully balanced in the following ways:

- Explain the usefulness of both sources.
- Evaluate the **usefulness** of each source in two areas – **content/context** of the source and **nature/origin/purpose**.
- Analyse the **limitations** of each source in the same two areas – **content/context** and **nature/origin/purpose**.

Include a conclusion that summarises the usefulness of each source. In some cases the two sources might be useful because they give similar views of an event.

Ideas for your answer Copy the table below and use key words to complete each section. This is a good way of planning your answer.

	Source D	Source E
Usefulness of content and context		
Limitations of content and context		
Usefulness of nature, origin and purpose		
Limitations of nature, origin and purpose		

Examine the usefulness of each source in turn.

1 Source D is useful because of its content and nature. It gives us the views of a top German commander who is writing in a diary and would probably be giving his honest opinions.

2 Now consider the limitations of Source D. It only mentions some of the problems (you would need to mention some that are missing) and is written by a commander who may be making excuses for his own failings.

3 Now you will need to do the same for Source E. A few hints: How useful are the contents of the source? What problems can you actually see? What type of source is it? Does this make it less or more useful? What limitations does it have as a source of evidence of the problems of the German armies?

4 Now a conclusion: in this case the two sources are useful because they show different problems faced by the German armies. In what other respects are they useful?

d) Study all the sources.
  'Operation Barbarossa failed because it was badly planned.'
  Use the sources, and your own knowledge, to explain whether you agree with this view.   *(12 marks)*

What is required? This question is the most important because it is worth twelve marks. The examiner wants you to reach a conclusion on the question using your own knowledge and by referring to most, if not all, of the sources.

  Low-level answers (1–3 marks) will make simple points using the sources and/or your own knowledge. The next level of answer (4–7 marks) will make developed statements in support of *or* against the view using the sources and/or your own knowledge. To reach level 3 (8–10 marks) you must make developed statements for *and* against the view using the sources and your own knowledge. To achieve the very top level (11–12 marks) you will have to do the following:

- ensure that your whole answer is focused on the question
- include an introduction that explains the view expressed in the question and how you intend to answer it
- give a balanced argument for and against the view
- use most, if not all, of the sources and your own knowledge to give this argument
- begin each paragraph with your argument and then back it up with your own knowledge and evidence from one or more of the sources – in other words integrate your arguments, own knowledge and evidence from the sources
- write a conclusion that gives a final judgement on the view in the question. Make sure this is consistent with what you have already written.

Ideas for your answer Copy the table below and use key words to complete each section. Use this as a plan for your eventual answer. Part of it has been completed for you.

	Supporting the view	Against the view
Arguments		Soviet winter
Own knowledge		Explanation of impact of Soviet winter
Sources		Source E
Conclusion		

1 In support of the view you will need to give a developed explanation from your own knowledge of the mistakes in planning, including the idea of a three-pronged offensive and the delay in starting the invasion.
2 You could use Sources A and C to support the view.
3 Against the view you need to explain from your own knowledge other reasons for the failure of the offensive, including the geography and poor communications of the Soviet Union and the attitude of the Red Army.
4 You could use Sources D, E and F to argue against the view.
5 For a conclusion decide whether bad planning was the only or the fundamental reason for the failure of Operation Barbarossa.

Practice questions

Now look at the following sources and questions adapted from the 1998 Paper 2 by permission of Edexcel. Have a go at answering the questions without any help.

Source A From a book about the Second World War published in Britain in the 1990s
When the first British troops arrived at Dunkirk, discipline nearly broke down altogether. For the first two days of the evacuation, order had to be kept by armed naval personnel. Even then soldiers were rushing the boats in their anxiety to get away. Large numbers of officers ran away and deserted their troops so as to get on to the earliest boat. Churchill said that Dunkirk was 'the greatest military defeat for many centuries'.

Source B From the memoirs of a British Army officer published in the 1970s. He was captured by the Germans near Dunkirk in 1940
My search-light battalion was sent to block the road into Calais. Only half of us had rifles. In addition, we had two machine guns, of First World War issue, and one anti-tank gun, which none of us had been trained to use. Before us we found the advanced reconnaissance group of an entire German armoured Division.

Source C An extract about events in France in 1940 taken from a book about the importance of that year for the history of the Second World War. The book was written by a British historian in the 1990s
The collapse of France was caused by the numerically superior and highly mechanised German army using waves of modern tanks in a new style of blitzkrieg warfare. The British army, let down by the French and betrayed by the Belgians, fought its way back to the coast, where it was evacuated by a fleet of small boats from the beaches of Dunkirk.

Source D A painting entitled *The Withdrawal from Dunkirk, 1940* by Charles Cundall, an official war artist with the British army. It was painted in 1940

Source E From the BBC six o'clock news bulletin on 31 May 1940. This was the first report about Dunkirk

All night and all day soldiers of the undefeated British Expeditionary Force have been coming home. From interviews with the men it is clear they have come back in glory. Their morale is as high as ever and they want to get back again 'to have a real crack at the Germans'.

Source F A table showing British army supplies used in France in 1939–40 and the supplies brought back to Britain

	Taken to France	Lost/used	Brought back
Guns	2,794	2,472	322
Vehicles	68,618	63,879	4,739
Motorcycles	21,081	20,548	533
Ammunition (tonnes)	109,000	76,697	32,303
Petrol (tonnes)	166,000	164,929	1,071

a) Study Source A.
What can you learn from Source A about the evacuation
from Dunkirk in 1940? *(4 marks)*

b) Study Sources A, B and C.
Does Source C support the evidence of Sources A and B?
Explain your answer. *(6 marks)*

c) Study Sources D and E.
How useful are these two sources as evidence about Dunkirk? *(8 marks)*

d) Study all the sources.
'Dunkirk was a defeat for Britain, not a victory.'
Use these sources, and your own knowledge, to explain
whether you agree with this view. *(12 marks)*

Summary and revision plan

Below is a list of headings which you may find helpful. Use this as a check-list to make sure you are familiar with the material featured in this chapter. Record your key words alongside each heading.

A Appeasement, 1938–39, and the role of Chamberlain
- ❏ Hitler and German expansion, 1933–37
- ❏ The policy of appeasement
- ❏ The events of 1938–39
- ❏ Criticisms of appeasement

B The outbreak of the Second World War
- ❏ Long-term factors
- ❏ Poland
- ❏ The Nazi–Soviet Pact, August 1939

C Reasons for early German success
- ❏ German success, September 1939–May 1940
- ❏ Dunkirk
- ❏ Reasons for German success

D The fall of France and the survival of Britain
- ❏ The fall of France
- ❏ The survival of Britain
- ❏ The Battle of Britain
- ❏ The Blitz

E Operation Barbarossa and the Eastern Front
- ❏ The German invasion of the Soviet Union
- ❏ Soviet recovery and Stalingrad

F The causes of the outbreak of war in the Pacific
- ❏ Reasons for the Japanese attack
- ❏ Pearl Harbor
- ❏ Early Japanese success, 1941–42

G Reasons for the defeat of Germany
- ❏ Long-term factors
- ❏ The Allied invasion of Normandy
- ❏ Allied advances, 1944–45

H Reasons for the defeat of Japan
- ❏ Battle of Midway Island, June 1942
- ❏ Long-term reasons for Japan's defeat
- ❏ The use of the atomic bomb

Conflict in Vietnam, c.1963–75

In the 1960s successive US presidents committed their armed forces to involvement in the conflict in Vietnam and supported South Vietnam in its attempts to stop communist invasion from the North. US tactics against the Viet Cong forces did not work and brought much opposition at home. This, in turn, led to a gradual reduction in US involvement in the late 1960s and early 1970s. Eventually the North triumphed and reunited Vietnam under communist leadership.

Key content   You will need a good working knowledge of these areas:

A Reasons for US involvement in Vietnam
B US tactics in Vietnam
C The tactics of the Viet Cong
D The impact of the war on the people of Vietnam
E The impact of the war on the USA
F The reasons for US defeat
G The consequences of the war for Vietnam and the USA

Key themes   You will be asked to show your understanding of some key themes:

● Why did conflict break out in Vietnam in the early 1960s?
● How and why did the USA become involved?
● How did each side fight the war?
● What criticisms were made of the use of napalm and other chemical weapons?
● How far was the American defeat due to the strengths of the Viet Cong?
● Why was there so much opposition to the war in the USA?
● How did this opposition affect the US war effort?
● What happened to Vietnam after the US withdrawal?
● Did defeat in Vietnam greatly change US foreign policy?

Source-based questions test both your knowledge of the topic and your source-evaluation skills. For example, look at this question adapted from the 2001 Paper 2, by permission of Edexcel.

Source A From an interview with a US airforce mechanic in 1983 who served in Vietnam in 1968

We were attacked at our base by the Viet Cong and there was chaos but by next morning it was over. As she did every day the old lady across the way came out to sweep her porch at 6 o'clock. An army sergeant jumped up with his rifle and tried to shoot her. He ordered a marine to shoot her with the high-powered machine gun. He said she was a Viet Cong.

a) Study Source A.
What can you learn from Source A about the actions of US forces in the Vietnam War in 1968?   *(4 marks)*

This question is testing:

· your knowledge of US actions in Vietnam in 1968
· your understanding of source skills, especially your ability to make inferences from a source.

We will look at this question in more detail at the end of this chapter.

A Reasons for US involvement in Vietnam

1 US involvement before 1954

Vietnam was part of the French empire until its occupation by the Japanese during the Second World War. Japan was defeated in 1945 and Vietnam was returned to the French. However, the Communist leader Ho Chi Minh led opposition to French control and declared Vietnam's independence in September 1945. This led to war between the French and supporters of Ho Chi Minh. The US president, Truman, gave $3 million to support the French. This was due to American fears of the spread of communism. In 1954 the French were defeated at Dien Bien Phu and agreed to a peace conference.

At the Geneva peace conference the following was decided:

• Vietnam would be temporarily divided in two along the 17th parallel (see the map on p.220).
• The North would be under the control of the communist regime of Ho Chi Minh.
• The South would be controlled by Ngo Dinh Diem, an anti-communist, Catholic politician.
• There would be a general election in 1956 for the whole of Vietnam to decide its future.

Communism in Vietnam, mid-1960s

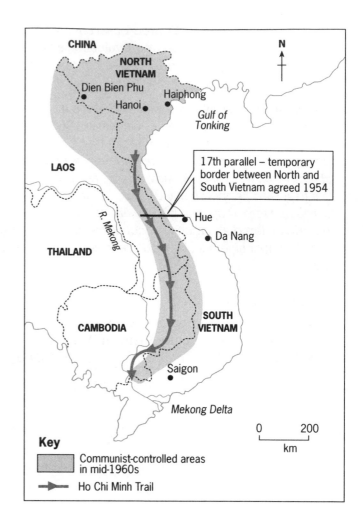

CHINA

NORTH VIETNAM

Dien Bien Phu

Hanoi

Haiphong

Gulf of Tonking

LAOS

17th parallel – temporary border between North and South Vietnam agreed 1954

R. Mekong

THAILAND

Hue

Da Nang

CAMBODIA

SOUTH VIETNAM

Saigon

Mekong Delta

0   200
km

Key

Communist-controlled areas in mid-1960s

Ho Chi Minh Trail

2 US support, 1954–60

The USA was determined to support South Vietnam against any possible take-over from the North. This was due to the domino theory – the USA feared that one by one, each country in Asia would fall to communism, like a row of dominoes. US support for South Vietnam included:

- $1.6 billion in aid between 1954 and 1960
- sending US military advisers in 1954 to help 'prepare' for the 1956 elections
- backing Diem's refusal to hold elections in 1956 in case the communists won.

Diem's corrupt government became very unpopular. Leading socialists, communists, journalists and trade unionists were arrested. Buddhists were excluded from top government positions. In the villages the traditionally elected councils were replaced by Saigon officials.

The National Liberation Front (NLF) was set up in opposition to Diem and soon controlled parts of the countryside in South Vietnam. It was given supplies and support from Ho Chi Minh and wanted to reunite North and South and to introduce economic and social reform.

3 US involvement during the Kennedy years, 1961–63

Kennedy did not like Diem but was determined to prevent the spread of communism from the North. The NLF, now known as the Viet Cong or VC, had grown to 16,000 members. The USA tried to counter its influence by:

- sending even more military advisers. By 1962 there were 11,000 training the South Vietnamese army, known as the ARVN.

• the 'strategic hamlets' policy in which hamlets supporting the Viet Cong were moved and replaced by new ones defended by barbed wire and the ARVN. This policy did not work as many South Vietnamese resented having to move. It increased support for the Viet Cong.

Diem's unpopularity grew. He imprisoned and killed hundreds of Buddhists, who he claimed were helping the communists. Some Buddhist monks burnt themselves in protest. Diem's anti-Buddhist policy lost him the support of the USA, and in November 1963 he was assassinated by his army generals.

4 Greater involvement under Lyndon Johnson

After Kennedy's assassination in 1963, the new president, Lyndon Johnson, was preoccupied with domestic reforms in the USA. However, the situation changed in August 1964 with the Gulf of Tonkin incident. An American naval craft, the *Maddox*, was attacked by North Vietnamese gunboats. Johnson was furious and persuaded Congress to give him the freedom to take whatever action was necessary in Vietnam. President Johnson now committed combat troops to Vietnam.

5 Views of American involvement

One view is that American involvement was a natural development of the domino theory and US fears of communist expansion in Asia. Hence there was a gradual build-up of US military personnel in Vietnam in the 1950s and early 1960s.

A different view is that the USA was trying to impose its own values and beliefs across the world – to create its own areas of influence which included Vietnam. Communism was simply an excuse to hide American imperialism.

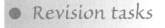

● *Revision tasks*

1 Using a timeline trace the growing US involvement in Vietnam from 1945 to 1964.
2 What were the following:
   a) Domino theory
   b) NLF
   c) ARVN
   d) Gulf of Tonkin incident?
3 Which view do you accept of reasons for the US involvement in Vietnam? Use key words to explain your answer.

B US tactics in Vietnam

The first US combat troops arrived in South Vietnam in March 1965. Three weeks earlier the USA had begun 'Operation Rolling Thunder'.

1 Operation Rolling Thunder

This was the codename used for the US bombing of North Vietnam. By the end of the war the US Air Force had dropped more bombs on Vietnam than all the countries had dropped during the Second World War. This operation was designed to destroy roads, railways and Viet Cong bases in North Vietnam, and especially the Ho Chi Minh Trail. This was the supply route from North to South Vietnam for the Viet Cong.

Saturation bombing did not flush out or destroy the Viet Cong. It had little effect against the guerrilla tactics used by the Viet Cong. By the end of 1965 there were 180,000 US troops in South Vietnam but the Viet Cong had not been defeated.

2 Search and destroy

The Americans used search-and-destroy tactics to try to flush the Viet Cong out of the countryside. They used helicopters which landed close to Viet Cong-controlled villages in the hope of getting into the village before the Viet Cong could arm themselves. This was not easy because:

- it was difficult to distinguish the Viet Cong from the normal Vietnamese people
- the US soldiers found the conditions very difficult due to the heat, the jungle and mosquitoes.

Civilian casualties in search-and-destroy raids were very high. This made the US and South Vietnamese forces even more unpopular with the peasants.

3 Chemical weapons

The Americans decided to use chemical weapons to try to flush the Viet Cong out of the jungles. These weapons included:

- Agent Orange which destroyed hundreds of thousands of hectares of forest and crops. Exposure to Agent Orange caused cancers, birth defects, etc. Both the Vietnamese peasants and the US forces were affected.
- Napalm, an incendiary weapon, which contained petrol, chemicals and phosphorus, and burnt the skin right to the bone.

These tactics did not work. As well as destroying much of the countryside and killing and wounding thousands of civilians they:

- turned world opinion against the USA for using such inhuman weapons
- alienated even more of the population of South Vietnam, who turned to the Viet Cong.

● *American tactics evolved and changed during the course of the war in Vietnam, from saturation bombing, to search and destroy, and the use of chemical weapons. None of these was successful in defeating the Viet Cong. Indeed, in most respects they had the opposite effect. They alienated the people of Vietnam and increased their support for the Viet Cong.* ●

● *Revision tasks*

1 Make a copy of the following table and use key words to explain the methods used by the USA and why they did not work.

Method	Explanation	Limitations
Operation Rolling Thunder		
Search and destroy		
Chemical weapons		

2 What was the Ho Chi Minh trail?

C The tactics of the Viet Cong

The Viet Cong copied the methods that had been used by Mao in communist China. This involved a combination of guerrilla tactics and trying to win the support of the people of South Vietnam.

1 Guerrilla tactics

- Guerrilla tactics were ideal in jungle conditions. The Viet Cong were able to make booby traps, carry out ambushes and sabotage US bases and then disappear into the jungle. As most of the population supported the Viet Cong it was almost impossible to detect them in the villages.
- The Viet Cong built thousands of kilometres of tunnels and complex underground shelters to avoid US air raids and reduce casualties. Often US troops were killed by booby traps.
- The Viet Cong had much support in the villages, and those who did not support them were terrorised into providing shelter and food.

2 Outside aid

The Viet Cong were supplied by the North Vietnamese via the Ho Chi Minh Trail. Other communist countries, such as the USSR and China, gave at least 6000 tonnes of supplies per day to North Vietnam to fight the USA.

3 The Tet Offensive, 1968

In 1968 the Viet Cong launched a surprise offensive during the Tet (New Year) Festival. They attacked 36 cities and even reached Saigon where, for a short period of time, they held the US embassy. They were eventually forced to retreat with very heavy losses. In many respects this was a military victory for the USA but, in the long term, it had a disastrous effect on the attitudes of Americans, especially witnessing their own embassy under attack.

4 Vietnamisation

The advances made by the Viet Cong in the Tet Offensive so shocked the American public that President Richard Nixon (who took office in 1969) decided to introduce the policy of 'Vietnamisation'. This meant training the Vietnamese army to fight on its own with US arms and supplies, and withdrawing US troops. Between 1969 and 1971 about 400,000 troops were withdrawn.

At the same time, however, Nixon bombed the neighbouring countries of Laos and Cambodia and sent in US troops to destroy the Viet Cong supply lines and bases there.

Finally, Nixon began peace talks aimed at ending the conflict in Vietnam. The Paris Peace Agreement of January 1973 signalled the end of direct US intervention in the conflict. The US promised the South Vietnamese $1 billion of military equipment to enable the South to defend itself against the North.

● *The Viet Cong used very effective tactics based on guerrilla warfare and the use of an underground tunnel network. American tactics helped, by driving the civilians of South Vietnam into supporting and hiding the Viet Cong. The Tet Offensive of 1968 marked the beginning of the end of direct US involvement in Vietnam due to its impact on the morale of the American people. However, in many respects, the offensive was a failure for the Viet Cong.* ●

● *Revision tasks*

1 Use a few key words to explain the guerrilla tactics used by the Viet Cong. Why were they so effective in this conflict?
2 Why was the Tet Offensive of such importance to the USA and the Viet Cong?
3 What was meant by 'Vietnamisation? How far was it carried out by Richard Nixon? Use key words to record your answer.

D The impact of the war on the people of Vietnam

The war had a devastating effect on the people of Vietnam. More than a million civilians were killed.

1 North Vietnam

The people of North Vietnam suffered from bombing, shelling and chemical warfare. Hanoi and Haiphong were badly damaged. Conscription was introduced so that soldiers could be sent to the South to help the Viet Cong.

2 South Vietnam

This was the battlefield between the Viet Cong, supported by troops from North Vietnam on one side, and the ARVN and US soldiers on the other. Villages were often attacked and terrorised by both sides. The use of chemical weapons and widespread bombing left towns and cities in ruins and was an environmental disaster for the countryside and people. Today large numbers of Vietnamese born at the time of the war have birth defects due to the chemicals that entered the water supply. Over 2 million hectares of forest were destroyed by chemicals. As a result Vietnam, once a major producer of rice, had to import food.

3 The reunification of Vietnam

The Paris Peace Agreement of 1973 left the South to fight alone against the Viet Cong. It could not withstand the forces of North Vietnam and was soon defeated. In 1976 Vietnam was reunited.

● *Revision task*

1 Using a few key words summarise the impact of the war on the people of South and North Vietnam.

E The impact of the war on the USA

The war in Vietnam had a far-reaching impact on American society.

1 US soldiers

Young American men were drafted (conscripted) into the US army, with the average age of US soldiers being nineteen. By 1968 there were 535,000 US troops in Vietnam.

- US casualties in the Vietnam war were high. More than 47,000 were killed in action and nearly 11,000 died of other causes. Over 300,000 were wounded.
- Many of the American troops had no enthusiasm for the war and did not understand what they were fighting for.
- A substantial number turned to drugs and began smoking marijuana and using heroin. In 1971, 5000 soldiers were treated for wounds and 20,000 for serious drug abuse.
- Some officers were even killed by their own troops. They were shot in the back or blown up by hand grenades thrown into their tents.
- A great number of soldiers deserted. Some American teenagers left the USA to avoid being drafted into the army.

2 The US public

Opposition to the war began as early as 1964. This was for several reasons:

- Some people opposed American involvement and the death of US troops in a war which they felt did not directly affect the USA.

- Martin Luther King opposed the war because of the disproportionate number of Black American casualties.
- Others believed the USA was spending far too much money on the war – money that should be financing Johnson's reforms. Opposition grew when taxes were raised in 1967.
- Newspaper and television coverage brought horrific scenes from the war into people's living rooms. It was impossible to ignore what was happening.
- Many Americans were shocked at the number of US casualties and the tactics used by their armed forces, including the use of chemical weapons and search and destroy.
- The Tet Offensive shocked many Americans, especially the sight of the US embassy being attacked.
- When news of the My Lai massacre emerged in 1969, there was even more opposition. This had happened a year earlier, when US forces led by Lieutenant William Calley entered the village of My Lai, suspected of hiding the Viet Cong, and killed 347 unarmed civilians.

There were many anti-war protest meetings in 1967. In April 1967 massive anti-war parades were held in major cities.

3 Student protests

The war in Vietnam coincided with the growth of student protest movements. There was widespread trouble at American universities. Students protested against the war and the draft system. Some burnt their draft cards (notifying them of their call-up to the army) or fled to avoid the draft. In 1968–69 4000 students were arrested. In 1970 four students were killed in clashes with the National Guard at Kent State University in Ohio.

● *The war had a massive effect on the USA. This was mainly due to the impact of television coverage. Casualties, atrocities, the death of civilians and the impact of chemical warfare could be seen in most homes in the USA. Strong anti-war protests contributed to Nixon's success in 1968 and his decision to introduce a policy of Vietnamisation.* ●

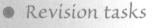
● *Revision tasks*

1 Make a copy of the following table and use key words to explain the reasons for the opposition of each group to the war.

Group	Reasons for opposition
US soldiers in Vietnam	
US public	
Students	

2 What impact did the following have on opposition to the war:
  a) television coverage
  b) the Tet Offensive
  c) the My Lai massacre?

F The reasons for US defeat

The USA was defeated in Vietnam for several reasons.

1 Viet Cong strengths

- the use of guerrilla warfare and a defensive system of underground tunnels
- working with and gaining the support of the people of South Vietnam
- an efficient supply line from the North along the Ho Chi Minh Trail
- assistance from China and the Soviet Union
- skilful propaganda, portraying the US as foreigners interfering in South Vietnam.

2 US weaknesses

- tactics which seemed to lack coherence and clear planning
- unenthusiastic soldiers
- inability to deal with the guerrilla tactics of the Viet Cong
- alienating the South Vietnamese people through heavy-handed tactics
- difficulty in coping with the conditions in Vietnam, such as the jungle and heat
- the weakness of the army of South Vietnam.

3 The importance of public opinion

It is difficult to measure the impact of public opinion on the war.

- It influenced Nixon in his decision to introduce a policy of Vietnamisation.
- It badly affected the morale of new recruits as well as those fighting in Vietnam, many of whom did not understand US motives for involvement.
- On the other hand, often more than half the US public supported the war.

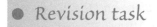

Revision task

1 Was it American public opinion that led to US defeat in the war in Vietnam?

G The consequences of the war for Vietnam and the USA

1 Vietnam

The war brought massive destruction to North and South Vietnam with 2.5 million casualties. On the other hand the country was reunited. After reunification Vietnam followed communist economic policies. Many of the South Vietnamese did not want to remain in this reunited country and fled in any kind of vessel possible. These refugees became known as the 'boat people' .

2 The USA

- The war prevented the building of Johnson's 'New Society' because money was diverted to the war effort.
- US prestige abroad fell and the US government later became unwilling to involve itself in any international conflict.
- On the other hand it encouraged the USA to seek accommodation with the communist world. Nixon followed a policy of détente with China and the USSR.
- The domino theory was disproved. There was no mass communist take-over of countries in South-East Asia.

Revision task

1 Copy the following table and use key words to explain the main effects of the war on the two countries.

Effects on the USA	Effects on Vietnam

Revision session

The aim of this revision session is for you to see how you can apply your knowledge of Conflict in Vietnam *c.* 1963–75 to answer source-based questions.

Examination questions

Below are examples of source questions from the 2001 Paper 2, adapted by permission of Edexcel.

Source A From an interview with a US airforce mechanic in 1983 who served in Vietnam in 1968

We were attacked at our base by the Viet Cong and there was chaos but by next morning it was over. As she did every day the old lady across the way came out to sweep her porch at 6 o'clock. An army sergeant jumped up with his rifle and tried to shoot her. He ordered a marine to shoot her with the high-powered machine gun. He said she was a Viet Cong.

Source B From a book about the conflict in Vietnam published in 1983

When the marines went into the village of Thuybo, the peasants, mostly old men and women, ran around in panic. The marines looked all over for Viet Cong and burnt huts and blew up underground shelters. The captain of the marines said that no more than fifteen peasants were killed.

Source C A photograph showing a US soldier guarding Viet Cong suspects in the mid-1960s

a) Study Source A.

What can you learn from Source A about the actions of the US forces in the Vietnam War in 1968?

(4 marks)

What is required? This question is testing your understanding of a source and your ability to interpret what it says. Try to make at least one inference from the source. In other words, read between the lines of what the source says.

Ideas for your answer
- To encourage you to make an inference or inferences you could start at least one sentence with 'This source suggests that...' or 'This source shows that...'.
- One possible inference could be that the US troops killed many civilians.

b) Study Sources A, B and C.

Does Source C support the evidence of Sources A and B about the actions of the US forces in Vietnam? Explain your answer.

(6 marks)

What is required? This question is asking you to compare the information in Source C to that in Sources A and B. A simple answer that compares the sources at their face value will only achieve level 1 (1–2 marks). An answer that makes developed statements about similarities or differences between two or three of the sources will reach level 2 (3–4 marks). For level 3 (5–6 marks) you need to:

- ensure you directly compare Source C to Source A and Source C to Source B, in other words, refer to all three sources
- look for similarities and differences between them in information, tone and attitude
- ensure your comparisons are developed and precisely explained.

Ideas for your answer
1. Begin by explaining the information/attitude/tone of Source C. It shows a US soldier guarding Vietnamese suspects who seem to be women, children and the elderly.
2. Now compare Source C to Source A.
   a) Does Source C support the views of Source A? Yes, because both show US troops' suspicion of Vietnamese civilians, especially the elderly.
   b) Are there any differences? Yes, because Source A goes further than Source C in suggesting that US soldiers shot civilians.
3. Compare Source C to Source B.
   a) Does Source C support the evidence of Source B? Yes, because Source B mentions the actions of US troops in a village suspected of supporting the Viet Cong. Fifteen peasants were killed and the village was burnt down.
   b) Are there any differences? Yes. Source B shows US troops going further in their actions against the civilians in Vietnam than Source C does.
4. Now write a conclusion summing up your answer to the question, and giving a judgement as to how far Source C supports Sources A and B.

Source D A photograph of South Vietnam's Chief of Police executing a Viet Cong officer in Saigon, February 1968. Film of the execution was broadcast on television news bulletins all over the world and this photograph was also published in newspapers worldwide

Source E From a book about the Vietnam conflict by T. Powers written in 1973. Powers was a journalist who covered the anti-Vietnam and civil rights movements in the years 1964–68
The riot in the New York district of Harlem in 1964 was followed by the more serious uprising in the Watts district of Los Angeles. The riot in Newark in 1966 saw 26 people killed and 1200 injured. Overcrowded schools, unemployment and the like were common features in these cities. Part of the mood was the failure of President Johnson's war on poverty – the obvious explanation was the cost of the war in Vietnam.

Source F From a note sent by Robert McNamara, the US Secretary of Defence, to President Johnson in October 1966
The picture of the world's greatest superpower killing or injuring 1000 civilians a week, while trying to pound a tiny backward nation into submission, is not a pretty one. It might change the picture that the world has of the USA.

c) Study Sources D and E.

How useful are these two sources as evidence about why the Vietnam War became unpopular in the USA?

(8 marks)

What is required?   A simple statement on the content or nature of the sources will achieve no more than three marks. More developed statements which lack balance, for example by ignoring the nature of the sources and/or their limitations, will reach level 2 (4–6 marks). To reach level 3 (7–8 marks) you need to ensure that your answer is fully balanced in the following ways:

- Explain the usefulness of both sources.
- Evaluate the **usefulness** of each source in two areas – **content/context** of the source and **nature/origin/purpose**.
- Analyse the **limitations** of each source in the same two areas – **content/context** and **nature/origin/purpose**.

Include a conclusion that summarises the usefulness of each source. In some cases the two sources might be useful because they give similar views of an event.

Ideas for your answer   Copy the table below and use key words to complete each section. This is a good way of planning your answer.

	Source D	Source E
Usefulness of content and context		
Limitations of content and context		
Usefulness of nature, origin and purpose		
Limitations of nature, origin and purpose		

Examine the usefulness of each source in turn.

1 Source D is useful because of its content and nature. It shows a street execution of a Viet Cong suspect, which shocked people in the USA and across the world. The film of the incident was shown on American television and greatly influenced attitudes to the war.

2 Now consider the limitations of Source D. It only gives us one photograph of one execution. It is difficult to gauge the impact it had and only explains one reason for growing opposition in the USA.

3 Now you will need to do the same for Source E. A few hints: How useful are the contents of the source? What reasons are suggested for the war's growing unpopularity? What type of source is it? Does this make it less or more useful? What limitations does it have as a source of evidence about the unpopularity of the war in Vietnam?

4 Now a conclusion: in this case the sources are useful because they show different reasons for the unpopularity of the war. In what other respects are they useful?

d) Study all the sources.

'The USA was unable to win the war in Vietnam because it could not gain the support of all the South Vietnamese people.'

Use the sources, and your own knowledge, to explain whether you agree with this view. *(12 marks)*

What is required? This question is the most important because it is worth twelve marks. The examiner wants you to reach a conclusion on the question using your own knowledge and by referring to most, if not all, of the sources.

Low-level answers (1–3 marks) will make simple points using the sources and/or your own knowledge. The next level of answer (4–7 marks) will make developed statements in support of *or* against the view using the sources and/or your own knowledge. To reach level 3 (8–10 marks) you must make developed statements for *and* against the view using the sources *and* your own knowledge. To achieve the very top level (11–12 marks) you will have to do the following:

- ensure that your whole answer is focused on the question
- include an introduction that explains the view expressed in the question and how you intend to answer it
- give a balanced argument for and against the view
- use most, if not all, of the sources and your own knowledge to give this argument
- begin each paragraph with your argument and then back it up with your own knowledge and evidence from one or more of the sources – in other words, integrate your arguments, your own knowledge and the evidence from the sources
- write a conclusion that gives a final judgement on the view in the question. Make sure this is consistent with what you have already written.

Ideas for your answer Copy the table below and complete each section using key words. Use this as a plan for your eventual answer. Part of it has been completed for you.

	Supporting the view	**Against the view**
Arguments	US search and destroy tactics	
Own knowledge	My Lai massacre	
Sources	Sources A, B and C	
Conclusion		

1 In support of the view you will need to give a developed explanation from your own knowledge of how the US tactics alienated the people, especially the search-and-destroy tactics and the use of chemical weapons.

2 You could use Sources A, B and C to support the view.

3 Against the view you will need to explain, using your own knowledge, other reasons for the failure of the US war efforts, such as the strengths of the Viet Cong.

4 You could use Sources D and E to argue against the view.

5 For a conclusion decide which was the most important reason for US defeat – failure to get the support of South Vietnamese civilians or other reason(s).

Practice questions

Now look at the following sources and questions adapted from the 2000 Paper 2, by permission of Edexcel. Have a go at answering the questions without any help.

Source A From a history textbook about the Vietnam War published in Britain in 1991

In 1965, David Miller publicly burnt his draft card and was sentenced to 2½ years in prison. His action inspired others and, throughout the USA, Anti-Vietnam War groups organised meetings where large groups of young men burnt their draft cards. Between 1963 and 1973, 9118 men were prosecuted for refusing to be drafted.

Source B From an interview with a US soldier, who returned home from Vietnam in 1967

I was walking down Telegraph Avenue, San Francisco. I was in uniform – I was spat on by passers-by. A gang of guys threw their peanuts at me. I went into a bar and some long-haired, bearded guys wanted to fight me. They shouted – 'You kill any women? You kill any kids?' I didn't understand why they were saying this.

Source C A photograph of anti-war demonstrators outside the Pentagon (US Military Headquarters) in October 1967

Source D A graph showing the number of US soldiers killed during the Vietnam War. The figures were produced by the US government

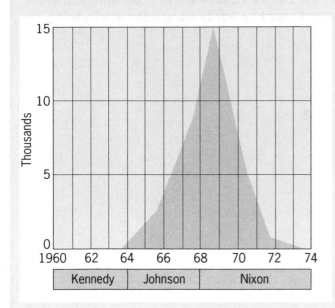

Source E Ho Chi Minh, leader of North Vietnam, speaking in a radio broadcast to the people of North Vietnam in 1967

Vietnam is thousands of miles from the USA. The US government has committed war crimes. Half a million US troops have resorted to inhuman weapons. Napalm, poisonous chemicals and gases have been used to massacre our people, destroy our crops and villages. We will never submit to force and never accept talks under threat of bombs.

Source F From an interview with a US army officer who finished his tour of duty in 1970. He was interviewed in the 1980s

I had lost confidence in the way the war was being fought. I believed that our soldiers needed the most experienced leadership they could get. The system was that the officer went to Vietnam, got a few months' experience and then moved on. A new guy with no experience would be put in his place as company commander. Obviously he is going to lose more lives while he learns. This wasn't the way to respect the lives of our young men or to fight a war.

a) Study Source A.
What can you learn from Source A about opposition in the USA to the Vietnam War? *(4 marks)*

b) Study Sources A, B and C.
Does Source C support the evidence of Sources A and B about opposition in the USA to the Vietnam War? Explain your answer. *(6 marks)*

c) Study Sources D and E.
How useful are Sources D and E as evidence about why there was opposition in the USA to the Vietnam War? *(8 marks)*

d) Study all the sources.
'Inexperienced leadership and poor military training were the main reasons why the USA was not successful in the Vietnam War.'
Use the sources, and your own knowledge, to explain whether you agree with this view. *(12 marks)*

Summary and revision plan

Below is a list of headings which you may find helpful. Use this as a check-list to make sure you are familiar with the material featured in this chapter. Record your key words alongside each heading.

A Reasons for US involvement in Vietnam
- ❏ US involvement before 1954
- ❏ US support, 1954–60
- ❏ US involvement during the Kennedy years, 1961–63
- ❏ Greater involvement under Lyndon Johnson
- ❏ Views of American involvement

B US tactics in Vietnam
- ❏ Operation Rolling Thunder
- ❏ Search and destroy
- ❏ Chemical weapons

C The tactics of the Viet Cong
- ❏ Guerrilla tactics
- ❏ Outside aid
- ❏ The Tet Offensive, 1968
- ❏ Vietnamisation

D The impact of the war on the people of Vietnam
- ❏ North Vietnam
- ❏ South Vietnam
- ❏ The reunification of Vietnam

E The impact of the war on the USA
- ❏ US soldiers
- ❏ The US public
- ❏ Student protests

F The reasons for US defeat
- ❏ Viet Cong strengths
- ❏ US weaknesses
- ❏ The importance of public opinion

G The consequences of the war for Vietnam and the USA
- ❏ Vietnam
- ❏ The USA

Glossary

alliances agreements made between two or more countries for a particular purpose, for example, to help each other if they are attacked

appeasement giving in to the demands of an aggressive country as a way of keeping the peace, for example, Chamberlain's attitude to Germany in the 1930s

armistice an end to fighting in a war, but not necessarily the end of the war itself, for example, the armistice of 1918 ended the fighting in the First World War, but the war itself did not officially end until the Treaty of Versailles was signed

autocrat a ruler who holds absolute power in a country and does not have to explain their actions to anyone else. A good example would be the Tsar of Russia

blitzkrieg German for 'lightning war'. It involved the use of tanks and motorised troops to achieve speed and surprise

Bolsheviks literally translated from Russian this means 'the majority'. The Bolsheviks were the highly disciplined communists led by Lenin

coalitions usually means a situation where different political parties inside a country work together, either because they agree on one particular issue or because they are both opposed to some other group

collectivisation the process in Stalin's USSR in the 1930s of bringing small farms together to create larger ones, which were meant to be more efficient

colony a country under the control of another more powerful country

conscription compulsory military service in the army; most countries in Europe had a system where young men spent two to three years in the army

containment a foreign policy aimed at containing the political influence or military power of another country, for example, the American policy to stop the spread of communism during the Cold War

détente the relaxing of tension or hostility between nations, for example, the improvement of relations between the USA and the USSR at the end of the 1960s

dictatorship of the proletariat see *proletariat*

Great Powers those countries that led the world in economic and political terms in the period before the First World War

guerrilla a type of soldier who uses surprise hit-and-run tactics and generally does not wear a uniform, making them hard to identify. They are usually politically motivated

Iron Curtain the guarded border that divided the communist countries of eastern Europe from the Western democracies, from 1945 until 1989

isolationism a policy of not taking part in international affairs

lebensraum territory claimed by a country on the grounds that it needs more space to grow and survive, for example, Hitler's claim to lands in eastern Europe

nationalism a feeling of patriotic support and pride for one's country

Ostpolitik a term first used to describe Willy Brandt's attempts to improve relations with European communist countries, especially East Germany, in the 1960s and 1970s

plebiscite vote by the people of a state or region on an important question such as a proposed union with another country

prohibition   the name given to the law enforced in America in the 1920s that made alcohol illegal

proletariat   workers who sell their labour for wages. In Marxist theory, the *dictatorship of the proletariat* was a stage in the revolution when the workers would have to oppose the attempts of the bourgeoisie to stop the socialist revolution

proportional representation   a system of voting in which all of the votes cast in an election are counted and political parties receive seats in proportion to the number of votes they receive. This system was used in Germany after the First World War

protectionism   economic policies followed by a country to protect its own industries and products from overseas competition, for example, by charging import duties on goods from abroad

radicals   people or groups (sometimes within other groups) who hold extreme political views, for example, the Nazis could be described as a radical party

Reichstag   the German parliament

reparations   compensation for war damage paid by the defeated nation, for example, Germany after the First World War

satellite   a country or region controlled or dominated by a foreign power

socialism   a political doctrine that supports democracy and greater government involvement in society and the economy

superpowers   a term used to describe the Soviet Union and the United States

tariff   a tax on foreign goods that makes them more expensive and therefore less attractive to customers

Viet Cong   a term used to describe the Vietnamese communists who fought the French and later the Americans